The Best American Short Plays

2013–2014

The Best American Short Plays

2013–2014

edited with an introduction by
William W. Demastes

APPLAUSE THEATRE & CINEMA BOOKS
An Imprint of Hal Leonard Corporation

The Best American Short Plays 2013–2014
Edited with an intoduction by William W. Demastes

Copyright © 2015 by Applause Theatre & Cinema Books (an imprint of Hal Leonard Corporation)

Published in 2015 by Applause Theatre & Cinema Books
An Imprint of Hal Leonard Corporation
7777 West Bluemound Road
Milwaukee, WI 53213

Trade Book Division Editorial Offices
33 Plymouth St., Montclair, NJ 07042

Printed in the United States of America
Book interior by UB Communications

ISBN 978-1-48039-548-0 [paper]
ISSN 0067-6284

www.applausebooks.com

contents

introduction

The Times They Are A-Changing

William W. Demastes

Uncertain seems to be the watchword of today's world, filled as it is with surprises, shocks, and even a few delights. Uncertainty brings with it fear and insecurity, and a nostalgic longing for the good old days. But for some, uncertainty means opportunity, and along with that opportunity comes the prospect of change for the better. Fifty years ago, Bob Dylan inserted a catchy phrase into our cultural consciousness: The times they are a-changing. The 1960s did in fact mark changes of all sorts for our world, many good and even revolutionary. It was an amazing time marked by triumph and tragedy both great and small. But think about how much more times have changed in the half-century since Dylan's declaration. Things not even envisioned by science-fiction visionaries are now part of our daily fabric. Technology has transformed our lives by placing information of all sorts literally at our fingertips. It has made us far more efficient in the workplace. And it has provided us the opportunity to share our lives with anyone at any time from any distance. Of course, this is not all good. Rapid pace and shrinking distance have reduced opportunities to reflect and contemplate. They have cut out times for creative play, for daydreaming, and so many other not-for-profit enterprises that make life worth living.

Then there are all those other changes, the ones that somehow have made us more alienated from one another than ever before. It is fortunate today that political adversaries remain unarmed, as oppositional political enmity has torn our country into enclaves of fear and mistrust. Race relations have reached both new highs and new lows. Sex and gender issues have received unprecedented public exposure, again for good and ill. And religion (traditional as well as New Age) continues its struggle against erosions of faith, leading to visions of godlessness and attendant despair. The triumph of tearing down the cold-war wall has brought on innumerable unintended negative consequences, opening the way for countless brush-fire tyrannies, and making the world in many ways more dangerous than ever before since we can't even be sure who our enemies are, or what they want, or why they hate us.

But in this world of uncertainty, acts of kindness, almost miraculously, find ways to break through. Generosity hasn't gone underground, altruism is not a dirty word, and love remains as coveted as ever. These are the energies that Dylan called forth in 1964, invoking leaders of all stripes to turn to conciliation rather than holding on to policies of self-interest.

Looking back at the last fifty years since Dylan's landmark declaration provides us another opportunity to reflect upon how the last half-century has brought about changes utterly unforeseen by anyone looking. We can see that indeed the times have changed, both for good and for ill. It's pretty apparent to most of us that reflection is not something strongly encouraged in our hurly-burly culture. But this volume asks that you do exactly that: reflect upon so much that has changed in the last half-century, or perhaps even in the last decade. Knowing where we came from is a major step toward knowing where we're headed.

This volume of *The Best American Short Plays* takes a look at our changing times, keying in on reflections about relational difficulties that in many ways are at the heart of all that is right and wrong with the world. Opening this volume is a series of plays produced in a single New York City venue (The Nuyorican Poets Cafe) appropriately entitled *Nine Signs of the Times*, produced by Daniel Gallant. Another collection of plays follows, entitled *Summer Voices 2014*, performed at the Stage Door Repertory Theatre in Anaheim, California. Smart and inventive, these collections capture the spirit of the times, some embracing the unknown future by looking forward, others embracing the times by reflecting upon the past. These collections are further complemented by a range of plays from around the country by playwrights likewise observing and digesting the signs of the times. Together the plays of this volume work as a time capsule for this uncertain world during these uncertain times, capturing the fears and longings of a world on the verge and in the midst of big changes, hopefully for the better but quite possibly for the worse.

Johnny & Rosie

Quincy Long

Quincy Long

Productions include *People Be Heard* at Playwrights Horizons; *The Only Child* at South Coast Rep, Costa Mesa, California; *The Lively Lad* at New York Stage and Film and The Actors Theatre of Louisville; *The Virgin Molly* at the Atlantic Theatre and Berkeley Rep; *The Joy of Going Somewhere Definite* at the Atlantic Theatre and Mark Taper Forum. *Joy* was optioned by Icon Films and was published by Dramatists Play Service, as were *People Be Heard* and *The Lively Lad*. Current projects include *Buried Alive*, a one-act opera adapted from an Edgar Allan Poe short story, commissioned by American Lyric Theatre in New York, produced in 2014 by Fargo Moorhead Opera, to be produced in 2016 by Fort Worth Opera; *Daughters of Io*, a play, and *The Cup*, an opera, both commissioned by Theatre Mon Dieu in New York City. Long is a graduate of the Yale School of Drama, is from Warren, Ohio, and lives in New York City.

··· production history ···

Johnny & Rosie was part of a presentation of monologues and one-act plays under the title *Nine Signs of the Times*, a benefit for New York's Nuyorican Poets Cafe's education programs, April 11–13, 2014. Technical director Samuel Chico, music by Michael Gallant, produced by Daniel Gallant, directed by Kathleen Dimmick.

JOHNNY   Dean Imperial

ROSIE   Penny Balfour

characters

JOHNNY, an emotional mobster.

ROSIE, his commonsensical moll.

location

An apartment in the big city.

time

The 1930s.

• • •

JOHNNY   [*Paces.*] You sure now, Rosie?

ROSIE   Yeah, Johnny.

JOHNNY   No snapshots, no movies, no nothin', promise?

ROSIE   I promise to God.

JOHNNY   Can't be any of that, okay? Got a thing about that. And don't ask.

ROSIE   I won't ask.

JOHNNY   No boyfriends with cameras?

ROSIE   Nope.

JOHNNY   No baby pictures on bearskin rugs?

ROSIE   I was a baby, who knows?

JOHNNY   I come to find out you lied to me....

ROSIE   Then you can kill me, okay?

JOHNNY   I wouldn't never do that.

ROSIE   I know how you mob guys do.

JOHNNY   Not to our wife. Girl we take home to our mother? Girl we're gonna celebrate our anniversaries wit' down the years, huh?

ROSIE   Yeah.

JOHNNY   Huuuuh?

ROSIE   Ah, Johnny.

JOHNNY   Long as there ain't naked pictures somewheres.

ROSIE   Like I said—

JOHNNY   Okay, okay.

ROSIE   You want a affidavit of it?

JOHNNY   I want word of honor there ain't pictures you fornicatin' somebody on a deck of cards, or in the smuts, or what happened wit' Harry the Hat's girl showin' up in that stag pitcher, everybody laughin'.

ROSIE   Hey, it ain't like I'm a virgin, ya know.

JOHNNY   I don't care about that. You can do it with dingoes in Times Square all I care. I just don't want it showin' up anywhere on—

ROSIE   On film, I know, I know. There's no pictures, Johnny!

JOHNNY   Good.

ROSIE   And no dingoes neither, just for the record.

JOHNNY   Makes my skin crawl, the thought of seein' some picture poppin' up.

ROSIE   I mean, could be there's a painting maybe.

JOHNNY   A what?

ROSIE   There was a guy once I sat for.

JOHNNY   Whatya mean, sat?

ROSIE   I mean he paid me to sit.

JOHNNY   What, on his face?

ROSIE   No, not his—

JOHNNY   What, then!? What!?

ROSIE   Sit, sit—pose for a painting, you jackass!

JOHNNY   You mean like a naked painting?

ROSIE   They don't call it naked. They call it nude.

JOHNNY   Ah, fuck.

ROSIE   You couldn't even tell it was me, Johnny.

JOHNNY   Rosie!

ROSIE   Looked like a Cyclops with boobs.

JOHNNY   That's even worse!

ROSIE   God, I looked somethin' awful.

JOHNNY   No, no, don't you see? He was painting your inside self! Things I don't even know about you! Things even you don't even know about you! That's what they do, them guys!

ROSIE   What guys?

JOHNNY   Artists! Artists! I seen a movie one time!

ROSIE   What movie?

JOHNNY   I don't know! It was some movie with what's-his-name—him and that Vivien somebody—and her face was burnt in a fire but inside she was—no, no, it was the other—she was beautiful outside, but inside she was rotten, so the painting come out lookin' all burnt-lookin' and, and, and—how could you do this to me, Rosie?!

ROSIE   I didn't even know you! He made one painting, one time! I was in high school, and it paid better than babysittin'! Now leave me alone, you big dope!

JOHNNY   Okay, okay, so where is this thing, this painting? A museum someplace?

ROSIE   How should I know?

JOHNNY   Guys linin' up to look at *you* and laugh at *me*!

ROSIE   Doubt it's in any museum. Guy wasn't no artist. He was a doctor.

JOHNNY   A medical man?

ROSIE   A professor. Liked to paint on the side.

JOHNNY   This egghead have a name?

ROSIE   Muldoon, I think.

JOHNNY   Doctor Muldoon, huh?

ROSIE   Had a place down on Gossamer he liked to hide out from the wife and paint girls from the neighborhood.

JOHNNY   Nailing poor little butterflies to the wall, that son of a bitch!

ROSIE   Liked to call them his twins.

JOHNNY   Call who what?

[*She points to her breasts, one at a time.*]

ROSIE   Sacco. And Vanzetti. Or was it the other way around? His wife was a commie.

JOHNNY   Jesus Christ! I'm gonna. I'm. I'm goin' down there!

ROSIE   You won't find him, Johnny. Took him a job at some girls' college up in cow country. Prob'ly in heaven up there.

JOHNNY   Up where?

ROSIE   I dunno, who knows?

JOHNNY   The college, Rosie. Where's it at?

ROSIE   You ain't goin' up there.

JOHNNY   You try an' stop me!

ROSIE   You'd stand out like a thumb, place like that!

JOHNNY I can't stand it, Rosie!

ROSIE Johnny-with-a-rod-in-his-pants showin' up at a college fulla girls!

JOHNNY I don't care, I don't care! I can't stand the idea this fool got you up on the wall above of his bed! Lookin' up at you! Dreamin' of you! Makin' love wit' you!

ROSIE Okay, Johnny—

JOHNNY Havin' his old age anniversary hump wit' you 'stead of his ugly communist wife! I just can't stand it, Rosie! I can't stand it!

ROSIE Shh shh, it's okay, baby. It's okay.

JOHNNY It *ain't* okay!

ROSIE Yeah it is. Yeah. You know why? 'Cause Rosie's gonna be right by your side in this here.

JOHNNY *What?*

ROSIE You and me, Johnny—come 'ere.

[*Patting the couch.*]

Come on.

[JOHNNY *sits.*]

You an' me, we find out this college an' go up there, okay? We stay at a inn wit' quilts. We walk in the woods together. We take in the leaves, the moon, the stars. We find this Muldoon, get the painting back, bring it home here, hang it up over our bed, an' get married, huh? Whaddya say?

[JOHNNY *bursts into tears and throws his head onto* ROSIE*'s lap.*]

JOHNNY Ah, Rosie!

[ROSIE *strokes his head, soothing him.*]

ROSIE Hey, Johnny Johnny whoops Johnny whoops Johnny Johnny Johnny…Johnny?

[JOHNNY*'s asleep.*]

• • •

The Wet Echo

Clay McLeod Chapman

Clay McLeod Chapman

Clay McLeod Chapman is the creator of the rigorous storytelling session *The Pumpkin Pie Show*. His plays *Rest Area*, *Miss Corpus*, and *The Tribe* trilogy—*Homeroom Headhunters*, *Camp Cannibal*, and *Academic Assassins*—are published by Disney/Hyperion. He wrote the screenplays for *The Boy* (with Craig Macneill), *The Trouble with Dad* (with Glenn McQuaid), *Late Bloomer* (Sundance 2005), and *Henley* (Sundance 2012). His works for theater include *Commencement* and *Hostage Song* (music/lyrics by Kyle Jarrow). He has worked on the comics *The Avengers*, *Amazing Spider-Man*, *Edge of Spider-Verse*, and *Ultimate Spider-Man Adventures*. He is a writing instructor at the Actors Studio MFA Program at Pace University. Visit him at: www.claymcleodchapman.com.

··· production history ···

The Wet Echo was part of a presentation of monologues and one-act plays under the title *Nine Signs of the Times*, a benefit for New York's Nuyorican Poets Cafe's education programs, April 11–13, 2014. Technical director Samuel Chico, music by Michael Gallant, produced by Daniel Gallant, directed by Clay McLeod Chapman.

SIR EDWARD PLEASANT   Abe Goldfarb

MADAME LILITH VERMILLION   Fig Chilcott

EDWARD   The petrified remains of Frances Xavier von Schwarzenberg were discovered sitting in a perfectly upright position at the snowy peak of Mount Pelvoux. The sun-bleached bones of the late Lieutenant Benjamin Banks were discovered scattered across the sandy outback of the then-unknown *Terra Australis*, years after his expedition's disappearance into that grainy wasteland. For as long as men possess that burning urge to venture into the unknown, laying claim to that uncharted terrain wherever it may be found—there will be daredevils such as myself searching this earth, yearning to find that nameless space and call it their own. *Anonymous no more!*

Mark my words the world will remember the name of Sir Edward Pleasant!

Explorer. Pioneer. Discoverer of that final frontier!

Few dare travel where I have embarked—and none have ever returned. You will not find this incomprehensible continent on any map, for no topographer has survived the journey to detail its dimensions. It remains a most amorphous terrain, shapeless and strange, its exact latitudes still a mystery to man. I myself was not conscious of its occupancy upon this globe until Madame Lilith Vermillion exposed me to its entrance, granting me safe passage through her ivory-toned thighs—her pale legs like two lusty tusks on a most sensual elephant. And what a foreign world it is, my friends! The heat of the Amazon is nothing compared to the climate I find myself sweltering within now, possessing a density like no other. Such muggy atmospherics! Even sound seems to be hampered within this environment. When I first entered this nether-region, staring down into its darkened corridors, my initial impulse was to give a good bellow from the lungs—

Hello! Is anyone down there?

It was then, heaven help me—that I was first met with…*the wet echo.*

Helloooo. Is anyooooone down theeeere?

Such a slurpy reverberation! These were my words, yes. That was my voice, for sure. And yet, somehow—the tenor had changed, perverting itself, like a boomerang bringing back something altogether foreign from along its flight. Something *slippery.*

LILITH *Don't talk to the damn thing, Edward.*

EDWARD *Sorry—sorry.*

LILITH *Kiss it already!*

EDWARD Even my mustache has fallen prey to these soggy surroundings! The twines of my handlebar are now soaked in such a strange condensation. Sucking on my upper lip, I was stunned to discover the moisture had a tanginess to it. Thank goodness for this new world and the bizarre fruit it bears! For I have derived sustenance from its damp climate for days now. Has it been days already? Time has contorted itself into the most obscure proportions. My God—how long have I been down here?

LILITH *Don't be so bashful, Sir Pleasant. You'd think there was a continent between us.*

EDWARD *Edward—please. Call me Edward.*

LILITH *Edward?*

EDWARD *Yes, madam?*

LILITH *There's something I want to show you, Edward…*

EDWARD I first came upon the cave drawings some time ago. I have spent my days in the deeper recesses of this region, venturing further into its vast catacombs. It was merely by chance that I even discovered these primitive illustrations of some lost civilization adorning the borders beside me. These bizarre symbols seem to narrate a tale hereunto untold to man.

At first I believed I had the honor of laying claim of this land—but now I fear that this land may in fact have been laying claim to me all along.

Were Lilith only here to lead me through this tangle of intertwining tunnels. What would she think of her poor explorer now? May God forgive me for my hubris! I am finally willing to admit to myself that I am lost. Absolutely lost!

LILITH *Shall I draw you a map, Sir Pleasant?*

EDWARD *I can't seem to locate the—*

LILITH *Just keep looking, Edward.*

EDWARD *There?*

LILITH *Further up.*

EDWARD *There?*

LILITH *No—up. Up.*

EDWARD *Here?*

LILITH *There.*

EDWARD *Like that?*

LILITH *Slower. Slower…*

EDWARD *This?*

LILITH *Steady, steady. There.*

EDWARD *I can't seem to get the hang of—*

LILITH *Stop talking, Edward. Just—yes. Yes! Just like that.*

EDWARD *Like this?*

LILITH *That's it, Edward! That's it.*

EDWARD *Really now?*

LILITH *Now faster, Edward. Faster!*

EDWARD *If you say so, madam…*

LILITH *Yes, Edward! Yes! Yes! Yes!*

EDWARD I am writing now in the hopes that my words will reach the next explorer who dares enter this region. My only audience is you, dear pioneer! You—who have descended into these vast catacombs for glory! For the sake of fame! Let my story be a warning to you…I found the first bone—*a femur, I believe*—further down the corridor. I nearly tripped over its tibia, patting at the ground before coming upon the rest of the skeleton. I felt the contours of a rib, an ulna, the very metacarpals of what had been a man's hand slipping through my fingers like grains of sand. Most haunting of all, however—from the dim glow, I discovered what could only be described as the ruins of a once mighty empire. Here, before me, was a temple as monumental as any shrine the Aztecs ever erected! The number of men, the sheer amount of years it must've taken to construct such a colossal sanctuary—these ruins had been here for centuries! Right under our noses all along!

Man has no rule over this realm. Though it bears no name, though there is no flag demarcating another countryman's discovery—we were not meant for this wilderness!

What's left of me now I pray I never have to see. May sunlight never strike this sallow skin, laced in blue veins. Eyes brimming in a white blindness. Possibly a pinkness lingering within the pupil, but not a pigment more. Every last scrap of fabric hanging off the body has long since deteriorated. Now as naked as the day we were born.

The world has taken shape around us, gentlemen. The continents have all been mapped. The mountains all scaled. What undiscovered country that still remains will be explored before the end of this very century. I daresay we discoverers have become an endangered species unto ourselves.…

This has become our home now. There are many of us down here. I daresay dozens—if not hundreds of unmoored explorers. All of us lost, living in some sort of larval harmony. We're all looking for a way out! Searching blindly for our next meal, eating the weaker pioneers.

Crying out for help—the sound of our voices resonating through these channels, over and over again. Lean in and you might just hear...

The wet echo.

• • •

This Side of
New York

Caridad Svich

Caridad Svich

Caridad Svich is a playwright and translator. She received the 2013 National Latino Playwriting Award, the 2012 OBIE for Lifetime Achievement, and the 2011 American Theatre Critics Association Primus Prize. Her plays include *12 Ophelias, Iphigenia Crash Land Falls...*, and *The House of the Spirits* (based on the Isabel Allende novel). She holds an MFA in playwriting from the University of California, San Diego.

··· production history ···

This Side of New York was part of a presentation of monologues and one-act plays under the title *Nine Signs of the Times*, a benefit for New York's Nuyorican Poets Cafe education programs, April 11–13, 2014. Technical director Samuel Chico, music by Michael Gallant, produced by Daniel Gallant.

CLAIRE   Kristen Williams

HENRY   Daniel Gallant

[*Lights reveal* CLAIRE *and* HENRY. *Silence.*]

HENRY   must've been—

CLAIRE   two years ago—

HENRY   three? don't remember now.

CLAIRE   you were—

HENRY   i was—

CLAIRE   telling a story.

HENRY   isn't that what i'm supposed to do?

CLAIRE   what do you mean?

HENRY   well, i mean, isn't that what people do…here?

CLAIRE   not always.

HENRY   but most of the time.

CLAIRE   yes, but we weren't like most.

HENRY   we pretended we weren't but really—

CLAIRE   and now? what are we?

HENRY   i don't know. people.

CLAIRE   just people.

HENRY   familiar.

CLAIRE   i don't know how i feel about that.

HENRY   sorry?

CLAIRE   about being familiar. i don't think i like that.

HENRY   why? it's the best.

CLAIRE   is it?

HENRY   absolutely.

[*Pause.*]

CLAIRE   i don't get it.

HENRY   what's not to get? you know something, someone already…it makes things easier, you know. comfortable. what? you don't think—?

CLAIRE   …i'm not sure.

[*Pause.*]

HENRY   'cause it's me. is that why? you can say it. 'cause i know i was, you know…something of an asshole, but…i'm not really. i mean, i was just in a certain place then. y'know? you don't have to say it. i know. i was. definitely. asshole. i admit it. there. i've said the words.

CLAIRE   you're absolving yourself then?

HENRY   excuse me?

CLAIRE   this saying things out loud. a form of absolution?

HENRY   i'm not Catholic.

CLAIRE   i didn't say you…

HENRY   just saying the words. that's all. getting them out there. does good. in the world. don't you feel good?

CLAIRE   about what?

HENRY   oh. come on. you know what i mean. saying things. getting stuff that's inside, been inside…out. there…it makes you feel good.

[*Pause.*]

CLAIRE   why do you do that?

HENRY   huh?

CLAIRE   say words for me?

HENRY   i don't.

CLAIRE   look, i think maybe this isn't…i mean, sometimes you think one thing but then another thing…but then you're there, here and…it's clear that that thing you thought of just wasn't…what you wanted.

HENRY   huh?

CLAIRE   this. here.

HENRY   we can go somewhere else.

CLAIRE   no.

HENRY   …Claire.

CLAIRE   don't.

HENRY   what is it?

CLAIRE   you were fierce.

HENRY   i'm not fierce. i've never…

CLAIRE   …you can be.

HENRY   …you want me to be. okay. let's be fierce. let's fucking…burn everything down. come on. right here. in front of the whole world.

[*Lit match near to skin.*]

CLAIRE   what are you…?

HENRY   you think they care? those people? fuck them. they don't care. they want us to burn. so, let's give it to them. come on.

CLAIRE   what are you…?

HENRY   tits…ass…torso…lips…hard up…hard core…fuel injected…speed demons…racing to the split…

CLAIRE   are you quoting something?

HENRY   what?

CLAIRE   those aren't your words.

HENRY   words are words.

CLAIRE   that's some kind of song.

HENRY   so, maybe it's a song. so what? it's just us, we're just…whatever, capturing a thrill. times past. times spent. times dreamt about. fucking mainline on the hard line.

CLAIRE   i don't remember you like this.

HENRY   i was always like this.

CLAIRE   no. you were different.

HENRY   nice, you mean? like i sat here and told nice stories. quiet stories. stories about rabbits and fields and reading Whitman under some tree?

CLAIRE   no.

HENRY   what then? come on.

CLAIRE   [*Pulls away.*] don't…

HENRY   Claire….

[*Pause.*]

CLAIRE   …how bout we take away the familiar?

HENRY   how's that?

CLAIRE   like we never knew each other. never met. no past.

HENRY   …strangers.

CLAIRE   not necessarily. people cross each other all the time. they don't meet. but they're not strangers. they're just not familiar.

[*Pause.*]

HENRY   could make animals of each other.

CLAIRE   we are animals.

HENRY   fish.

CLAIRE   there are all kinds of possibilities.

HENRY   sometimes i think when we cross each other,
   when our glances pass and we don't say anything,
   but we look nevertheless, at how we're dressed,
   at how we're taken aback by the flutter of an eyelash, say, or how you
      sometimes look just like a boy i once knew
   when i had a past way back somewhere
   that we won't let ourselves access now
   'cause we prefer to delete things from our lives
   it's easier to live this way…in deletion. completion. comfortable, i
      suppose.
   a kind of strange comfort.
   like animals in some beautiful zoo of our own making.
   but nevertheless, sometimes i think, yes,
   when we cross each other, and our glances pass
   in this purposefully anonymous here,
   how vile you are, i think, how sublimely vile in some secretive and
      gorgeous way.
   and you see, these words, as i say them to you
   without knowing you, fish to fish, let's say,
   well, they could be mine.
   they could be completely my own thoughts
   spoken true,
   released in that out there kind of way
   i may have once described
   and yet, maybe they're someone else's words
   that i've stolen from somewhere,
   some song, some book, some dream.
   and there's no way for you to know
   whether what i say is real.
   and i suppose—what?—that makes you feel…

CLAIRE   perfect.

[*Pause.*]

HENRY   tell me. and what if i want to remember?

CLAIRE   i slap you.

HENRY tit for tat.

CLAIRE just a slap. no before to it.

HENRY just after.

CLAIRE like all stories.

HENRY bloody aftermath.

CLAIRE yes.

HENRY what if you want to remember?

CLAIRE then you…let me.
  you watch me lost in some kind of remembrance
  and you do nothing. you just wonder what might be occupying my
      mind momentarily. like we do with all those
  who drink their tall glasses of pink
  while over there some poisonous gas,
  some awful stinking mess flares up
  and destroys half a village or two
  and hundreds or thousands lose their homes
  and hands and who knows what all that gets stuffed in some
  dusty suitcase filled with blood. y'see?
  you just let me remember for a moment. that's all.
  you let me remember how my country was smashed.

[*Pause.*]

HENRY i suppose i was hoping for some kind of…

CLAIRE warm bowl in your hands?

HENRY i like your face. i've always liked your face.

[*Pause.*]

CLAIRE here.

HENRY what?

CLAIRE come here.

HENRY like we've never met.

CLAIRE   we haven't.

HENRY   which means if i said i was sorry—

CLAIRE   it wouldn't mean anything.

[*Pause.*]

HENRY   so, what do we…?

CLAIRE   kiss.

HENRY   first kiss?

CLAIRE   yes.

HENRY   we could get lost.

CLAIRE   we already are.

[*They kiss.*]

[*The whisper of Cat Power's cover of "New York, New York" is heard from some part of the somewhat restored city.*]

• • •

Alt-Visions, Kiss Before Clouding

Daniel F. Levin

Daniel F. Levin

Daniel F. Levin is delighted to rejoin with past collaborators for *Nine Signs of the Times*, first produced at the Nuyorican Poets Cafe. His play, *Hee-Haw: It's a Wonderful Life*, a counter-telling of the holiday classic from a bitter Sam Wainwright, also originated at the Nuyorican, where it was called a "delightful surprise" by the *New York Times*. Recent credits include *Spandex the Musical* (Off-Broadway, 777 Theatre), and a staged reading of *To Paint the Earth* (New Jersey Rep). Levin has held fellowships from the Dramatists Guild and MacDowell Colony and is the recipient of the Richard Rodgers Development Award for New Musicals. For more info, visit: www.levintheatricals.com.

···production history···

Alt-Visions, Kiss Before Clouding was part of a presentation of monologues and one-act plays under the title *Nine Signs of the Times*, a benefit for the Nuyorican Poets Cafe's education programs, April 11–13, 2014. Technical director Samuel Chico, music by Michael Gallant, produced by Daniel Gallant, directed by Daniel F. Levin.

GARRET ZOND   Tyler Bunch

[GARRET ZOND *sits reflectively. It's roughly seventy years after the Joining. Intro music is "Between Two Worlds" by Metrik.*]

GARRET   [*Takes a drag on electronic cigarette.*] And there was this new platform. iVision. This was something, separate, like…software? Anyone?

[*Shrugs.*]

I'm talking seventy years ago.

I got up in the morning, I kissed her shell—yes, at that point there still was under-shell…And I dropped to work…I think I was working on shrimp formula, or something, and before I came home, I imported…iVision! I got home, and all the sudden, Raven, who was, as her name maybe implies, a brunette, with very dark lashes, was, all the sudden, a redhead. And Raven had been slight and slim, but now, all the sudden, she's very curvy, she's such a…female…she *looks* to me, opposite but she's still…her. And that of course was the algorithm.

Remember, in the morning I had been seeing matter. That's why the transition, if you lived through it, was so insane!

[*Pause.*]

We put on music and talked…we had Chinese flavor at 2 a.m. We…at one point, we just looked at the solar system. We talked about where we wanted to go. We were floating all night and we didn't know where the hell we were going to land. I had brought home a crystal rose for her, and we pretended it was monitoring us, and if we didn't keep up the act that we were lovers, we would be

clouded. So I would kiss her all over. And then, after five minutes...
I'd nod to the rose, and say, "We have to kiss before clouding." And
she'd say, "We just kissed!" and I said, "They're very dull. We have to
overdo it just to convince them we're the most basic lovers!" My God,
she laughed. We ended up out on the colony lawn, in a sack, our
bodies pressed to each other, no shell, sweating, loving, heaving, and I
wanted her...so badly. And I was nervous again.

Then after a few months, I stopped being nervous. And I started to
think about black-haired Raven. She was very ironic, more so than
Red-Haired Raven, who could be kind of mushy, I thought. I missed
her.

So I went back.

Plus I still had red-haired Raven programmed. So I went back and
forth. Don't get me wrong, it was definitely confusing sometimes.
One time Black-Haired Raven pointed to the crystal flower and said,
"Kiss before clouding!" but that of course had been Red-Haired
Raven's thing, so it didn't really mean anything from Black-Haired
Raven, even though to her it did. I guess I thought that was just the
price one pays...for newness. It was so exhilarating. Even when I'd
miss one Raven, I knew she'd be back. I felt very safe, very loved, but
still excited. I felt like I could stop...searching.

But accustomization is a bitch. Does anyone even know what I mean
when I say accustomization? Alright, I'm old. So pretty soon on weeks
where I was supposed to switch from Black-Haired Raven to Red-
Haired Raven, or vice versa...no butterflies. Nothing. That was when
I went to randomization. Remember that the original iVision only
refracted on a central genetic line. But this was years later. Now it
could randomize, which I ended up doing daily...then multiple times.
So I would turn away from Raven, and turn back, and...Raven! I
mean, you can't become accustomized to that! But it was also
exhausting. I couldn't ever relax.

[*Pause.*]

I couldn't ever go to the bathroom. And there was one day, before I
set minimum holds, where I just saw, like thousands of noses, and one
giant, pulsing Cyclops eye. Even after the minimums...I missed just

having…at least for a week, my partner. I was going to end it. I decided to be with just her first image. I—I was actually in the process of extracting. I literally was going to go back to matter—

But when I got home, she had cleared out all of her things. She looked very Midwestern then—dirty blond, very sweet…and a little sad. And she just said, "I don't know who you are anymore."

"Yes you do."

She made for the door. I wasn't trying to hurt her. I blocked her. She tried to get around me, but she didn't know the room. It turns out she was using iVision for habitat variety and she couldn't see the furniture. The crystal rose pierced between her plates. The way she looked at me. The way all of them looked at me. Surprise, fear, a wince, a fluttering of eyes, then nothing.

I put her up on the cloud that night and buried her behind the pod.

I fully understand why I'm being clouded now that this is all in the open.

[*Starts to reach for a tube.*]

I do think it's important, though, to remember that there was a time when people saw each other…literally, and traveled with each other, through life, aging.

On the night she ended, I wasn't trying to hurt her. You can scan for full accuracy. I was trying to go back to loving just her. Please consider that when designing my searching "metadata."

That's all. How do we do this?

[*Lights fade to black. Music is "Give Up the Ghost" by C2C—cued to begin after the line "That's all."*]

• • •

I Didn't Want a Mastodon

Halley Feiffer

Halley Feiffer

Halley Feiffer is a playwright and actress. Full-length plays include *I'm Gonna Pray for You So Hard* (Atlantic, dir. Trip Cullman) and *How to Make Friends and Then Kill Them* (Rattlestick, dir. Kip Fagan). Her work has been developed by Second Stage, New York Theatre Workshop, LAByrinth, the Eugene O'Neill National Playwrights Conference, and elsewhere. Commissions include Keen Company, Manhattan Theatre Club, and Jen Hoguet Productions. She co-wrote and starred in the 2013 film *He's Way More Famous Than You* and co-created the web series *What's Your Emergency* (both directed by Michael Urie). She currently writes for the Starz series *The One Percent*.

···production history···

I Didn't Want a Mastodon was produced by Core Artist Ensemble at the Barrow Group Studio Theater in New York City as part of Fresh Shorts; September 21–23, 2012. Cast: Rachael Lee and Matt Mundy. Directed by Michael Padden.

It was also produced by the Nuyorican Poets Cafe in New York City as part of *Nine Signs of the Times*, April 11–13, 2014. Technical director Samuel Chico, music by Michael Gallant, produced by Daniel Gallant, directed by Christina Roussos.

DANI Diana Stahl

HENRY Sanford Wilson

Later, it was produced by IAMA Theater Company at the Three of Clubs in Los Angeles as part of IAMAfest; November 7–16, 2014. Cast: Melissa Stephens and Will Greenberg. Directed by Eli Gonda.

···

[*Lights up, abruptly, on* DANI's *apartment. It's a neatly furnished one-bedroom in New York City. In the foreground is the living room area; in the back the kitchen, separated from the living room by a counter.*]

[*On the coffee table are a pack of cigarettes, some matches, an ashtray, some candles, and a glass sculpture of a mastodon, about the size of a bread box.*]

[DANI *and* HENRY *stand on either side of the coffee table.* DANI *is an attractive but messy-looking woman in her mid- thirties; she wears yoga pants and a light scarf.* HENRY *is a sort of nebbishy-looking fellow in his late thirties; he wears glasses and a corduroy blazer.* DANI *is smoking a cigarette fiercely.* HENRY *is looking at his feet.*]

HENRY What.

DANI What *is* that.

HENRY [*Softly.*] A mastodon.

DANI [*Tight pull on cigarette.*] Uh-huh.

HENRY [*Softly.*] I blew it for you. Out of glass.

DANI [*Ashing her cigarette.*] Why did you blow me a fucking *mastodon*, Henry?

HENRY I thought—

DANI [*Interrupting him; stamping out her cigarette in the ashtray.*] You know what? Don't speak; I'm too angry to listen to you right now.

[*She crosses to the kitchen. HENRY looks at his feet, adjusts his glasses. DANI pours water into her teakettle and puts the kettle on to boil. They are both silent for some moments. Then, flatly—*]

Did you want tea.

HENRY [*Without looking up.*] Sure.

DANI Your usual kind?

HENRY Em. What kind are you having?

DANI CALMING.

HENRY [*Taken aback; then—*] All right. Then I'll have Calming too.

DANI Perfect.

[*They stand there. Silence. Then—*]

It'll just take a minute to boil.

HENRY All right.

[*Sitting down on the couch.*]

DANI I didn't say you could sit down.

HENRY [*Standing back up.*] I'm sorry.

DANI You can sit down.

HENRY [*Sitting back down.*] Thank you.

DANI No problem.

[*They sit/stand there. Silence. Then—*]

HENRY [*Looking around a bit.*] Did you do something to your apartment? It looks—bigger.

DANI Maybe it's the mastodon.

HENRY [*Laughs.*] He-he.

[*Notices DANI is not laughing.*]

Oh.

[DANI *gets two mugs out for the tea.*]

DANI   Honey?

HENRY   Yes?

DANI   Do you WANT HONEY?

HENRY   Oh. I thought—

DANI   What.

HENRY   Nothing.

DANI   What did you think? That I was calling you Honey?

HENRY   No. Yes.

DANI   [*Laughs.*] That's very funny.

HENRY   [*Giggles, despite himself.*] Heh, that rhymes.

　　[DANI *is stony-faced; then, so is* HENRY.]

　　Sorry.

DANI   Did you *want* honey? In your *tea*?

HENRY   [*Getting it.*] Oh! Ohhhh. Em, sure.

DANI   Great.

　　[*She squirts some honey from a bear-shaped plastic bottle into one of the mugs. The bear makes a farting sound as the honey is squirted.* HENRY *laughs.* DANI *stares at him. He stops laughing. She pours water from the teakettle into the two mugs.* HENRY *laughs again, nervously.*]

　　[DANI *brings the two mugs into the living room.*]

　　What are you laughing at.

HENRY   Em.

DANI   "Em"?

HENRY   Um. You know.

DANI   [*Handing* HENRY *his tea.*] I don't know. Please explain.

HENRY   Dani....

DANI [*Sitting on the couch, as far away from* HENRY *as she can.*] Henry?

HENRY Please.

DANI [*Blowing on her tea.*] Uh-huh?

HENRY Nothing.

DANI Huh.

HENRY Yeah.

[*Beat. They both blow on their tea. They each take a sip. Silence. Then, regarding the tea.*]

Thank you.

DANI For what.

HENRY The tea?

DANI You're welcome.

[*Beat.* DANI *blows, sips her tea.* HENRY *looks at* DANI.]

HENRY Why are you so mad at me?

DANI Excuse me?

HENRY Why are you so mad at me?

DANI Huh.

HENRY I mean—

DANI Really?

HENRY I mean, I know why you're mad at me.

DANI Good!

HENRY I mean, I know that; I just—if you're—I mean—I mean....The mastodon...I mean...Why...I don't know.

[*Beat. Sips of tea. Then—*]

DANI Good sentence.

HENRY [*Laughs, despite himself.*] Thanks.

DANI [*Blows on her tea.*] Why are you laughing.

HENRY [*Finally a bit exasperated.*] Because you make me laugh, Dani. Even like this, even in this—the bleakest of circumstances, the—I don't know…You make me laugh.

[*A faint trace of a smile on DANI's face. They look at each other, a beat. Soft silence. Then, softly, gently.*]

Why are you so mad at me?

DANI [*Getting up.*] Oh, Lord.

HENRY What?

DANI Here we go, playing the victim. You're always the victim, aren't you.

HENRY I don't understand.

DANI Oh, HERE we go, playing the "I Don't Understand" Game—you *never* understand, do you?

HENRY Em.

DANI Oh, HERE WE GO, playing the "Em, Em, Em" Charade—it's always, "Em, Em, Em" with you, isn't it? Why can't you just say "UM" like every other goddamn American?!

HENRY Huh.

DANI Uh-huh.

HENRY Em.

DANI Oh?

HENRY Huh.

DANI Right. That's what I thought.

[*Silence. They each take a sip of tea. Then—*]

HENRY [*Softly; gently.*] I thought you'd like it.

DANI What.

HENRY The—

DANI The *mastodon*?

HENRY [*Looking down at his lap.*] Yes.

DANI [*Blowing on her tea.*] Huh. And what would make you think that?

HENRY Em. *Um.* A couple reasons.

DANI [*Blowing harder.*] Such as?

HENRY Well. It's a mastodon.

DANI Uh-huh?

HENRY It's an unusual subject.

DANI That it is!

HENRY And I thought you might like that; you like unusual things....

DANI Huh!

HENRY That time we went to the Brooklyn Museum—

DANI [*Turning away from him.*] Oh, God.

HENRY You were drawn to the art that had the most unusual subjects....

DANI [*Turning back; bitingly.*] Oh *really*.

HENRY You were—like that pop art sculpture of a toothbrush....Or that painting of a woman who was—who was...masturbating....Interesting, unusual subjects, to see, in art....

[*Beat.*]

DANI Go on.

HENRY And...and I thought the mastodon might fit into that category.

DANI How thoughtful!

HENRY [*Ignoring her sarcasm.*] Its teeth, for instance.

DANI Do tell.

HENRY Its teeth are shaped like—well, the people, at that time, thought the teeth resembled, um, breasts? Because they're pointy, and sort of rounded? And so that's why it's called the mastodon? "Masto"—like breast, like in a mastectomy? And "don," which means tooth....

DANI [*Intrigued, despite herself.*] Huh.

HENRY And I thought that might be interesting. And also…

DANI Uh-huh?

HENRY Well. I blew it for you. And I thought that might mean something.

DANI And what would that *mean*, Henry?

HENRY Well, it might mean like I loved you, or something like that.

[*Beat.*]

DANI Well, *that's* cute.

HENRY [*Softly; almost mumbling.*] I'm not trying to be cute.

DANI [*Biting.*] Awww. Too bad. 'Cause you're so cute. You're like a cuddly little bear, you're so cute.

HENRY Please. Dani. Stop.

DANI [*Acid.*] What.

HENRY You're being cruel.

[*This stops her. She stops. A beat. She takes a sip of tea. Silence. Then, softly—*]

I love you.

DANI [*Turning away from him, heading back into the kitchen.*] Okay.

[*We see, from the back, that DANI is wiping a tear away from her eye as she walks back into the kitchen.*]

HENRY Listen, Dani—

DANI [*Whipping back around on him; exploding suddenly.*] Don't tell me to *listen*, Henry! Don't tell me to *ever listen*! Okay!? I don't *listen* to you. You *listen* to me. That's not how it goes, and you know it. Yes, we're equals, but *not* after what you did, so you *listen to me*, okay!?

[*Beat.*]

HENRY [*Taken aback; softly.*] Okay.

DANI [*Not taking her eyes off him.*] Okay.

[*She glares at him for a beat. Then, she turns and heads into the kitchen. She pours the rest of her tea down the drain, places the cup in the sink.*]

HENRY [*Not knowing what else to say.*] You're done with your tea, already?

DANI I'm not *done*, Henry; I just didn't *want* it anymore.

HENRY Oh.

DANI [*Leaning on the counter.*] It wasn't doing a very good job CALMING me.

HENRY [*Taken aback.*] All right.

[*Beat.*]

DANI Do you find that *your* tea is *calming* you?

HENRY I don't know.

DANI Then don't *judge* me for how *my* tea affected *me*, okay?

HENRY Okay.

DANI Okay. Good.

[*Beat. Then DANI comes back into the living room. She sits on the couch, as far away from HENRY as she can manage. A beat. DANI exhales. Then—*]

Listen. I'm s—I'm—sorry. You did something terrible, terrible, *terrible*, and I can't forgive you for that and I won't, but, that said, you're right, I'm being cruel. So. I own that. I accept that. I'm gonna try not to be. I don't like being like that....

[*Wipes another tear off the corner of her eye.*]

So I'll try not to be. For me. Not for you. Just—for me. Because I don't like myself when I'm like that.

[*Wipes a tear off the corner of her other eye.*]

HENRY It's okay.

DANI I don't need you to say it's okay; I just need you to know that I'm aware that I'm acting somewhat—that I could be acting—*calmer*, so to speak.

[*Beat.*]

That's why I chose that tea.

[*Beat.*]

But it didn't work.

[*Beat.*]

I think those calming teas are all bullshit, actually.

[*Beat.*]

Also I haven't done my yoga practice in two days and I think it's really getting to me.

[*Beat.*]

I don't know, I'm just—*off*. So. Just. This isn't. You know I'm not.

[*She cries.*]

Oh, God....

[*A beat.* HENRY *doesn't know what to do, say. They both sit there. Silence, aside from* DANI*'s crying. Then—*]

HENRY   Can I tell you the real reason I wanted to blow that mastodon for you?

DANI   I don't know.

HENRY   Please?

DANI   [*Wiping away tears; sniffling; sitting up straighter.*] Okay. Fine.

[*Beat.* HENRY *smiles.*]

HENRY   It's because I listened to what you told me.

DANI   [*Sniffling; wiping; softly.*] And what was that.

HENRY   About how I needed to find some new activities. In my sobriety.

[*Beat.* DANI *is moved, despite herself; tries not to show it.*]

DANI   Oh?

HENRY   Yes. And this was one of them.

[*Beat.*]

DANI Blowing glass?

HENRY Yes. I've been taking a glass-blowing class for over a year now. It's what I do on Wednesday nights.

DANI No, you—I thought—

HENRY I know, you thought I went to a men's meeting, but if you look in the Meeting Book, you'll see, there is no men's meeting on Wednesday nights in our neighborhood; I don't even know if there's one in all of New York City. But there's a glass-blowing class, down at the New School, and that's where I learned to blow glass, and finally, to make sculptures, like this. It was our final project, to do anything we wanted. And we had made vases and ornaments and even a sculpture of a small bird. But this is what I wanted to do. And I asked the teacher if it was all right and he said fine, just as long as I thought I could handle it, and I told him I was nervous but that I thought I could, that I was making it for the most special person in my life, for my dear dear dear loving wonderful sweet kind compassionate adorable sweet sweet friend Dani, and he said Then go ahead, make a mastodon, and I said Okay I will, because I had told him I wanted to maybe make a mastodon for you because I had recently read that Harvard had a 12,000-year-old mastodon in one of its museums, and I just loved that word—*mastodon*—it just intrigued me, I don't know; it sounded important and yet also silly, and when I found out why it was called that, you know, about the—breast teeth, I just—I giggled so much; I thought it was so funny; it reminded me of you. And I knew I wanted to blow *something* for you, and I thought that might be a good subject, so I researched the mastodon and I found what it looked like and I thought it was sort of majestic and yet also kinda goofy, and I thought, I don't know, that you'd sorta get a kick out of it, and I thought it'd look really nice here on your coffee table, and it does. So I made it, and this was before—well, you know…I mean, I didn't make it so you'd forgive me; I mean, I made it just out of—love…for you.…Not like as a consolation, gift…or something.…But it took six weeks and it was very challenging and I'm not saying that so that you'll feel bad for me and forgive me; I just want you to know a lot of work went into it, a lot of blood and sweat and even tears, I cried a couple times, thinking of you, and thinking of your face when you saw it, and imagining what your reaction might be, and I smiled, and I cried, with gratitude, for my friendship with you, for knowing you, for my Higher Power having brought you into my life, how grateful I was to know you and be able to be near you almost every day and watch you and listen to you and learn from you, how fortunate I am to have a friend like you whom I so admire, who I'd give anything to be more like, to have qualities you have like your strength and your wisdom and your compassion—your ability to give of yourself to others as if you were giving to yourself, your hours and hours you spend in service with others, giving freely of what has been given to you, and your tenderness, and your capacity for gratitude, yourself, how you never take anything for granted, how you are always thankful and so humble, when you receive a compliment, how you are always so gracious and humble, all these things, and so many more, so many, many more, I admire so much about you. And I thought all these things while I made the mastodon, I blew and shaped and I thought about you, and I cried with gratitude. And in this last week, of course, I cried the most, I cried the most, to think of what I did, what a silly, stupid, foolish and irrevocable mistake I made, and how the worst part was the people whom it affected, and most of all you, the one person I admire most of anyone I have met in this rather lonely city, and really of all the people I've met in this rather lonely world, and how I hurt you, my one dear lovely loving sweet true friend, how I've hurt you and I am so, so sorry, I can't tell you how sorry I am, except to give you this mastodon.

[*Beat.*]

DANI   Thank you.

HENRY   You're welcome.

[*She comes closer to him. She leans in, slowly, and kisses him on the cheek.*]

DANI   [*Soft; close to him.*] I can't say I forgive you.

HENRY   I understand.

DANI   But I'm softened by what you've said.

HENRY   I'm glad.

DANI   Now please get the fuck out.

HENRY   Really?

DANI   Just kidding; wanna fuck?

HENRY   Really?

DANI   Just kidding; I don't know—where do we go from here?

HENRY   I don't know; maybe we eat breakfast?

DANI   I don't know; I feel like I should kick you out actually.

HENRY   Really? Why?

DANI   Because it's nice that you apologized and that was a very moving speech you just made and I do like this mastodon very much and I do appreciate how much work you put into it and I can see how much you love me and how bad you feel about what you did, but you did sleep with my A.A. sponsor, so I don't really know if it's a great idea for me to whip up some eggs and bacon for us and enjoy a nice hot breakfast with you while we watch the freshly falling snow, you know?

[*Beat.*]

HENRY   [*Getting up.*] All right.

DANI   Wait, where are you going?

HENRY   I'm gonna leave.

DANI   Oh.

HENRY   Isn't—isn't that what you want me to do?

DANI   [*Starts to cry again.*] I don't know!

[*She cries; it is sad and pathetic. HENRY approaches her, gently, and very, very gently takes her in his arms. She lets him. She collapses into his arms. She digs her fingers into him. He lets her. She wails. He listens. He strokes the back of her head. She lets him. Some moments. Then sniffling—*]

Let's just go get drunk.

[*Beat. Pulling away.*]

Just kidding.

[*She wipes her nose with her hand. They look at each other. She takes a drag of her cigarette, exhales. Then they lunge for each other, devour each other ferociously in a passionate kiss. They kiss and kiss and kiss. They make their way down to the couch. DANI stubs out her cigarette in the ashtray while still devouring HENRY with her lips. They begin to undress each other, hungrily. DANI rips off HENRY's blazer; HENRY tears off DANI's scarf and shirt. DANI moves down to HENRY's feet, kisses his ankles as she tries to get one of his shoes off. She finally wrenches it off, and it goes flying!—Into the mastodon. The mastodon falls to the ground and shatters. A beat. They stop what they are doing. They turn. A beat.*]

HENRY Em.

DANI Huh.

HENRY Well.

DANI Wow.

HENRY Huh.

DANI Yeah.

HENRY I—I…

DANI Huh…

[DANI *turns to* HENRY.]

DANI & HENRY I am so, so—

DANI Don't.

> [HENRY *puts a finger on her lips, gently. He kisses her, sweetly, softly, lusciously. She falls into the kiss. Then—they break away. A beat. Then* DANI *rises, crosses to the shattered mastodon on the floor. Inspects it. She picks up a piece.*]

This piece was preserved pretty well.

HENRY What is it?

[*A beat.* DANI *inspects it.*]

DANI I think it's—the breast…tooth…

HENRY [*Smiles.*] Perfect.

> [DANI *returns to the couch, holding the breast-tooth. She hands it to* HENRY; *he looks at it, turning the breast-tooth over in his hands.*]

I'll take it to class next week and put a hole in it and then we can put a string thought it and use it as a Christmas ornament.

DANI [*Beams.*] That's a great idea.

HENRY It's almost Christmas.

DANI Our first Christmas together.

HENRY [*Somewhat wistful, all of a sudden.*] Our mastodon never got to see a Christmas.

DANI [*Moved.*] Our mastodon?

HENRY [*Smiles; strokes* DANI's *hair.*] Our.

[*A beat. He sets the breast-tooth down on the table. A beat. He looks at* DANI, *adoring her. She loves him back with her eyes. Then—*]

DANI What do we do now?

[*A beat.*]

HENRY [*Smiles.*] We clean it up.

[*A beat. They smile. Then they both get on their hands and knees and begin picking up the pieces of the mastodon, smiling.*]

• • •

iBaby

Laura Shaine Cunningham

Laura Shaine Cunningham

Laura Shaine Cunningham leads a diversified life as an author, playwright, and journalist. She is the author of nine published books, including two acclaimed bestselling memoirs, *Sleeping Arrangements* and *A Place in the Country*. Both memoirs first appeared in the *New Yorker* magazine and were excerpted in the *New York Times* and the *London Times*. She is the winner of many awards, including two NEA grants, two NYFA fellowships, a Yaddo fellowship, and a Ford grant. Her plays are widely produced and anthologized. *Beautiful Bodies* leads a dual life as a play and a novel.

··· production history ···

iBaby was part of a presentation of monologues and one-act plays under the title *Nine Signs of the Times*, a benefit for the Nuyorican Poets Cafe's education programs, April 11–13, 2014. Technical director Samuel Chico, music by Michael Gallant, produced by Daniel Gallant, directed by Laura Shaine Cunningham.

DOULA   Daniela Dakich

MEL   Maja Wampuszyc

cast

2 F or 1 F, 1 M

MEL, pregnant, faces the ultimate challenge of birth.

DOULA, midwife (can also be M).

EXPECTANT MOTHER

···

[*Midnight, at the Steve Jobs Memorial Birthing Center. A fluorescent-lit birthing room, outfitted with a birth table, angled like a dentist's chair but with widespread foot stirrups for the pregnant woman and a stool for the birthing assistant, in this case a DOULA to crouch to deliver the baby. Enter, huffing, puffing, holding her back, is the pregnant woman, MEL, a pretty woman in her thirties, about to deliver prematurely. MEL is very stressed; she doesn't "show" much pregnancy, just a "baby bump" under her spandex. DOULA wears surgical scrubs and latex gloves: She is calm and prepared to do her professional duty; no matter what happens, no matter how unusual the birth.*]

DOULA   Remember your breathing. Count the breaths. Breathe with me and everything will be fine.

[*She demonstrates Lamaze breathing.*]

MEL   I didn't expect to go into labor…I thought I had a month to go…everyone said I look small…for eight months.

DOULA   Not for your body type, for this type of pregnancy….

MEL   I really worked out the whole time. Crunches. Leg lifts. I ran. I swam. I went to the gym. I want to be in shape even right after the birth….

DOULA You will be! This should be a relatively easy birth.

MEL You can tell that? I feel weird....Like my pelvic bones...are creaking...and a strange liquid came spilling out of me....On the subway. At 14th Street. I was so lucky, it stopped right here...and you answered your cell phone....

DOULA Of course, I answered my cell phone. Actually, I wasn't surprised to hear from you....I had a feeling you would go into labor about now.

MEL [*Panting.*] Wait...another contraction! Should I push?

DOULA No. No. Not yet. Get in the chair. You might have a spontaneous delivery...we never know....

MEL A spontaneous delivery? What's that?

DOULA When the baby just pops out...they often fall into the toilet bowl.

MEL What an entry.

[MEL *undergoes another contraction.*]

DOULA Breathe, breathe, breathe! I am going to see how dilated you are....Please get on the obstetrical chair....

[*With effort,* MEL *climbs on.*]

MEL OUCH! Whew—

[*A breath.*]

That was a nasty one. But everyone says it is worth it—when you hold your baby afterward. And God knows, I want this baby! I am lucky to get her, I know that!

DOULA The conception wasn't so difficult.

MEL Thanks to you. But I wasn't entirely happy it was *artificial.*...I tried the old way, so many times, and it just wasn't happening so I googled "How to Get Pregnant Fast" and I saw your website—that you both implant and deliver, I thought—"This is my chance. One-stop shopping..." and you take Visa and MasterCard. And the donor's profile was so terrific—"brilliant, accomplished in electronics" There seemed like nothing he couldn't do. But you know…I did have a little affair the night after you inseminated me…just to add a bit of human desire to the mix. And I kept up some pretty heated exchanges in e-mail and on the phone.…I wanted to be in a state of estrous.…I understand that improved my chances to start and maintain a pregnancy.…

DOULA   No question.…The hormones probably helped a lot. The lubrication, the contractions of orgasm…speeding the sperm to implant and embed…then the cells to grow…and multiply. Think of all that input, helping this baby come into the world.…Truly a little miracle baby.

[DOULA *is examining her, and* MEL *reacts, with small cries of pain and sensitivity.*]

MEL   Omigod, that hurts. I don't think I can get this out.

DOULA   Of course you can. No one has ever *not* delivered! Just remember—the pain ends and you have a baby. Ooooh…you are dilated enough *but* I think the baby turned sideways and you may have a breech.…

MEL   Do something. I can't go on like this.

DOULA   I don't like forceps…they can do so much damage.

MEL   Right now, all I care about is getting this out. Do what you have to do. Tell me I can push.…

DOULA   Alright, I think I turned it enough…now PUSH. PUSH. PUSH. It is alright to grunt, to let go. To make rude sounds! This is natural birth and I have seen and heard it all before…! It's crowning…your baby is crowning.…One more big push and we have her.…

MEL   Awwwghhhh!

[MEL *keeps screaming.*]

DOULA   Scream. It's helping! Okay…I got her.…

[*A ring tone sounds. Maurice Chevalier singing "Thank Heaven for Little Girls."* DOULA *catches the baby and wraps her in a receiving blanket or towel.*]

MEL   Oh my God.…Is she alright? Does she have all her fingers and toes?

DOULA   She has everything she needs. She is the best baby I have ever seen! So tiny and light.…Let me get her score. One ounce, three inches long, responds to touch…a perfect ten on the Apgar scale.

MEL   One ounce, three inches? That's so tiny. You're joking. That's her hand measurement or something?

DOULA   She is tiny but perfect…and she is all *pink*.

MEL   Let me see her. Put her on my breast. I have to see her.

[DOULA *shows her the baby*.]

MEL   [*Screaming*.] This isn't a baby…it's a cell phone.

[*Cell phone starts to cry, a baby cry*.]

DOULA   She is your iBaby. The latest model. A smart baby. You are so lucky! Your iBaby phone, LG-1 , first generation, combines a mobile phone, a widescreen iPad, with the retinal eye—pioneering revolutionary software you control with your fingers.…You can watch hi-definition movies not just with her but on her.…*Awww*…LG-1 [*Little Girl 1*.] is crying for her mama. Hold her. She wants a cuddle and she wants you to put on her little cover…it is best to keep her swaddled.…

[*Baby crying with musical tones*.]

MEL   This is ridiculous. I gave birth to a cell phone? How? Why? What was in that syringe? It was supposed to be…sperm.…

DOULA   Well, it came frozen from Steve Jobs.…It is guaranteed to be brilliant. You are so lucky, really—you won't have to bother with diapers, feedings.…You don't have to hear her cry at night, you can put her on "mute."

MEL   I wouldn't mind diapers and feedings. You mean I had a cell phone in my womb for the past eight months?

DOULA   Yes.…Let me program her…and

[*Cutesy sing-song*.]

what are you naming your baby?

MEL   Nothing. Send it back.

DOULA   We can't. It was special order. Pick her up for God sake.

MEL   No. I'll…I'll put it up on eBay.

DOULA   No one wants a used cell phone that has been up your uterus for eight months. Aside from that, she comes pre-programmed only to respond to your touch. You really are lucky. She will be a help instead of a dependent. Just think: no babysitter, no nanny, no expensive private schools…no college tuition. You just upgrade every year.…You have a Great Life Plan with Verizon Wireless. You are on the Verizon Wireless iBaby Plan for eighteen years, during which you are responsible for her maintenance.…

[*iBaby cries, buzzes.*]

Uh-oh, I am seeing a foreign program here that inserted a corrupt file. You said you slept with a man?

MEL   Yes…I slept with a man. I met him in a chat room; he seemed promising…then his e-mails became…increasingly erotic…and disturbing and I blocked him.

DOULA   You have to tell me, be honest—I see here that he said he felt "so wonderful when he penetrated you"?

MEL   Oh God. Hey, I deleted that…!

DOULA   Oh, Mel…I am also an electronic doula, I can retrieve everything. It's right here, on March 1…three calls and…more.… Admit, admit it…what did he do to you on March 1, at 7 p.m. and again at 11:30 p.m.? *And would you please pick up your baby?*

MEL   [*Burning with shame.*] He texted me. You mean you can get pregnant from being texted?

DOULA   You sure can…but I think there is more you need to tell me, if I am to reprogram your iBaby?

[*The following dialogue takes the heightened form of a courtroom drama,* DOULA *interrogating a reluctant witness,* MEL.]

MEL   I am too ashamed to tell you. It was his idea, not mine. He told me to…to place my phone between my legs…at my *you know*, actually, and then he called and well, yes…of course, the heat and vibration made me more receptive.…

DOULA   And then?

MEL   You know what happened then…I…I listened to this idiot, this creep, this perv and…

DOULA   And what happened then?

MEL   I don't want to say. It wasn't my idea! I would never have thought of such a thing!

DOULA   What happened then?

MEL   You must know?! Alright.…It…it rang…it rang inside me.

DOULA   Text or voice? And what did that cause to happen?

MEL   [*Low, ashamed.*] Voice.

DOULA   And what did the voice say?

MEL   I don't want to repeat it. At first, it was just…obscene.

DOULA   Don't be ashamed. We all get carried away. And what did the Voice say within you?

MEL   I said…I said it was…obscene…but then…then…it said, "I …I love you."

DOULA   [*Hurriedly to get to the next interrogatory question.*] It's alright, you don't have to repeat the obscene part—it said it loved you and then, then what happened? You had an orgasm, did you not?

MEL   I wouldn't call *that* an orgasm.…It was an internal shuddering fall, a…a cataclysm of metal and plastic and flesh such as I have never known; the bone cage within me, rattled…then…a series of electric shocks—sparks! I couldn't tell pleasure from pain.

DOULA   Sometimes, they are the same. Admit it, for the first time in years, you came!

MEL   No! Something entered and something left!—*It was cyber rape. I knew getting texted was trouble and now this.*

DOULA   You say that…after the fact. Come on, Mel. You took a big bite out of "the Apple," you gave in to Little Mac.…

[*Her voice turns Biblical. She is talking about her God, her Jesus.*]

He went unto you and the software and the soul were one.

[*Sigh.*]

MEL   [*Whimpering.*] Make it go back the way it was before I went on Gmail. I don't understand this.…It frightens me. It's like those "abductions" when you get probed by aliens.…

DOULA   We don't have to wait for "aliens" now.…

MEL   It…but it is happening now. To me. Inside me. I was raped by Google, and it inserted its worm, its virus into me. And now, I am forced to bear his/its offspring.…Can't you do a "system restore"?

DOULA   Don't worry, Mel. It's not so bad. I am installing a firewall in your uterus now so no other alien system can implant. And I have the technology to reprogram your iBaby and she will be just like you in every way except her appearance.…*She needs you to hold her, touch her NOW.*

MEL   Yeah, but how can she proceed in life? And look after her old mother when the time comes? The way I looked after mine.

DOULA   Don't worry, she can learn all she needs to know to succeed— she will surpass you by light-years…and save you the usual college tuition costs…by eighteen, all the kids are cell phones anyway…so you are no worse off than the other mothers, except you have the smartest phone and she will have invested for you and obtained incredible assets.…In your old age, she can hire home aides, buy you into assisted living. Whatever it takes. You have nothing to fear…and…

[*Her voice softens.*]

She is programmed to love…and needs your love.…

[*iBaby cries, a soft melodic cry.*]

MEL   She has a sweet ring tone.…

[*She takes the wrapped cell phone, cradles her, rocks her, kisses her.*]

[MEL *sings.*]

"Hush, little Baby, don't you cry…Mama's going to buy you…"

[*The music plays, the song accompanying* MEL *as she sings to her iBaby.*]

[*Fade to black.*]

• • •

Diminished Then Augmented

Daniel Gallant

Daniel Gallant

Daniel Gallant is the Executive Director of the Nuyorican Poets Cafe, as well as a writer, producer, actor, and teacher. He previously served as the Director of Theater and Talk Programming at the 92nd Street Y's Makor and Tribeca centers. He has produced theater and music events at venues including Summerstage, Town Hall, Brooklyn Museum, Joe's Pub, Abrons Arts Center, and the DR2 Theater. His work has been featured in the *Wall Street Journal*, the *New York Times*, *Crain's New York*, the *Daily News*, and the *New York Post*; on MTV, NBC, NY1, CBS, Univision, the BBC; and in anthologies from Vintage Books, TCG, and Applause.

···production history···

Diminished Then Augmented was part of a presentation of monologues and one-act plays under the title *Nine Signs of the Times*, a benefit for the Nuyorican Poets Cafe's education programs, April 11–13, 2014. Technical director Samuel Chico, music by Michael Gallant, produced by Daniel Gallant, directed by Daniel Gallant.

TANGLE   Tyler La Marr

CARDIZ   Edward Columbia

GURBIN   Daniel Gallant

A subsequent film version of the play featured Brian MacDonald in the role of Tangle, with Edward Columbia and Daniel Gallant reprising their roles from the premiere.

characters

CARDIZ

GURBIN

TANGLE

···

[*Lights rise on* CARDIZ; *he sprawls in a chair, with* GURBIN *standing at his side.*]

CARDIZ   So where is this guy?

GURBIN   You're awaiting Tangle. He's going to ask and you're going to answer.

CARDIZ   Tangle? He's that prick in the hat?

GURBIN   Yeah—but what a hat.

CARDIZ   I hear it never leaves his head—man even sleeps with it—and never takes his shades off, never answers the phone, never moves from the corner.

[*Pause.*]

They also say he bets the over/under. Like religiously.

GURBIN   If all you heard is true, and even if it ain't, I'm sure he has his reasons.

CARDIZ I'm used to more responsive guys.

GURBIN He ain't our usual. He came down from somewhere northern, made a name and built some books.

CARDIZ He fly the family flag?

GURBIN He does now. Freelance, but I'm told he's loyal.

CARDIZ I'll believe it when.

GURBIN He want a slice of deep dish?

[*Pause;* GURBIN *yells toward the corner.*]

I said, "He want a slice of deep dish?"

[TANGLE *enters, wearing a hat and shades. He is quiet and watchful. He surveys the room.* GURBIN *is quiet, hulking, and jacketed.* CARDIZ *defiantly lounges at the small table, under a single light.* TANGLE *approaches* CARDIZ.]

CARDIZ You the fuck in charge?

[TANGLE *doesn't answer. Casually removes his hat, takes a seat across the table, hat in lap.*]

TANGLE You want a drink? Seltzer? Beer?

CARDIZ Nope. Don't want for nothing.

TANGLE You best be sure. That drink's the last thing we're giving you. From then on, it's going to be you giving us everything.

[*A pause.*]

CARDIZ Sprite with lime.

[GURBIN *departs to fill the order.*]

TANGLE Most people are honest most of the time. Dishonesty is stressful, and stress causes a physical reaction. You must know all this, because you seem very confident.

CARDIZ Yup.

TANGLE For a while, money was disappearing. We couldn't figure out how. The best minds in the cartel and the wisest consultants were assigned to plug the leak, or to find its source—even just a cessation of theft would have been a blessing. But for the life of them, the boss and all his counselors couldn't figure out the problem.

CARDIZ   Where's my soda?

TANGLE   So they called me. I'm not with the Family. I'm from another place, up north, less noisy. I'm very focused.

CARDIZ   Where's my soda?

TANGLE   I don't recall—what sort of soda did you want?

CARDIZ   I said Sprite with lime.

[*Pause.*]

TANGLE   When I enter an interrogation room, I may have had a fight or lost a lover or won the lottery, but I leave all of that outside. I only bring my hat, my focus, and my strategy into the room with me.

CARDIZ   It true you always bet the over/under?

TANGLE   I don't always anything—that's how you lose a fortune.

CARDIZ   Why the fuck am I here?

[*Long pause.*]

TANGLE   Let's call the boss by his name. I can do that, I'm an outsider. Let's call him Bondola. All of Bondola's staff and dozens of his freelancers, they knew Bon was terribly concerned about the leak, the theft, the missing revenue. They let their fear of Bondola influence their investigations, so they overlooked some subtle leads. I didn't give a crap about Bondola's priorities, and I'm not in his pocket.

CARDIZ   You don't work for Bondola? I wondered why the fuck I'm here, but why the fuck *you* here?

TANGLE   I have some theories, about cartel structure, best practices, oversight, workflow. I proposed to Bondola that I try out these theories when he has a lost cause or a worst-case scenario. I trade my expertise for the right to experiment.

CARDIZ   So which am I, lost cause or worst case?

TANGLE I think perhaps I see a small chink in your armor. Look at my eyes—they're dead. Yours are trembling. You don't like the sound of Bondola's name. It burns you just a bit, huh?

[*Pause.*]

Bondola's crew was eager to please, so they looked for complex answers that were pleasing and ignored simple answers that were unpleasant. No such bias clouds my outlook. You're the nephew.

CARDIZ Of who?

TANGLE Of who. You tell me. Name all your uncles and your aunts.

CARDIZ I want my soda.

[*Pause.*]

TANGLE Aunts Jenine, Suzanne, Maria, Margaret. Uncles Vernon, Roman, James, Bernard. Who am I forgetting?

CARDIZ Fuck knows. I ain't met a person you just named.

TANGLE Maria raised you when your mom ran south with a mechanic, and Jenine taught you to read.

CARDIZ Don't know.

TANGLE Roman taught you to box, so Bernard wouldn't fuck you up. It's okay if you got water in your eyes. Let's call 'em allergies.

[CARDIZ *shrugs, crying silently.*]

CARDIZ James beat Maria, till I interceded, put James in the ER with a roundhouse.

TANGLE And yet none of these aunts or uncles is your most important relative. The one you emulated, one whose name kept your chin high when every punk at PS18 roughed you up, then when you fought back at school and did time in juvie. The name you could have always shouted in a bar brawl or a drug bust or in solitary, but you never did because you meant to make it on your own, because you knew they'd call you weak if you cried out for help.

[CARDIZ *looks at the ceiling, shoulders heaving.*]

CARDIZ   I did my time, I met one of Bondola's lieutenants in the joint, I didn't let on my connection, I impressed the guy with my talents and my personality. He hired me for a crew, and a week after I was released, I worked a job. I did so well, the crew met with Bondola afterwards. He raised a glass of bubbly, and we all raised ours, and I waited for his praise and congratulations. He walked right by me. Didn't say a word, or look my way, or mention me or pat me on the back. He hugged my jail pals, complimented his own lieutenant, acted like I wasn't even there.

[CARDIZ *hides his eyes with both hands.*]

TANGLE   And that's when you began to steal from your uncle Bondola.

CARDIZ   Fuck.

TANGLE   The irony, kid, is that Bon knew exactly who you were, realized precisely what you'd done for him and understood the sacrifices you had made to get on that crew without using his name. But that champagne reception was the next-level test, to see how well you'd handle yourself when he was in the room with all of his lieutenants. And you cracked.

CARDIZ   What the fuck?

TANGLE   You wanted overt praise when your rank and accomplishments did not yet merit them. You disciplined yourself so well for so long, but you cracked at the most crucial moment.

CARDIZ   Fucking Bondola could have fucking said a word of praise. He ain't never once acknowledged me.

TANGLE   In public? No. In private, regularly. Your crew members knew you were Bon's nephew. Everyone knew. That's why they overlooked you when they started hunting for the thief.

CARDIZ   [*In disbelief.*] That's not—how…

TANGLE   You never heard that he acknowledged you to his troops? Such a loss and such a pity.

CARDIZ   [*Croaking.*] Where's my soda?

GURBIN [*Appearing from the shadows.*] Here, motherfucker.

[GURBIN *yanks* CARDIZ'*s head back and pours the contents of a soda can down the suspect's throat.* CARDIZ *struggles, but* GURBIN *has* CARDIZ'*s shoulders pinned against the seat. The soda spills all over* CARDIZ, *the table, and the floor. Once the can runs dry, the guard shoves* CARDIZ *forward onto the table, yanks his hair back so he stares at* TANGLE.]

We shared with you, now you share with us. Where's the capital you stole from your uncle?

[*Lights shift;* TANGLE *sits with* GURBIN *an hour later.*]

TANGLE You didn't have to douse him with his drink. Now we won't know if the confession was for real. He made it under duress.

GURBIN [*Laughing.*] He made it under my fist.

[TANGLE *is silent;* GURBIN *sobers up.*]

I hear you, Tangle, but you can't expect us to give up on tried and true methodology just because you're from a different neck of the woods.

TANGLE Your tried and true don't work. How many times you followed up on a confession you retrieved that way and found it to be false?

GURBIN Fuck if I know.

[*Pause; he reflects.*]

Often. But sometimes it gives us useable intelligence.

TANGLE Let me try something on you. Gurbin, you are banished from the cartel unless you cough up the name of the driver who jacked a delivery of gears on Tuesday.

GURBIN How the fuck'd you know about that?

TANGLE You're banished unless you name the name.

GURBIN Fuck. It was someone or other. Gregory Filanpre.

TANGLE And if I followed up that lead, I'd find out that Gregory wasn't even in the car because he's laid up on meds at his brother's house from a tactical mistake he made during a previous hit that wasn't sanctioned by Bondola.

GURBIN Fine, I lied. Because you ain't Bondola and you ain't gonna kick me out of fuck-all. A real threat would produce a real answer.

[*After a pause,* TANGLE *methodically unzips his jacket and draws a handgun from an interior pocket. Tangle shoots near* GURBIN's *feet, and* GURBIN *jumps back. Then* TANGLE *aims for* GURBIN's *head.*]

TANGLE You mean nothing to me, and the loss of you would cost me zero. Who was the driver?

GURBIN Fuck. You're one crazy fuck. The driver. Fucking…Bizra Tim drove the car.

TANGLE Wrong.

[TANGLE *shoots near* GURBIN's *feet,* GURBIN *jumps again, and* TANGLE *aims again for* GURBIN's *head.*]

You ruined my interrogation of Bondola's nephew. Your value to the cartel is plunging. Shall I continue?

GURBIN [*Shivering.*] It was Bizra drove the car.

TANGLE You're trying to work out an angle from which you could win my gun.

[TANGLE *shoots to* GURBIN's *right side.*]

You aren't going to tell me who really drove it, are you?

GURBIN I fucking told you! Bizra drove it! Why you got to shoot me up?

[TANGLE *raises his gun to* GURBIN's *head.*]

You won't tell me who really drove that car, because the fact is, you don't know. Had you owned up to not knowing, you would not be in this high-stakes situation. But under duress, you tell me what you think I want to hear. You give me two false names because you think a name will satisfy me. This is how others respond to your violence, so this is how you respond to mine. But you don't know who drove the car. You don't know because the driver…was me.

[TANGLE *looks at* GURBIN *and fires.*]

[*Lights down.*]

• • •

Old Boyfriend

Neil LaBute

Neil LaBute

Neil LaBute writes for both stage and screen (big and small). His works include *Bash*, *Mercy Seat*, *The Shape of Things*, *The Distance from Here*, *Fat Pig*, *Autobahn*, *This Is How It Goes*, *Reasons to Be Pretty*, *In the Company of Men*, *Your Friends & Neighbors*, *Some Velvet Morning*, *The Money Shot*, *Ten X Ten*, *Full Circle*, *Reasons to Be Happy*, *In a Dark Dark House*, *Dirty Weekend*, and the upcoming *Billy & Billie* and *The Way We Get By*.

··· production history ···

Old Boyfriend was part of a presentation of monologues and one-act plays under the title *Nine Signs of the Times*, a benefit for the Nuyorican Poets Cafe's education programs, April 11–13, 2014. Technical director Samuel Chico, music by Michael Gallant, produced by Daniel Gallant, directed by Rajendra Maharaj.

WOMAN   Kaitlyn Schirard

···

[*A* WOMAN *in her twenties looking at us.*]

WOMAN   I saw an old boyfriend yesterday. It was probably—no, that's not right. It was the day *before* yesterday. Two days ago now. That's when I saw him.

[*Beat.*]

I shouldn't make it sound like it was some sort of . . . it wasn't a *reunion* or that kind of thing . . . it was just this little moment. Kind of like a . . .

[*Beat.*]

He was driving and we were both stopped at a light and I was sitting there, I'm glancing down at my phone—not texting or anything like that, I promise you I wasn't, I try not to do that because it really is dangerous, terribly dangerous, and I know a girl who died that way. In college. Texting. She wasn't doing it but she was reading one that was sent to her. Just going along in her little car . . . she had one of those Mazda Miatas, which are just tiny . . . and she looked down to check a text she received (this has all been verified by the police) and she flipped her car on a bad turn about twenty miles out of town. Right over on its hood, and that killed her instantly . . . not certain if she had the top on or not but I'm not sure that would've mattered—Karen had a soft top convertible, not the hard shell type, so there wasn't really any hope for her after she did that. She died. Because of a text that some guy she was going with at the time sent to her. You know what it said? "I DON'T KNOW."

[*Beat.*]

No, I'm not saying…I *do* know what it said, I'm not being coy…it said those words: I DON'T KNOW. He was responding to something she had written to him earlier in the day…like, four hours earlier when he was in class, and he was just answering her back right then, and he wrote: "I DON'T KNOW." The authorities tracked down on her phone what she'd asked him and it was this. She had written to him—they'd only been out maybe three times together, and she had texted him this: "SO, DO YOU LIKE ME OR NOT?" Karen had just put it out there…which was *so* like her…and asked the guy where they stood and that's what he wrote her back. The truth. I DON'T KNOW.

[*Beat.*]

Of course no one's sure if she ever read the thing…if she actually saw what he wrote to her…but she did receive it. She did *click* on it. So who knows? I've always wanted to believe she didn't read it…that she died just trying to hold her phone and drive and it was an accident that was stupid and should've been avoided but I don't know for sure. No one does. There's just too many other things that might be true if she did see that text…stuff that I don't want to be real or want to have happened, if in fact she actually knew how that guy felt. You know? Because Karen used to *really* fall hard for people—boys—and I don't know what she might've done if she put herself out there like that with someone and then they wrote back to her "I DON'T KNOW." I don't wanna believe that she would've…you know…but anything's possible and I also don't want to put that on *him*. That kind of guilt for having written what was probably just the truth—the truth based on him and her and how long they'd been dating at that point—and who wants to carry that around for the rest of their life? Not him. I'm sure he wouldn't want to. Not me, either.

[*Beat.*]

But I suppose I do. A little…

[*Beat.*]

See, the reason he was unsure about whether he had any feelings for Karen was because at that same moment he was dating another girl. *Me.* Obviously. I mean, obviously you've figured that out by now…or just did. And I knew that she liked him and that meeting guys—or *keeping* guys, really, keeping them was more specifically her problem—but I was young and I didn't really care and I liked him so I just did that. I dated him, too, and so we kept it a secret—from her, at least—and that was that. He sort've had the best of both worlds there for a little while…being around Karen, who was a nice person and had a cute car…plus some kind of trust fund—maybe not that, maybe not something as elaborate as a "fund" but money of some kind, not just living off financial aid or student loans like the rest of us. She had all that so he did, too…and he also had me. Someone on the side that he could play with and be with and…just…whatever. The guy was seeing both of us at the same time and I knew it and didn't care and she didn't know a thing about it and so…that was the story. He'd go back and forth with us, sometimes straight from one of us to the other—and I mean, in the same night. But it wasn't gross, it wasn't dirty…he had this *way* about him that was just sort of boyish…likable and tender and…God, funny as well, he could really make you laugh…

[*Beat.*]

We both liked him. At that point, and I mean at the beginning point, there wasn't really any harm being done. Didn't seem like it to me, anyhow…but yes, she *technically* met him first and so…should I not've gone out with them for a meal on one occasion or talked to him when we ran into each other on campus or that type of thing? Maybe…maybe so. Isn't that what friends do—they're supposed to watch out for each other? But I didn't…I did not do that and/or want to or even feel some nagging pain in my side telling me there was something morally wrong with what was happening. And there were others, too…we didn't know that, at the time, Karen or me, but there were a few other girls that he was involved with, too. A *few. Quite* a few. Which is not really for me to judge, I don't think, and he was not the only guy that I would go out with—or even *slept* with—during that semester, either, but I think it was a much bigger deal for Karen. I feel like it was for her, or would've been, if she'd known.…

[*Beat.*]

Maybe she *did* know. Maybe she did—maybe that's even why she sent that text to him in the middle of a school day when she could've just as easily talked to him that night...asked him flat out, to his face. That's how *I* would've done it....

I mean, if I'd cared.

[*Beat.*]

I honestly don't know what was going on with her at that moment or during that day, so we're just speculating to think that there is any validity to the idea that Karen may or may not've spun out of control and crashed her car on purpose. The police couldn't say and the coroner couldn't tell and none of her friends or family or school officials felt like this was anything other than a tragedy that was bound to happen to a young girl who was texting someone while she was driving a sports car on a decidedly dangerous and twisty road. And so that was that. She died that day, Karen did, and no one's even felt the need to ask any questions or raise their eyebrows or request further investigations into the case.

[*Beat.*]

It was hard to go on, of course. I mean, not as a person—I'm sorry...I made that sound very maudlin but that isn't what I meant—of *course* I could go on with my life. Of course I could. I had to...that's what you do. It just is. I mean him and me; as a couple, or whatever it is we were—I never bothered to *text* him to find out, never once—but that's who I mean. The two of us. We had been sneaking around the whole time, really, ever since we first decided to go see a movie together without her, without Karen...and once she died...well... didn't seem like the right time to suddenly come out as this big romantic partnership with him and so we kept going on—for a little while, at least—but it began to drop off like those things do, like this probably would've done anyway, even if such a bad thing hadn't happened. But it had and so it was doubly doomed, I think. Whatever it is we'd found in each other. He quit calling...or calling very often...and I did the same or one of us would go after the other for a week or so and then give up, date other people...it was not a big thing, really. Very normal and nice and doomed to failure, like most every love story you see in college or high school. That's just what happens.

[*Beat.*]

But that was him, sitting there at the light. Next to me in his car…nearly ten years later and in a different *state* even. Just by a fluke of coincidence were we ever there together, even just for these few little seconds.

[*Beat.*]

I started to roll down my window, to wave to him…but I didn't. I let it go. What would I say to him? Make him pull over or follow me to a Denny's and have a meal together, talking about old times and all that?

See who is now married or has kids or doesn't and why? Or sleep together even—I was in town on business so he might be, too—but what would be the point of that? None. There would not be one…except for the act of doing it. Proving to ourselves that we are still here. Still around. *Alive.* So I drove off. Turned my head and drove away.

[*Beat.*]

. . . that's it. That's the end of the story.

[*She stops talking for a moment. Looks at us. Nods. Looks away.*]

• • •

Between

John Guare

John Guare

John Guare's plays include *Free Man of Color* (Pulitzer Prize finalist), *3 Kinds of Exile*, *The House of Blue Leaves* (NY Drama Critics Circle Award), *Six Degrees of Separation* (NY Drama Critics Circle Award; London's Olivier Award Best Play), *Landscape of the Body*, *Lydie Breeze*, *Two Gentlemen of Verona* (Tony Award), and *Atlantic City* (Oscar nomination). He won the 2003 PEN Master Dramatist Award, 2004 Gold Medal in Drama from the American Academy of Arts and Letters. He is a council member of the Dramatists Guild and co-editor of the *Lincoln Center Theater Review*.

··· production history ···

Between was part of a presentation of monologues and one-act plays under the title *Nine Signs of the Times*, a benefit for the Nuyorican Poets Cafe's education programs, April 11–13, 2014. Technical director Samuel Chico, music by Michael Gallant, produced by Daniel Gallant, directed by Adam Mace.

A Dennis Henriquez

B Licia James Zegar

In June 2014, TBTB Theater Breaking Through Boundaries produced *Between* in New York as part of an evening called Power Plays. *Between* was directed by Ike Schambelan. A was played by Pamela Sabaugh, B by Melanie Boland. The TBTB production toured Japan in October 2014.

Between was performed by Stockard Channing and John Guare and directed by Jack O'Brien at Neue House in New York City on November 3, 2014.

··· •••

[*A restaurant. A man. A woman. Or not. Two people.*]

A To be here.

B To be here.

A The walls.

B The textures.

A The ambience.

B To use that word.

A *Am-bi-ence.*

B *Am-bi-ence.*

A You got us a reservation.

B *Une Res-er-va-tion.* It's a day.

A That's exactly what today is. A day. No more. An occasion for a memorable meal. But nothing else.

B Don't be—

A If anyone saw us. Don't turn around

B Are we being looked at?

A Over there. Don't look. They've lowered their eyes and lifted their menus over their mouths.

B Like geishas.

A They're not geishas. You did it. You looked.

B He's a truck driver. He's a truck driver who's struck it rich.

A Do you think they could guess who we are?

B Why are you so self-conscious? Can't people just have dinner?

A Oh yes. People can.

B But not us.

A I would say not.

B You think they're trying to figure out who we are? Vanity, vanity.

A Is it business?

B A date?

A An anniversary? Look at them. Here to mark an anniversary? And I wouldn't have given it ten minutes.

B Do we look a married couple?

A Or are they saying this is a first date.

B We've just met?

A Recently.

B At our age?

A High school sweethearts.

B You think they'd say that?

A Trying to rekindle the past.

B Are we?

A   Do we look as if we have a past that was worth rekindling.

B   Then trying to imagine a future

A   Hoping to imagine a future. The waiter looked at us. Those people are looking at us. Don't look up. She turned away.

B   Are we worthy of scrutiny? I thought we looked completely invisible

A   To whom?

B   To the naked eye?

A   How can an eye be naked? Can the naked eye ever see what's really going on? Does naked eye mean it sees deep into your soul—the real you? Or does the naked eye just see through our clothes. Like an airport scanner. Or is the naked eye always disappointed?

B   Are you finished?

A   Talking?

B   Your plate. Your food.

A   Let me dawdle. Let me savor.

B   The time.

A   Is Time on the menu? Cancel that side of Time? What do they say in diners? Eighty-six the Time? Hold the Time. As if.

B   I'm just trying to ease—

A   When we leave here, everything shall be different.

B   I want it to be easy. I brought you here.

A   You chose well. This restaurant. These walls. That texture. This light. A place to mark an event. If we lived here, we'd be home now.

B   You can't live in a restaurant.

A   Why not? Why not? Why in God's name not? If I lived in this restaurant I might like myself. The *Me* that's here. They say it's the food on the menu but people come here to find the *Me* we each dreamed of being. A *Me* I can live with. A *Me* who speaks in quiet tones. Who looks around with gentle curiosity. Who never impinges on another table. One who doesn't need. One who raises an eye, a hand. A minion appears to ensure our happiness.

B   But unfortunately our real life happens outside the restaurant.

A   Real life? Isn't this real? Me here. You there. This is the *Me* I'd hoped to be.

B   And what are you when you're not—

A   Not in this ambience? A damn good question. When I was a child, my mother would say, "If people outside knew what you were really like, they wouldn't like you so much." "What am I really like?" I'd ask. "People break my heart when they praise you. I want to tell them if you knew what my praiseworthy child was really like, you wouldn't— you wouldn't—" and she'd pause. "Wouldn't what?" I'd ask. She'd go on: "If you knew what my child was really like, you wouldn't break my heart, which is what you do when you praise my child. If you knew what my praiseworthy child was really like. If you knew…"

B   What were you really like?

A   That's what I'd say. "What am I really like?" She'd sigh. "I would rather you were a monster outside so when the world came to my doorstep to condemn you I could say, 'My child may be horrible in the outside world but if you knew what my child was like at home, if you knew the pleasure, the kindness. If you knew the real child the way I know.' But I can't say that. I can't tell anyone what you're really like." "But what am I really like?" She'd say, "Wouldn't you like to know." "Yes! Yes! As a matter of fact, yes! I would I would like to know." "Then I'll tell them what you're really like." "No!" I'd cry. "Don't tell them what I'm really like!" "Oh. So you know." "No! I don't! Please! Tell me." "Why should I tell a street angel, a house devil what they're really like?" "What am really I like?" "Wouldn't you like to know."

B   Did she ever tell?

A   She took the answer to her grave.

B   "Street angel. House devil." We'll put that on your tombstone.

A   No. Put "What am I really like?" "Wouldn't you like to know?" But what would she have told them?

B   Did she even know?

A   She knew something. She had given birth to me. I feel comfortable here. I can take the truth. I ask you here in this place where I am the *Me* I would like to be. What am I really like? I'd like to know that once.

B   As you say. A damn good question. I wish I could help.

A   I hoped you could.

B   Are you finished?

A   Let me dawdle in the ambience.

B   Do you hate me?

A   Why should I?

B   Do you love me?

A   Why should I?

B   Will you love me?

A   Again?

B   After. Can you forgive me?

[*Pause.*]

A   Who the hell are you?

B   Someone who is trying to be of help.

A   Stop diminishing me with your goodness.

B   I'm not trying to—

A   What's the real you?

B   I don't think I'll tell you.

A   Tell me the worst thing you've ever done in your life? Make me hate you or be repelled or look at you with a dropped jaw.

B Why?

A It'll make all this more bearable if I hate you.

B That's so easy. The Valley of the Kings.

A As in Egypt?

B I was a student. Years ago. Hitchhiking. Daring to hitchhike. Europe. The Middle East. No strife back then. A world that said look at me. Learn from me. Take me. Enjoy me. Egypt. December. Empty. No tourists. A hitchhiker I had met told me not to miss a recently discovered tomb in the Valley of the Kings. I went there. Asked. Got lost. Asked a man with a camel. I found it. No ticket takers. No guides. Open door. I stepped into the dark. Found the stairs. Held on to a rickety bannister going way below ground level. Down down down. The air was stale. No, not stale. Ancient air that no one had breathed for thousands of years and now was being inhaled by me. I loved the tombs. The Egyptians had a marvelous sense of proportion. Very geometric. Very comforting.

A The tomb. You're in a tomb.

B Oh yes, the tomb. I walked down down down. I heard voices. A single naked light bulb dangled from a beam. It lit the image of a human figure with the head of a bird painted on the wall. What was—a tour group led by a guide speaking English stood under a single light bulb. The guide deciphered the images. This tomb, this king. See his bird head. That is his *Ba*. We all have a *Ba*. Our personality. Our character. See this figure holding out his hand in welcome? That is his *Ka*. The life force. The part of us that is immortal. The two parts of a human—his personality, his life force separated at death. The *Ba* would meet the *Ka* on the other side of the underworld. And be reunited for eternity. I was entranced. The guide suddenly stopped. Someone is listening to this talk who has not paid to be on the tour. This person is stealing information that was purchased by you. I will not go on until that intruder leaves. The group turned and glared at me. I begged pardon and went to another part of the tomb which went lower and lower. The air was stale. Another single light bulb showed me the wall paintings. Which was the *Ba*? Which was the Ka?

The tour appeared—the guide started explaining the paintings—see the *Ba* united with the Ka—I listened from behind a column. He saw me—I will not continue speaking until everyone who has not paid good money to be on this tour leaves the tomb—the group turned to me. Silence. Rage. I capitulated. I felt for the stairs and went up and up and up and up. I could hear the guide's voice growing fainter and fainter below. *Ba Ka Ba Ka*. I stepped out of the black tomb into blinding Egyptian sun. I looked around the Valley of the Kings. No one was around. I saw the light switch. I clicked it off. Screams below. I slammed the door shut and went to find someone dependable like King Tut.

A You turned off the lights and slammed the door?

B What right did they have to exclude—what right did they—Every now and then I hear those voices from that tour pleading: Turn on the lights. Open the door. Give us air. Please—let us out! I still hear them. I wake up. Are they still down there? So many times I've felt that I'm in a tomb breathing ancient air. The opposite of this place. The lights turned off. Flights of stairs. A lack of oxygen. A locked door.

A You did that?

B I'd do it again. Shall we have one more course?

A That's a famous unsolved mystery in Luxor.

B What are you saying? Keep your voice down.

A The dead tourists. December? All those years ago? A deserted part of the Valley of the Kings? A recently discovered tomb. Twenty-eight people found dead—suffocated.

B No!

A It's been one of the most famous unsolved mysteries in the annals of tourism.

B What are you saying?

A That's you? All these years later in this restaurant to solve a baffling crime that's crossed over into legend. Twenty-eight bodies at the top of the stairs died pounding against the locked door. No one heard.

December. No tourists. No air. The sun baking down. The heat. Who was the monster who had locked them in? Oh God—you? Horror. You had committed that crime. That is the worst thing I ever—I believe the Egyptian government offered a reward for information leading to—that should come in handy covering the bill for this meal.

B   You're joking.

A   I wish. Do you have constant anxiety gnawing at you?

B   I was a student. It doesn't count.

A   This crime would explain that constant anxious gnawing at your innards. Do you have bad luck?

B   From time to—yes. I do.

A   Your legendary bad luck is payment for this crime. The naked eye sees. I finally see you.

B   Don't look at me.

A   Everyone in this restaurant is staring at you. They see you. They slide their chairs away from this table. A cringing busboy. I thought I was the center of their attention. But it's you. Everyone sees your crime.

B   I was young.

A   Go back to Egypt. Confess. You have no choice.

B   Isn't there a statute of limitations?

A   Not in Egypt.

B   Oh God—

A   I'm kidding you.

B   What are you saying?

A   Keep your voice down. Smile. My pathetic attempt to inject levity into this—what is this meal? Lunch? Dinner? Supper? An event. We came here. We weren't hungry. We needed time before—before. Of course you didn't kill them. At least that I ever heard. If you had, the Egyptians would've quashed a story like that. The Egyptian government can't afford to have dead tourists on their hands. They depend on their tourists. As a restaurant depends on its clientele. Don't get any ideas. Don't think you can get up and turn off the lights and slam the door and leave. That won't work here.

B I didn't kill twenty-eight people?

A None that I ever heard of. Bravo, very good story.

B It's not a story. It's the truth of me.

A It makes me not like you.

B I'd lock that door again if I had the chance.

A And yet here in this ambience you're a paragon. Restaurant angel. Desert devil.

B Please.

A Tell me more about the *Ba* and the *Ka*.

B I've told you all I know. It's ancient times. This room. This texture. This light. This ambience.

A When I die, will you be my *Ka*?

B It's time we—

A When you die, will I be you *Ka*?

B It's time we—

A Time we

B Time we

A Just a moment more. Don't leave. This room.

[*They reach their hands across the table.*]

• • •

A Match

John Bolen

John Bolen

John Bolen is a novelist/playwright/actor living in Southern California. He has been published by Applause in *Best American Short Plays 2010–2011* and *Best Monologues from Best American Short Plays, Vol. 3*. He has also been published by Independentplay(w)rights, Indigo Rising, Scars Publications, The Write Place at the Write Time, OC180news, Eunoia Review, and *YouthPLAYS*. John Bolen's plays have been produced in theaters throughout the U.S. Bolen is also the Producing Artistic Director of the New Voices Playwrights Theatre & Workshop.

··· production history ···

A Match was first performed August 2–17, 2014, in the production Summer Voices 2014 at the Stage Door Repertory Theatre in Anaheim, California, directed by Jo Black-Jacob and starring Karen Wray and Sky Siegel.

setting

An upscale bar

characters

> **ELLIS**   Male, mid-thirties, the husband
> **DEEDEE**   Female, mid-thirties, the wife

• • •

[*It is 7:00 p.m. on a Wednesday night. DEEDEE is seated at a table for two in the bar. A wineglass sits before her, and a glass of water is at the other seat across from her. DEEDEE's purse is set on the table along with two cloth napkins. ELLIS enters, talking on his cell phone.*]

ELLIS   No, no, no! I am not going to let anything ruin this night.

[*Preoccupied with hanging up his cell phone, ELLIS accidentally trips. He is thrown into wild gyrations falling and trying to catch his balance. Despite the effort he still falls on his rear next to the table.*]

DEEDEE   [*Laughing.*] What the hell happened, Ellis? Oh God, get up. Everyone is going to be looking at you.

ELLIS   [*Angrily.*] There's nobody here.

DEEDEE   Well, the wait staff will see you. Get up.

ELLIS   I'm trying.

DEEDEE   Try harder. They're looking.

> [*ELLIS struggles to get up by grabbing the back of a chair, but it falls backward throwing him on his butt again. Laughing again.*]
>
> What are you doing?

ELLIS   I'm trying to get up, DeeDee. What do you think I'm doing?

DEEDEE   Just get up. It's embarrassing.

[ELLIS *manages to stand up, set the chair right, and sit down at the table.*]

ELLIS   Well, excuse me if I embarrassed you.

DEEDEE   Why are you being so huffy?

ELLIS   I'm not being huffy.

DEEDEE   Well, you're acting angry. What's the difference?

ELLIS   Huffy implies that I am being childishly angry. I am not. I am being maturishly angry.

DEEDEE   Maturishly? I don't think that is even a word.

ELLIS   Of course it's a word. What else would be the opposite of "childishly"?

DEEDEE   I'm not sure. I think you would have to say, "In a mature manner." You are angry in a mature manner.

ELLIS   Who would talk like that?

DEEDEE   People who know how to talk would. Anyway, I don't see why you feel the need to be angry.

ELLIS   I don't "feel the need to be angry." I am angry.

DEEDEE   Well, I certainly don't see any justification for that.

ELLIS   You don't see any justification? I fall and hurt myself, and all you can do is sit there and laugh?

DEEDEE   You didn't hurt yourself. Men don't hurt themselves.

ELLIS   How can you say such a thing?

DEEDEE   All my life, I've seen men fall down, smash their fingers, electrocute themselves, etcetera. And when you ask how they are, they always say, "I'm fine."

ELLIS   Just because the male of the species feels the need to act with a false bravado, it does not mean that we really do not hurt.

DEEDEE   And besides, how can you fault me for laughing? Isn't human pain the basis of comedy?

ELLIS Not my pain and not for you. This is a terrible way to start our date night. We finally get our first break from the kids and all you can do is laugh at me.

DEEDEE Well, sit back and relax. We'll enjoy our drinks and I have a table reserved in the dining room for 7:30 and we will have a nice meal.

[ELLIS *looks at the glass in front of him and then looks at* DEEDEE'*s glass of wine.*]

ELLIS So what did you order for me?

DEEDEE It's right there. Don't you see it?

ELLIS I can see a glass in front of me, but what is in it?

DEEDEE It's water. It's the middle of the week; you shouldn't be drinking any alcohol in the middle of the week. It's not good for you.

ELLIS I shouldn't have a cocktail, but what is that in front of you?

DEEDEE It's wine. You don't like wine.

ELLIS But it is alcohol. Didn't you just say having alcohol was bad?

DEEDEE Not wine. I can go on the Internet and show you a thousand studies about how drinking red wine is good for you. It has antioxidants and all manner of other positive effects on one's health. People who drink red wine live longer than people who don't. People who drink hard alcohol live shorter lives. It's a proven fact. Should I show you the studies?

ELLIS No, you don't need to show me the studies. Fine, I just won't have a drink.

DEEDEE You could have some fruit juice, although not too much. Studies have shown that the sugar content of juices is just as bad as...

ELLIS The water is fine.

DEEDEE Well, you don't have to be so huffy.

ELLIS I'm not being huffy.

DEEDEE Well, you don't have to be so angry in a mature manner, either. Who were you on the phone with?

ELLIS   It was the sitter. Seems our darling son put a frog he caught on the front table and now it's missing. I told her this is our first date night and I was not coming home to search for a frog. I told her to deal with it.

[DEEDEE *suddenly goes into a panic.*]

DEEDEE   My purse was on the front table. What if it climbed into my purse?

[DEEDEE *pushes her chair away from the table and jumps up to stand on the chair.*]

ELLIS   What are you doing? Get down. Someone will see you.

DEEDEE   [*Hysterically.*] I don't care. I can't stand frogs. I hate them. I hate them.

ELLIS   [*Laughing.*] You're really overreacting.

DEEDEE   Check my purse and see if it got in there.

ELLIS   I seriously doubt if it…

DEEDEE   Check it!

ELLIS   Alright! Okay! I'll check. But I seriously don't believe that a frog would…Well, I'll be.

[ELLIS *pulls the frog out of her purse.*]

DEEDEE   [*Screaming.*] Eeeeeeeek! Kill it! Kill it!

[ELLIS *is waving the frog around.*]

ELLIS   [*Laughing more.*] It's just a poor little frog.

DEEDEE   I don't care. Kill it! Kill it!

[ELLIS *is still waving the frog around.*]

ELLIS   [*Still laughing.*] I don't think I need to kill it. It's not moving. I think it got squished in your purse.

DEEDEE   Oh, gross, gross, gross! You have to make sure it's dead.

ELLIS   Oops!

[*The frog accidentally slips from* ELLIS*'s grasp and falls on the floor in front of* DEEDEE.]

DEEDEE Eeeeeeeeeeeeek!

[DEEDEE *jumps off the chair, lifts the chair up, and smashes the leg of the chair down on the frog multiple times. Then she sets the chair down and jumps up to stand on it again.*]

ELLIS [*Laughing so hard he is grabbing his sides.*] Offhand, I would say it is dead now.

[ELLIS *grabs a napkin, picks up the frog in it, and throws it offstage.*]

DEEDEE Are you sure?

ELLIS Yes, I am quite sure. Now get down from that chair. Someone will see you.

DEEDEE There is no one here.

ELLIS Well, the wait staff will see you. Now get down, it's embarrassing.

[DEEDEE *gets down, moves her chair to the table, and sits down.*]

DEEDEE Well, excuse me if I embarrassed you.

ELLIS You don't have to be so huffy.

DEEDEE I'm not being huffy.

ELLIS Well, you don't have to be so angry in a mature manner.

DEEDEE I'm in extreme anguish and all you can do is laugh?

ELLIS Human pain is basis of comedy, isn't it?

DEEDEE Not my pain.

ELLIS Besides, you weren't in anguish. Women aren't in anguish just because of some reptile. They put on this act, but if a man is not around, somehow the reptile gets squished, somehow the bug gets killed, somehow…

DEEDEE Just because some women put on an act doesn't mean I didn't truly feel repulsed. My brother used to put reptiles in my bed when we were young and it literally makes my skin crawl. I was in pain. I don't think this marriage is working.

ELLIS   Where did that come from?

DEEDEE   [*Yelling.*] It's obvious you don't love me when you are constantly being inconsiderate.

ELLIS   Lower your voice.

[*In a yelling whisper.*]

How am I being inconsiderate all the time?

[*Both* ELLIS *and* DEEDEE *are using a yelling whisper.*]

DEEDEE   You use the last of the toilet paper on the roll, and you don't put on a new one.

ELLIS   That's just silly.

DEEDEE   That's exactly what I mean. You blow your nose in the bathroom sink. That's inconsiderate.

ELLIS   What's so bad with that? It just rinses down the drain.

DEEDEE   Using that logic, you might as well piss in the shower. Oh God, please tell me you don't do that.

ELLIS   I don't, but you always leave your washed-out panties and pantyhose hanging in the shower. That's pretty awful to have to deal with.

DEEDEE   Oh yeah! Well, you leave hairs on the soap.

ELLIS   Jesus! How I hate you.

DEEDEE   I hate you back double.

ELLIS   Oh yeah! Well, you snore in your sleep.

DEEDEE   Oh yeah! You fart in your sleep.

ELLIS   I do not.

DEEDEE   You most certainly do.

ELLIS   Do I really?

DEEDEE   Yes, you do.

ELLIS   I had no idea. Why haven't you said something before this?

DEEDEE   [*Returning to a regular voice.*] There's nothing you can do about it. It's just one of those things a spouse has to put up with the person they love.

ELLIS   [*In a regular voice.*] So that means you love me?

DEEDEE   I guess I must.

ELLIS   I guess I must love you, too.

[*A voice comes over the intercom announcing, "DeeDee, party of two."*]

DEEDEE   Well, let's go in for dinner.

ELLIS   It's so nice to get a date night, isn't it.

[DEEDEE *takes* ELLIS*'s arm as they are exiting.*]

DEEDEE   It's nice to get away from it all, isn't it?

[*They stroll offstage, arm in arm.*]

• • •

And Baby Makes Four

A One-Act Play in Three Scenes

Frank Farmer

Frank Farmer

Frank Farmer, nephew of the late film star Francis Farmer, is both a professional actor and award-winning playwright whose plays have been produced in Los Angeles theaters from the American Renegade Theatre Company to the Zeitgeist Theatre Company, including Theatre West, Lonny Chapman's Group Repertory Theatre, and New Voices Playwrights at the Stage Door Repertory. A California "native son" born in Glendale, he received his BA from the University of Washington in Seattle and MA from Loyola University in Los Angeles. Farmer's many film and acting credits are listed on the Internet Movie Database. His theater credits include Off-Broadway, national tours, and regional dinner theaters in Texas, Colorado, and Florida.

···production history···

And Baby Makes Four was part of the New Voices Playwrights Theatre presentation Summer Voices 2014: Six One-Act Plays, held August 2, 9, 16, and 17, 2014, at the Stage Door Repertory Theatre in Anaheim, California. Directed by Geoffrey Gread.

> **JOHN**   Kim Kiedrowski
>
> **PETULIA**   Megan Tice
>
> **ANDREA**   Donna Jacques

characters

> **JOHN HIGGINS**   Retired executive, sixty-four
>
> **PETULIA RYAN**   Pretty, twenty-eight
>
> **ANDREA**   Striking, thirty-two

synopsis

A young lesbian's decision to have a child by a father of her choice is thwarted when he refuses to donate to a sperm bank, nearly forcing her to conceive "conventionally," much to the annoyance of her older partner.

setting

Two suggested locations: a coffee house, an apartment living room. No special technical requirements.

intended audience

Mature adults, no nudity, minor profanity. Of special interest to LGBT.

scene 1

[*At rise: stage right, the suggestion of a coffee house. A sign reads Java Joynt. A man in his sixties is sitting alone at a small table, sipping a latte and reading a business magazine. His name is* JOHN HIGGINS. *A pretty young woman named* PETULIA *approaches him.*]

PETULIA   Excuse me....

JOHN   Yes?

PETULIA Mr. Higgins.

JOHN Yes.

PETULIA Mr. John Anthony Higgins. The Third. I'm honored to meet you.

[*She extends her hand and he shakes it.*]

JOHN Why…thank you.

PETULIA I've been researching you. Fascinating.

JOHN Oh? And why, may I ask?

PETULIA For school. For my thesis.

JOHN A thesis for what?

PETULIA For my degree. In, uh, business administration. Captains of industry. America's greatest living CEOs.

JOHN Was. I'm retired now.

PETULIA But you're still on the board. You made Globalcon the third largest Internet broadband server in almost the entire world. The mergers, the acquisitions, the consolidations were all your babies, your decisions.

JOHN It was very much a team effort.

PETULIA But teams don't win unless they have strong leaders; strong leaders, like the grip of your hand. Strong yet sensitive.

JOHN Why, thank you, uh…

PETULIA Petulia. Petulia Ryan.

JOHN An Irish lass. Why this interest in corporate America?

PETULIA Corporate American *men*. The secrets of their success. Your success, Mister…may I call you John?

JOHN Please do.

PETULIA You exude a vital charisma that's extremely powerful. The secret to your success, I'll bet. It's overpowering. It's awesome.

JOHN Even at my somewhat advanced age?

PETULIA Not so advanced, just over sixty.

JOHN Sixty-four.

PETULIA You sure don't look it. I'll bet you still work out.

JOHN Occasionally. Not often enough, I'm afraid.

PETULIA Good genes.

JOHN I suppose so.

PETULIA For many, many generations....

JOHN What's the title of your thesis?

PETULIA My...oh, yes, my...my thesis.

JOHN The reason for this impromptu interview.

PETULIA "The Making of a CEO—A Profile of Excellence."

JOHN You mean profiles, don't you? Surely you're not devoting an entire graduate thesis to just one man, are you?

PETULIA Yes, that's my intention.

JOHN Miss Ryan...

PETULIA Pet. My friends call me Pet.

JOHN I would strongly suggest you include others. My resume isn't that extensive or remarkable.

PETULIA Oh, but it is. Did you know there's an entire website devoted to America's leading CEOs?

JOHN Yes. Such as it is.

PETULIA It even includes your resume.

JOHN I doubt if it's complete.

PETULIA Check it out. It's awesome.

JOHN Then why this interview?

PETULIA Oh, I've got all the corporate stuff, facts, figures, dates, you know. What I haven't got is the personal stuff. The real human you.

JOHN What "personal stuff" do you mean?

PETULIA Well, your family. Your kids.

JOHN I never had any.

PETULIA Why not? Let me guess, too busy achieving excellence.

JOHN Yes and no.

PETULIA She didn't want children?

JOHN Neither one did. Twice married, twice divorced. They wanted success. Until they tired of it. My fault as well. A price one pays for being a workaholic.

PETULIA Your kids would have been…wonderful.

JOHN Maybe. Maybe not. No guarantees, regardless our material successes. Many times money does nothing but corrupt relationships, be they with spouse or offspring….

PETULIA But that's in the parenting, John. Not in the genes. The DNA. The raw material of excellence. But without that…Have you ever considered donating to a sperm bank?

JOHN God, no. Whatever for? The world's overpopulated as it is. If more people adopted kids instead of churning them out, one after the other…

PETULIA But not of your quality! The world needs more John Higgins and if a woman knows her child will have those genes.

JOHN I've spent a lot of time in Third World countries, Pet. What's happening to children there is a crime against humanity.

PETULIA But the banks are important to women who haven't got…I mean…They pay you a hundred dollars for each time you donate. If it takes more than once, more money.

JOHN A hundred! Hmmm. Pet, money's the last thing I need.

PETULIA But your legacy, your legacy of excellence. Do you really want the Higgins line to end here?

JOHN It's a complicated issue. More than one side to it.

PETULIA Do you miss them?

JOHN Them?

PETULIA The children you never had.

JOHN To be brutally honest…many times.

PETULIA Never too late.

JOHN It first requires…

PETULIA I know. Wow, I've really gone off the track here.

JOHN No, that's quite all right. I haven't discussed this with anyone since…since a long time ago. When I was in college, matter of fact.

PETULIA Your first true love?

JOHN Yeah. We talked about having kids. Lots of them. But then we went our separate ambitious ways. Thanks for reminding me. Some memories are very sweet. How about you? Married?

PETULIA No man in my life.

JOHN You look a wee bit familiar. Have we ever…

PETULIA I used to work here part-time. You were always deep into papers or busy on your cell phone. Workaholic.

[*They both smile.*]

JOHN And just drank the coffee, never stopped to smell it. Or notice a pretty girl named Pet.

PETULIA Thank you, John. Better now than never.

JOHN May I take you to dinner tonight?

PETULIA Why, that would be lovely. Yes, of course.

JOHN Why don't I pick you up around…

PETULIA May I finish my interview now? At my apartment?

JOHN Your apartment?

PETULIA   Just a few blocks from here. My coffee's better than this.

JOHN   Well…how much more information do you need? That I can't give you right here?

PETULIA   Not that much, really. I promise I won't bite.

JOHN   A wise little voice in the back of my head is cautioning me, no, no, no. But another voice in another part of my head is whispering…

PETULIA   Yes, yes, yes?

JOHN   First let me cancel a very important appointment.

[*He punches some numbers on a cell phone.*]

Yes, this is John Higgins. I have a two o'clock tee time. I'm afraid I'll have to cancel it.…Yes, maybe later in the week. Thank you.

[*He replaces the phone.*]

PETULIA   Tea time?

JOHN   Golf, not the beverage. You don't by any chance play, do you?

PETULIA   No, but I'd love to learn. Maybe you can teach me sometime.

JOHN   I'd be delighted to.

[*They rise and begin to exit. She takes his hand as the lights fade.*]

scene 2

[*Lights up stage left on the suggestion of an apartment. A sofa and coffee table. Lying on it is a thick pile of bound papers.*]

[*A key is heard turning in a lock. A door opens and PET enters, followed by JOHN.*]

PETULIA   It's tiny but cozy. And rent controlled.

JOHN   Lucky lady.

PETULIA   Would you like a drink? You don't want any more coffee, do you?

JOHN   A drink of…?

PETULIA   All we ha…, I mean wine . All I have is wine. Red or white?

JOHN Merlot?

PETULIA Cabernet.

JOHN Fine.

PETULIA Sit down, I'll be right back.

[PET *exits to a kitchen.* JOHN *wanders around the room.*]

JOHN Lived here long?

PETULIA [Offstage.] Couple of years.

JOHN All alone?

PETULIA [*Offstage.*] I used to have a cat. But it ran away.

JOHN So what's your career track?

PETULIA [*Offstage.*] Oh, first things first. My thesis, my degree, maybe an entry-level gofer for a tech company, then…

[*She enters with two glasses of red wine.*]

…who knows? With your example I could go to the moon.

JOHN I understand it's very lonely up there.

PETULIA Not exactly vintage, but…

[*She gives him the wine, they touch glasses and drink. She sings.*]

"It was a very good year…"

[*Laughing.*]

A singer I'm not.

JOHN But pretty you are. So…what more do you want to know about me?

PETULIA Uh…what do you plan to do with the rest of your life?

JOHN That's not a captain of industry graduate student thesis question.

PETULIA Color me curious.

JOHN The honest truth?

PETULIA Unvarnished.

JOHN   I haven't the foggiest idea.

PETULIA   Much more to life than latte and golf. You're really a young man, John. Young and vibrant and virile and…

JOHN   Compliments will get you…whatever you want.

PETULIA   I want you to…

JOHN   To do what? What more do you need to know about me?

PETULIA   Nothing.

JOHN   Then why did you invite me up here?

PETULIA   Why did you invite me to dinner?

JOHN   Touché.

[*They're sitting very close to each other. Almost in unison, they set their wineglasses down and embrace in a kiss that begins to get very, very hot.*]

[*A key is heard turning in the lock. The door opens and a woman enters, striking, somewhat older than PET. Her name is ANDY. There's a moment of frozen tableaux as JOHN and PET break from their embrace.*]

ANDY   What the fuck…!?

PETULIA   [*Stricken.*] Andy!

JOHN   Andy?

ANDY   Who the hell are you?

PETULIA   You're supposed to be on location!

JOHN   Location? Pet, who is…?

ANDY   What's going on here?

PETULIA   Oh, Andy…Goddamn it!

[*Crying, PET exits to a bedroom. JOHN and ANDY stare at one another.*]

ANDY   Who are you?

JOHN   May I ask the same question?

ANDY   You're in my house.

JOHN You mean, Miss Ryan's house, don't you?

ANDY Our house.

JOHN You're Pet's roommate?

ANDY No, I'm Pet's mate-mate. She didn't tell you? Oh, dawns the light. You must be John Higgins. So are you going to do it?

JOHN Am I going to do what?

ANDY The sperm bank. For Pet's baby.

JOHN Oh, so that's what this is all about.

ANDY She didn't tell you?

JOHN No. Why don't *you* tell me.

ANDY Yes, I better do that. Uh, more wine?

[*He doesn't respond.* ANDY *goes into the kitchen and returns with the bottle of Cabernet and another glass.*]

This is…awkward, isn't it?

JOHN Very. What's going on?

ANDY Cutting right to the chase, we're two lesbian women who want to have a baby. And not just any baby.

JOHN My baby.

ANDY Yes. The plan was to have you donate to a local sperm bank. We both agreed you'd be the ideal…sperm. It looks like you were about to make a direct deposit.

JOHN So she bears my child, then sues me for millions in child support. Is that the scam the two of you are trying to run?

ANDY She didn't show you the papers?

JOHN What papers?

ANDY Oh, Jesus H.!

[ANDY *pulls a document from the file on the coffee table and hands it to* JOHN, *which he reads.*]

No claims, no demands, from birth to death. Notarized.

JOHN She's not a graduate student, is she?

ANDY No.

JOHN And I doubt if she's really gay.

ANDY Doubt no more. Pet's an actress, and a damn good one.

JOHN Aha. Quite a performance. I gather you're both in the business?

ANDY I'm a director.

JOHN A director! Yeah, right. Anything I might have seen?

ANDY Late-night cable infomercials. It's a foot in the door.

JOHN And may I further assume Petulia's one of your...

ANDY No. She has a recurring role on a soap. So the sperm bank route is out, huh?

JOHN Definitely. As well as any direct deposits.

ANDY What if I hadn't barged in?

JOHN But you did. Now if you'll excuse me, I have a date with a putting green. Interesting afternoon.

[*He starts for the door.*]

ANDY She wants your baby, John. Please reconsider.

[*He hesitates at the door, then abruptly exits. PET enters from the bedroom.*]

PETULIA What happened?

ANDY The shoot got scrubbed. So what was he doing up here?

PETULIA I changed my mind.

ANDY Why?

PETULIA He wouldn't do the bank thing.

ANDY So we do it with somebody else. What's the problem?

PETULIA I want *his* baby. His only.

ANDY You were going to let him knock you up right here on our couch?

PETULIA   Conceive, Andy. *Conceive*!

ANDY   Why didn't you wait till I got back so we could discuss it?

PETULIA   Because you wouldn't have agreed. Would you?

ANDY   Probably not. We agreed on the fertility bank. What changed your mind?

PETULIA   I want the baby to be conceived naturally. Conventionally. Like I was. Like both of us were.

ANDY   You still love me, don't you? Don't you?

PETULIA   Yes.

ANDY   What's done's done. Now let's get on with our life.

PETULIA   The baby was your idea originally, remember?

ANDY   And Mr. Higgins was yours. As long as he agreed to donate to the bank. Remember?

PETULIA   I've got to have the baby with him.

ANDY   Won't work, Pet.

PETULIA   And why not?

ANDY   I can't share you with someone else.

PETULIA   Because he's a he?

ANDY   Threesomes only work in pornos. What if the shoe was on the other foot? Would you be comfortable sharing me with someone else?

PETULIA   I want his baby, not him.

ANDY   I'm sure you heard him. He's history either way. So we go fishing in the gene pool for someone else. He isn't the only Mr. Right, Pet.

PETULIA   He's the only one I want.

ANDY   Then go get him. But don't you come back. Ever!

[*The two women stand facing each other, defiantly, as the lights slowly fade.*]

scene 3

[*The Scene I coffee shop. As at the opening* JOHN *is seated, sipping a latte and reading a magazine. A moment or two, then* PET *enters and slowly approaches him.*]

PETULIA   May I sit down?

[*He nods yes, she sits, and he continues reading.*]

I'm sorry I lied to you. It was a means to a very good end. At least I thought so.

JOHN   Apology accepted.

PETULIA   I don't know what more to say.

JOHN   Nothing more required.

PETULIA   You came back here.

JOHN   Why wouldn't I?

PETULIA   Because of what happened. Because of me.

JOHN   I've been stopping here for the past two years. One unpleasant incident is not going to change the quality of the coffee.

PETULIA   It would have been pleasant if only...

JOHN   All right, let's lay the cards right on the table. I was excited, turned on, I wanted you, right there on the sofa. But what about afterwards? Wham-bam-thank-you-sir? Don't slam the door on your way out? Just a one-afternoon stand? And what if it didn't happen? What if the little wiggly polliwogs didn't hit pay dirt?

PETULIA   "If at first you don't succeed, try, try again."

JOHN   God, you just won't give up, will you?

PETULIA   No. I want your baby, John.

JOHN   That was quite a performance. Andy's right, you're a very good actress

PETULIA   I wasn't acting. I was lying.

JOHN   About being a student. And desiring me?

PETULIA Yes.

JOHN Well, you convinced me, young lady.

PETULIA You have to be a good liar to be a good actor.

JOHN Only a truly honest person could admit that.

PETULIA I truly want your baby. But I don't want…

JOHN Complications. Right? Not to worry. It was just sex, nothing more.

PETULIA But it might have been more if Andy hadn't…

JOHN All right, all right. Yes, I would have wanted more. And more. And more. I may be old…older, but I'm not dead. You happened along just when I needed someone.

PETULIA Then it would have happened eventually, wouldn't it?

JOHN Possibly. Probably.

PETULIA You told me you missed having children.

JOHN I did. Still do. But I'm sixty-four. Much too old to be…

PETULIA You don't have to be a daddy. Just a, an uncle. Uncle John.

JOHN You're bound and determined to do this, aren't you?

PETULIA Yes.

JOHN A single mom, huh?

PETULIA If I have to.

JOHN I don't understand.

PETULIA Don't understand what?

JOHN Why a lesbian woman would want to have a child. A fatherless child.

PETULIA I only understand how I feel. I want to be a mother. I have to be a mother.

[ANDY *has entered and stands behind* PET, *who doesn't notice her.* JOHN *sees her but doesn't react.*]

JOHN What about Andy?

PETULIA We broke up. She was angry that we might become, well…involved.

JOHN Not just a business arrangement.

PETULIA That's all it would be but she won't believe me.

JOHN What if I agree to this artificial procedure? Think she'd have a change of heart?

PETULIA You would? You really would?

JOHN If I did…if you two really love each other…what would she say?

PETULIA I don't know.

JOHN Well, why don't you ask her.

[PET *turns, then slowly rises. The two women embrace.* JOHN *finishes his coffee.*]

Ladies, I shall give your…proposition some serious consideration. Uncle John. Hmmm. I'm actually rather flattered that you chose me and my…my genes. If it were a boy I think the name Anthony would be appropriate. And if a girl…perhaps Antoinette. So the Higgins family line would march on. Sort of. Uh, these sperm bank facilities…any one in particular?

• • •

Angel at My Door

John Franceschini

John Franceschini

John Franceschini became a playwright following a career as a pharmacist. His plays have been produced in Connecticut, Florida, Illinois, Kentucky, Maryland, Michigan, Montana, New York, Texas, Utah, Virginia, Washington, and at various venues in California. His play *It's Only a Minute a Guy* was published in Applause's *Best American Short Plays 2010–2011*. His play *Angel at My Door* was published in New Voices Playwrights' *Annual Anthology of Short Plays 2014*. Franceschini is a member of the Dramatists Guild of America, Orange County Playwrights Alliance, and New Voices Playwrights Theatre.

··· production history ···

Angel at My Door was part of the New Voices Playwrights Theatre presentation Summer Voices 2014: Six One-Act Plays, held August 2, 9, 16, and 17, 2014, at the Stage Door Repertory Theatre in Anaheim, California. Directed by Autumn Brown and starring Kim Kiedrowski and Amanda Petrocelly.

characters

JAKE   Cantankerous, despondent owner of a bookstore selling "used books." He is down on his luck and decides to take his own life. (Fifties–sixties.)

HOLLY   Cheerful, persistent, young woman is looking for a father figure. She purports to be a guide to the afterlife and wants to prevent Jake's suicide. (Late teens.)

···

[*Suggested "used books" bookstore with a table and chair. On the table are two piles of used books with a few displayed and an empty shoebox. At rise,* JAKE *is seated holding a handgun and looking dejected.* HOLLY *enters from stage right.*]

[HOLLY *mimes opening a door and enters the suggested bookstore and looks around.* JAKE *hurriedly puts the handgun in the shoebox.*]

JAKE   Come back another time, we're closed.

HOLLY   No, you're not.

JAKE   I said we're closed.

HOLLY   The sign on the window says, "Bookstore Open."

JAKE   I forgot to change it. Now get out.

HOLLY   How many people work here?

JAKE   What?

HOLLY   You just said, "We're closed." So there must be someone else here.

JAKE   It's a figure of speech.

HOLLY   Why don't you say, "I'm closed"? It's singular, not plural.

JAKE   What are you, taking a census? Now. Beat it!

HOLLY   That's the problem; people say one thing and mean something else.

[*Beat.*]

"I'll love you forever" and wham-o, a new flavor of the month comes along and overnight you become last year's cell phone.

JAKE   [*Gently.*] I'll make it plain for you. This is my bookstore and I'm asking you to please leave the premises.

HOLLY   Why? It's the middle of the day; you can't be taking a break for lunch; it's too late.

JAKE   Get out before I throw you out!

HOLLY   Ah, you gotta take a wiz, I get it. Go to the "head," no worries I won't steal any "used" books.

JAKE   Okay, that's it. I don't want to get physical but you forced my hand.

HOLLY   Hey, wait a minute! Is this how you treat customers? You sell books, don't you?

JAKE   You got any money?

HOLLY   You trying to size me up so you can charge more for one of your "old" books?

JAKE   All right, what book do you want?

HOLLY   That's better; but I still think you need a course in customer service.

JAKE   Just tell me what you want so you can scram outta here.

HOLLY   Don't your customers usually browse for a while?

JAKE   Not when the store is closed. It's now or never.

[HOLLY *moves stage right and mimes looking out a window.*]

HOLLY   I can't leave just yet.

JAKE Why?

HOLLY It started raining hard outside. I don't have an umbrella.

JAKE I've been open six hours with no customers and when one comes in; it's only to stay dry.

HOLLY My name's Holly. What's yours?

JAKE Pain in the ass. Are you one of those runaway kids who sleep under the freeway?

HOLLY Do I guess your name or do you tell me?

JAKE You're gettin' under my skin.

HOLLY Sir Issac Newton.

JAKE Just what I suspected, you're high.

HOLLY You ever been high?

JAKE Plenty of times.

HOLLY What'd you do, snort, mainline, pop a couple?

JAKE A natural high, one you kids wouldn't know about.

HOLLY Is it some kind of herbal stuff?

JAKE [*Reminiscing.*] Ever make love to the person you really love. Or come home from the war and see the smile on your mother's face. You get a feeling you wanna' hold on to forever. Now, that's a high.

HOLLY I haven't had those experiences.

JAKE Go build yourself a birdhouse; get a sense of accomplishment.

HOLLY I wanna' work here.

JAKE I see, you come in, don't spend any money and want me to give you some.

HOLLY I can hold a reading session for kids in the neighborhood. It'll build up foot traffic.

JAKE Did you shoot up before you came here?

HOLLY   I'm clean.

JAKE   Ninety-five percent of the kids today got more chemicals in them than an oil refinery.

HOLLY   Wow, you're down on "the people." What if they protested your store for capitalism? You know, set up a vigil outside like Occupy Wall Street.

JAKE   I wish they would, then the general public would think I had customers.

HOLLY   Harry, George, Charlie…feel free to interrupt me at anytime with your name.…

JAKE   … Are you waiting for your boyfriend so you can rob me? Homeless kids usually travel with a two-time felon.

HOLLY   I don't have a boyfriend.

JAKE   Doing it on your own? The loot is in a metal box under the counter. You won't find enough to buy a corn dog.

HOLLY   I'll learn the inventory in no time flat. You can pay me less than minimum wage like an undocumented worker.

JAKE   Got any references?

HOLLY   Just one but you can't contact him. I don't want him to know I'm looking for a new job.

JAKE   Why do you wanna leave? Get caught with your hand in the till?

HOLLY   You're a cynic.

   [*Beat.*]

   I need a change of pace. Ever do the same thing day in and day out?

JAKE   Look around. Do you see a circus going on in here? If you can't change the hand life dealt you, suck it up and march on.

HOLLY   I wanna connect with everyday people. Maybe hook up with the opposite sex. I'm ready to cruise in a convertible with my hair flying in the wind.

JAKE   What's your game?

HOLLY   No game, Jake, I'm here to help.

JAKE   How'd you know my name?

HOLLY   I have to do a background check before each assignment.

JAKE   Why did you ask me if you already knew?

HOLLY   Trying to develop rapport, you know, warm up to each other a little.

JAKE   Am I an object of curiosity for a school project?

HOLLY   I was told to be here, so I'm here. I only get the call when it's imminent.

JAKE   You working a deadline for a report?

HOLLY   I'm your guide, Jake.

JAKE   Guide for what?

HOLLY   To the hereafter.

JAKE   What in the world are you saying?

[HOLLY *places her hand on the shoebox.*]

HOLLY   I know you closed up shop to off yourself with a handgun.

[JAKE *quickly places some books on top of the shoebox.*]

JAKE   [*Angrily.*] What gives you the right to waltz in here and make such an outrageous statement!? Get out!

HOLLY   Your wife passed away recently, no family, you're feeling down; that's only natural.

JAKE   Thanks so much for the uplifting analysis.

HOLLY   It's like you said, "Suck it up and march on." I'll stay and keep you company. Help you build up the business, which is not exactly your strong suit.

JAKE   What makes you think I'm going to kill myself?

HOLLY   It's all in the dossier I downloaded.

JAKE   Let me see it.

HOLLY   It's not tangible in the way you understand. The info is sent directly to the memory cells in my brain.

JAKE   So you got no proof of anything.

HOLLY   You graduated from Michigan State with a major in English literature. When you joined a fraternity you had to soak you hands in red beet juice. Every Saturday your mom made your favorite breakfast of bacon, eggs, and pancakes....

JAKE   . . . Okay, okay, something's weird here. I'm not sure what it is but it ain't kosher.

HOLLY   I got it, why don't you pretend to adopt me. I'll be your daughter and live in the backroom. I can cook and sew for you.

JAKE   [*Empathetically.*] Your parents must be worried about you. What's the home number? I'll give them a call.

HOLLY   My parents died in an accident a long time ago.

[*Beat.*]

We can go for walks in the park and you can tell me about life.

JAKE   Sorry about your folks, any other family around?

HOLLY   I wish there were. Kinda lonely knocking about on my own. Could use some roots for a while, and enjoy a warm home life.

JAKE   Where are you living now?

HOLLY   Nowhere, Jake....

[*Beat.*]

Listen, we can read to each other at night, we can be like a family.

JAKE   I sense you're groping for something.

HOLLY   I want to change things for myself for a while.

[*Beat.*]

I can call you Dad. I can be the daughter you never had.

JAKE   I don't know anything about you. And the little I do raises red flags.

HOLLY   How do you get to know someone? You spend time with them, discuss issues, delve into their psyche. Come on, Jake, you can do it. I'll be a good friend for you.

JAKE   [*Concerned.*] Holly, you seem like a nice kid, have you ever talked with someone, I mean professionally? There's a clinic down the street.

HOLLY   What's your favorite book?

JAKE   What?

HOLLY   What book do you enjoy so much you've read it more than once?

[JAKE *picks up a book from the table.*]

JAKE   That's easy, *Galileo's Daughter*.

HOLLY   Tell me your impressions of it.

JAKE   It contains some very beautiful letters Galileo's daughter wrote to him. The simplicity and innocence of her devotion to him and expressed belief in God had a profound and soothing effect on me. It was as pure a love as one could ever be blessed to know.
[*Beat.*]
I have it right here.

[HOLLY *places her hands on the side of her head.*]

HOLLY   Open it to page one hundred and twenty-six, go to his daughter's letter at the lower part of the page. Look at the third sentence.

[JAKE *pages through the book.*]

JAKE   Now what?

HOLLY   "Above all, I want you to know how happy you made me by offering so lovingly to help our convent." Now go to page two hundred and ninety-eight and look at the first paragraph.

JAKE   How did you do that? How could you recite that exact sentence?

HOLLY   Just go to page two hundred and ninety-eight.

[JAKE *pages through the book.*]

"The grapes in the vineyard already looked frightfully scarce before two violent hailstorms struck and completed their ruination."

JAKE   Are you some kind of savant with total recall?

HOLLY   You can have that same feeling of serenity this book gives you for all eternity. Jake, it's the Jell-O.

JAKE   What are you talking about?

HOLLY   When we die, our energy blends into an ocean of energy. Think of being a single molecule in a bowl of Jell-O. You become connected to all the other molecules.

JAKE   What's that mean?

HOLLY   You receive all the knowledge there is throughout time.

JAKE   Who are you, kid? What do you really want?

HOLLY   To stop you from taking your life.

JAKE   What do my affairs have to do with you?

HOLLY   The boss looks down on people ending their life. They have to go through a long period of redemption before they can join the Jell-O.

JAKE   When you're dead, you're dead.

HOLLY   It's how you die. If you pull the plug on yourself, it'll be like taking a bus trip across the country with hundreds of stops along the way. But if you die a natural death, it's a jet flight to the Jell-O.

JAKE   I don't need conversion. Take your act somewhere else.

HOLLY   Each bus stop has an interrogator who will sweat you, Jake. Bright lights, hours of questioning with you sitting in a very uncomfortable chair.

JAKE   I'm done talking, you gotta leave.

HOLLY   And because I'm your guide I have to wait for you at each stop. I mean, talk about a downer for me.

JAKE   What do I have to say to get you to leave?

HOLLY   You've already made progress. You were gonna take your life five minutes ago. Now you're off the hook, make another choice.

JAKE   Okay, I'll play along. What happens if I don't pull the plug?

HOLLY   I live with you until you pass on.

[*Beat.*]

I'm usually sent to people on their death bed. I comfort and guide them into the hereafter. But this is different, you dodged a bullet, literally, plenty of time left.

JAKE   You got a good con going, kid. It sounds perfect. You almost got me believing you. What are you after?

HOLLY   To stay on earth for a little while.

[*Beat.*]

I never had a family upbringing. I was killed in the auto accident with my parents. I was an infant.

[*Beat.*]

I want a dog, go to the movies, fly a kite…I wanna know what it is to have a father.

JAKE   You're an adult.

HOLLY   They assigned me a physical form which would be non-threatening to you.

[*Beat.*]

You need a reason to stay and bide your time. Let's try it for two weeks. What do you have to lose?

JAKE   I'm worried about you, kid. You shouldn't be on the street tonight.

HOLLY   Please, call me Holly.

JAKE   Okay, Holly, I'll let you stay the night but first thing in the morning, I'm taking you over to the clinic.

HOLLY   I'll work in the store until then; the window display needs a lot of help and I can clean up the bookshelves.

JAKE   No playing rap music or chewing gum. Sleep on the cot in the backroom. We open at nine in the morning, sharp.

HOLLY   Jake, you said "we." You included me like I'm part of the family.

JAKE   It's a figure of speech.

HOLLY   If you say so, but I know better.

JAKE   I live upstairs; I'll heat up some soup for us.

HOLLY   We can read to each other tonight! Won't it be great!?

JAKE   [*Sarcastically.*] Oh yeah, it'll be wonderful; just what I was hoping would happen. You probably don't even need a book, just say it from your brain.

HOLLY   I just might do that.

[*Beat.*]

Can I call you Dad?

JAKE   Don't get carried away.

HOLLY   Dad?

JAKE   What?

HOLLY   Do I get an allowance?

JAKE   Why don't we see if you're still here after tomorrow?

HOLLY   I can wait until then, Dad.

JAKE   Stop calling me Dad.

HOLLY   It's a figure of speech…Dad.

[JAKE *looks up at the ceiling and stretches his arms out.*]

JAKE   Why me?

• • •

Boulevard of Broken Dreams

Lynne Bolen

Lynne Bolen

Lynne Bolen is a playwright, director, producer, and actor. She is a member of New Voices Playwrights Theatre and has served as an officer on the board of directors for several years. Lynne was a member of the former Vanguard Theatre Ensemble. Her plays have been produced at the University of Rhode Island, Stage Door Repertory Theatre, MUZEO, OC Pavilion Performing Arts Center, Chance Theater, Vanguard Theatre, Gallery Theatre, STAGEStheatre, Cabrillo Playhouse, Empire Theatre, and Mysterium Theater. Her play *Assumptions* is included in *Best American Short Plays 2011–2012*, published by Applause. She has directed over fifty plays and has produced dozens of shows. As an actor, Bolen has appeared in numerous stage productions and films. A graduate of UCLA, she holds an MBA and an MS.

··· **production history** ···

Boulevard of Broken Dreams was first performed in Summer Voices 2014 at the Stage Door Repertory Theatre in Anaheim, California, in August 2014. The play was directed by Karen Wray.

ROBERT HARRINGTON   Jeff Gilbank

KIMBERLY JOHNSON   Jasmine West

SQUIRE SMITH   Eric Davis

POLICE/JUDGE/PRINCIPAL   Sky Siegel

characters

ROBERT HARRINGTON   Twenty-seven and forty-seven, Caucasian, teacher.

KIMBERLY JOHNSON   Seventeen, Caucasian, student.

SQUIRE SMITH   Eighteen and thirty-eight, African American, student.

POLICE/JUDGE/PRINCIPAL   Three roles played by same actor. The actor's back should be kept mostly to the audience so the actor is not easily identifiable.

time

Spring 1984. Popular music hits underscore the play to indicate the period.

scenes

All of the mini-scenes should transition very quickly with no set changes except for setting and striking the tree(s), which denotes the park. The objective is a constant uninterrupted flow of events with actors moving on and off the stage.

···

scene 1

[*Park, Sunday night. A bench is downstage right. A second bench is center stage on an angle. There is a tree upstage left. ROBERT and KIMBERLY are sitting on the center bench.*]

ROBERT   Are you sure that you didn't see anyone you know?

KIMBERLY   [*Miffed.*] Do you have to keep asking me the same question every time we meet here? We're on the other side of town. We don't know anyone around here. If you ask me again, I won't meet you anymore!

ROBERT   [*Cozying up.*] I'm sorry. We can't be careless. If anyone were to see us…

KIMBERLY   We'd be toast, I know.

[*They kiss, and then he pulls her into a slow dance. ROBERT starts singing "Careless Whisper" by Wham! KIMBERLY joins.*]

KIMBERLY   Oooh, I love George Michael!

ROBERT   I don't know, there's something funny about him. He'll never last.

KIMBERLY   You're just jealous. George Michael is soooo cute!

ROBERT   Kimberly, you sound like a crazy love-struck teenager.

KIMBERLY   Well, maybe that's because I'm seventeen.

ROBERT   But you usually act like you're twenty-seven.

KIMBERLY   That would make me your age, you old man!

ROBERT   Dirty old man!

KIMBERLY   I love you anyway, *Mister* Harrington.

[*They kiss and then ROBERT breaks off suddenly.*]

KIMBERLY   What's wrong?

ROBERT   Someone is coming.

[*They move upstage and hide behind the tree(s). SQUIRE enters downstage, sits on a bench, and starts to read a book. His back is to them, so he does not see them.*]

KIMBERLY   Who is it? What is he doing?

ROBERT   He looks familiar.

KIMBERLY   Omigod, it's Squire.

ROBERT   Squire, from my English class? What the hell is he doing here on a Sunday night?

KIMBERLY   Ha! Looks like he's on the wrong side of the tracks.

ROBERT   Well, Miss Kimberly, not everyone's father is a corporate vice president.

KIMBERLY   I hate Squire. He always acts so superior.

ROBERT   [*Teasing.*] Sounds like you're jealous. Isn't he your big competition for the Class of '84 valedictorian?

[SQUIRE *looks up, as though he has heard something.*]

KIMBERLY   Let's get out of here. If he saw us together, he would like nothing better than to bring me down. We can still make it to the eight o'clock showing of *Ghostbusters*.

[KIMBERLY *and* ROBERT *exit. Lights fade to black. End of scene.*]

scene 2

[*Classroom, Monday morning.* KIMBERLY *and* SQUIRE *are sitting on the center-stage bench.* ROBERT *is downstage in front of them, in profile with his back to the audience.*]

SQUIRE   What's everyone all excited about?

[*The bell rings.*]

KIMBERLY   Didn't you hear about the robbery and double murder last night?

ROBERT   Kimberly, would you like to share with the class?

KIMBERLY   I was just telling Squire about the murders last night, Mr. Harrington.

  [*To* SQUIRE.]

Someone robbed the liquor store and shot the owner and the customer, who happened to be the mayor's wife. Everyone on *this side* of town is in an uproar. She lived long enough to say it was a black kid who did it.

ROBERT   Yes, it's a horrible tragedy. Another lady witnessed everything, so they'll get the guy real soon. There's nothing to worry about. Speaking of tragedies, let's continue on with our Shakespeare unit.

[*Lights fade to black.* KIMBERLY *and* ROBERT *exit. End of scene.*]

scene 3

[*Classroom, Monday afternoon.* ROBERT *and* SQUIRE *are finishing a conversation.*]

ROBERT   Thanks for staying after the meeting to help clean up.

SQUIRE   One of the perks of being the president! The Creative Writing Club is the best. It's great to have you as our club sponsor.

ROBERT   I really enjoy it. Our literary magazine will be quite special with the "Games of the XXIII Olympiad" theme.

SQUIRE   Yeah, it's going to be wonderful. Did you hear that Reagan is going to be the first U.S. president to attend the opening of the Summer Olympics? Well, I've gotta go toss some pizza now. See you tomorrow.

[SQUIRE *starts to walk away, when a* POLICEMAN *suddenly steps in, grabs him, throws him to the floor, and handcuffs him. The* POLICEMAN *mostly keeps his back to the audience.*]

What the hell?

POLICEMAN   Squire Smith, you are under arrest. You have the right to remain silent. Anything you say…

ROBERT   Officer, what are you doing?

POLICEMAN   Sir, back away. I am arresting this boy on suspicion of double homicide.

ROBERT   Homicide? What are you talking about?

POLICEMAN   Last night, he murdered Calvin Kinsey and Beverly Ward.

ROBERT   That's preposterous. He's my student.

POLICEMAN   A witness has identified Squire Smith as the murderer.

ROBERT   How did she identify him?

POLICEMAN   She said that the black boy who works at the pizza parlor shot those poor people.

SQUIRE   I didn't shoot anybody!

ROBERT   What time did it happen? Wasn't it 7:30 p.m.?

POLICEMAN   Around a quarter to 8.

SQUIRE   I wasn't even on this side of town then!

POLICEMAN   Save it for the judge. Come on, I'm taking you in.

SQUIRE   Mr. Harrington!

ROBERT   Don't worry, Squire. You're innocent, they'll let you go.

[*The* POLICEMAN *hauls* SQUIRE *off.* KIMBERLY *enters.*]

KIMBERLY   What's going on?

ROBERT   He's been accused of those murders last night.

KIMBERLY   Ridiculous! How can that be?

ROBERT   A witness identified him. She recognized the murderer as the kid from the pizza place.

KIMBERLY   But he was in the park when it happened.

ROBERT   Yes, Kim, we saw him at the same time the murders happened. We have to tell the police!

KIMBERLY   Robert, slow down. Think about it! If we tell the police, everyone will find out about *us*.

ROBERT   We have to do something.

KIMBERLY   We can't be Squire's alibi!

[*They look down and away from each other. Lights fade to black. They exit. End of scene.*]

scene 4

[*Courtroom, Tuesday.* SQUIRE *sits on the downstage bench, facing the audience.* ROBERT *and* KIMBERLY *sit on the upstage bench. The* JUDGE *enters and stands in front of* SQUIRE, *back to the audience.* SQUIRE *stands.*]

JUDGE Squire Smith, you are accused of the murders of Calvin Kinsey and Beverly Ward during the commission of a robbery. How do you plea?

SQUIRE Not guilty, Your Honor.

JUDGE Due to the special circumstances, the nature of the crime, and the parties involved, bail is set at five hundred thousand dollars.

ROBERT No!

SQUIRE Five hundred thousand dollars? Where am I going to get five hundred grand? I can't make bail.

JUDGE Defendant will be remanded to the county jail pending trial.

SQUIRE Your Honor, please. I'm innocent.

JUDGE Court adjourned.

[*The* JUDGE *and* SQUIRE *exit.*]

KIMBERLY Robert, get a hold of yourself! Are you crazy, shouting out like that?

ROBERT They're putting an innocent man in jail.

KIMBERLY A little time behind bars just might get rid of his cockiness.

ROBERT I've been waking up in the middle of every night, wracked with guilt. You hardly seem to care.

KIMBERLY We've discussed this over and over. You know there's nothing we can do without crucifying ourselves.

ROBERT This will destroy his dream of becoming a doctor.

KIMBERLY What about my dream of becoming an attorney? What about my plans to go to Harvard?

ROBERT We have to do something.

KIMBERLY   Oh, really? Like what? Shall I confess that I saw Squire at the park when I was kissing my teacher? Do you really want to lose your job and go to jail over some stuck-up guy who thinks he's smarter than everyone else?

ROBERT   Well…I suppose if we believe in the justice system, he will be released.

KIMBERLY   Absolutely! That's why I'm going to be a lawyer. There is no way an innocent man will be found guilty of murder.

ROBERT   Right. Justice will prevail.

[*They look down and away from each other. Lights fade to black. They exit. End of scene.*]

scene 5

[*Classroom, one month later.* KIMBERLY *is sitting on the center-stage bench.* ROBERT *is downstage in front of her, in profile with his back to the audience. The* PRINCIPAL *enters and speaks to* ROBERT.]

PRINCIPAL   I'm sorry to interrupt your class, Mr. Harrington, but I would like to make a couple of announcements to your students.

ROBERT   Of course.

[*To the students.*]

Class, Principal Anderson would like to say a few words.

PRINCIPAL   Good afternoon, everyone. I have a couple of announcements to share. First, as you know, it has been a month since your fellow classmate, Squire Smith, was arrested for murder and has been on trial.

ROBERT   What have you heard?

PRINCIPAL   I have known Squire for four years, and he is a fine, upstanding young man. Unfortunately, the mayor exerted pressure to accelerate the case because his wife was one of the victims of the crime. I am very sorry to inform you of the devastating news that Squire was found guilty.

ROBERT   [*Looks at* KIMBERLY.] Oh no!

PRINCIPAL   The verdict was based upon the testimony of just one witness. There was no evidence of robbery and no murder weapon recovered. This conviction is absolutely heartbreaking to me, as Squire is a hardworking honor student, ranked number one in the senior class.

ROBERT   The judge has to consider this during sentencing!

PRINCIPAL   I visited Squire in jail, and I promised him that I will do everything I can to help fight this injustice. Sadly, he will not be returning to school for graduation, so my second announcement is that the valedictorian for the Class of '84 will be Kimberly Johnson.

KIMBERLY   [*Jumps up and raises both arms, fingers in the Victory sign.*] Yes!

[KIMBERLY *looks left and right smiling, then at* ROBERT, *who shakes his head.* KIMBERLY *crosses her arms and sits down. End of scene.*]

scene 6

[*Park, same night.* ROBERT *is pacing in front of the center-stage bench, taking swigs from his flask.* KIMBERLY *enters.* ROBERT *reaches to kiss her, but she backs away.*]

ROBERT   What's wrong, Kim?

KIMBERLY   That was really risky, calling me at home.

ROBERT   I need to talk to you. How else could I contact you?

KIMBERLY   What if my mother or father had answered the phone instead of me?

ROBERT   I would have hung up.

KIMBERLY   That's really stupid, Robert.

ROBERT   Listen, they didn't answer, you did, and now you're here. That's all that matters.

KIMBERLY   I told my parents I was going to the library. I'm getting so tired of lying all the time. Why did you need to see me tonight?

ROBERT   [*Grabs her hand.*] Come here, Kim.

KIMBERLY   [*Pulls away.*] You know, Robert, I didn't like the way you looked at me in class today. It felt so condescending.

ROBERT   We just found out that Squire was convicted of murder, and you celebrated. It was pretty callous.

KIMBERLY   I get to be valedictorian, and all you care about is Squire? You should have congratulated me in front of all the students.

ROBERT   It was awfully bad timing, Kimberly. Squire was number one in the class, someone falsely accused him, and now he'll be going to prison unless we do something.

KIMBERLY   Do something? There is nothing we can do!

ROBERT   We have to corroborate his story that he was in the park at the time of the murders. I will feel guilty for the rest of my life if we don't do the right thing now.

KIMBERLY   Is it the right thing to ruin our lives? Who do you care more about, Squire or me? He is not so important that you need to ruin my life and yours. My parents would be devastated and probably disown me, and then how could I afford to go to Harvard?

ROBERT   I can tell the authorities I saw Squire without involving you.

KIMBERLY   Nobody will believe you now, after he's been convicted, saying you saw Squire in the park. They would ask why you didn't come forward earlier, why you let your student suffer through a murder trial. You would have no credibility as a witness.

ROBERT   I have to try. How can I do nothing and let someone go to prison when I know he is innocent?

KIMBERLY   They would ask what you were doing alone in the park, on the other side of town. They would get you to admit that I was there with you. If it came out that you and I are lovers, you would undoubtedly lose your job and be sent to jail. What about your dream of writing the great American novel? Would being in jail inspire your poetry? And after you got out of jail, you could never teach again, and it would be impossible, being a sex offender, to get a job.

ROBERT   [*Takes a swig.*] Stop getting carried away. I wouldn't tell anyone about you, so I wouldn't lose my job and go to jail.

KIMBERLY   You really think you could stand up against cops and attorneys who break people every day? You're not a good liar. When they press you, you will tell them about us. Think about it. Everyone, and I mean everyone, will know that you, a trusted teacher, had sex with your minor student. Do you really want to be branded a child molester?

ROBERT   God, you're cold-hearted.

KIMBERLY   I'm not cold, I'm pragmatic. I'm a survivor. My life—our lives—and the lives of many other people, are more important than just Squire's.

ROBERT   It isn't fair. He's a good person.

KIMBERLY   Bad things happen to good people all the time.

ROBERT   You know, our relationship is wrong on so many levels. Why did we ever get together?

KIMBERLY   You used me, and I used you. But it was fun while it lasted.

[*She turns to walk away, but* ROBERT *grabs her arm.*]

ROBERT   So that's it, you're willing to forego your morals and ethics and let an innocent person suffer?

KIMBERLY   Actually, I'm not worried about Squire, he's smart, and he'll be just fine. But you're weak, Robert. I am worried about you. *Don't be stupid.*

[*They stare at each other for a moment, then* KIMBERLY *abruptly exits.* ROBERT *starts to follow her, then stops and takes another swig. Lights fade to black. End of scene.*]

scene 7

[*The beginning of "Boulevard of Broken Dreams" by Green Day plays, indicating the time period change to 2004.*]

[*Park, afternoon.* ROBERT, *looking like a bum, is sitting on the center bench with a newspaper, snoozing.* SQUIRE *walks by, stops in front of* ROBERT, *and then sits.* ROBERT *wakes up.*]

SQUIRE   [*Points to newspaper.*] Too bad about Ronald Reagan passing away. Fortieth president of the United States.

ROBERT   Yeah, I know who he was.

SQUIRE   Sorry, that's not what I meant. I was just trying to remember when he was the fortieth president.

ROBERT   He was president from 1981 to 1989.

SQUIRE   The 80s. Yeah.

[*He glances at* ROBERT.]

Excuse me, but you look like…are you Mr. Harrington?

ROBERT   I'm Bob.

[*Beat.*]

Yes, Squire, you recognized me.

SQUIRE   You remember me? It's been twenty years.

ROBERT   Of course. I'll never forget you.

SQUIRE   I suppose I'm fairly notorious.

ROBERT   [*Takes a swig from flask.*] In the last twenty years, not a day has gone by that I haven't thought about you.

SQUIRE   I'm not sure what you mean. Mr. Harrington…are you okay?

ROBERT   Yeah. What about you? I didn't know you were out of prison. How did you get out?

SQUIRE   You didn't know?

ROBERT   I've been…out of touch.

SQUIRE   It's all thanks to Mr. Anderson—our principal—

ROBERT   Yeah, I remember him.

SQUIRE   Mr. Anderson became my champion and advocate. He helped me to attend college and get my degree through distance learning. He was relentless in his efforts to prove my innocence. DNA testing finally got me exonerated, and then Mr. Anderson helped me land a job.

ROBERT   Good ole Mr. Anderson.

SQUIRE   He's a good person. But what about you? You live here now?

ROBERT   You needn't be so diplomatic, Squire. Yes, I'm homeless.

SQUIRE   You were a great teacher. You were my favorite teacher. What happened?

ROBERT   [*Takes a swig.*] I didn't do anything.

SQUIRE   Something must have happened to get you to this state.

ROBERT   I didn't do anything, and I couldn't live with it. I drank to forget, and I lost everything.

SQUIRE   You didn't do anything? Sorry, I don't understand.

ROBERT   Sometimes *not* doing something is far worse than doing something.

SQUIRE   Tell me about it. I spent fifteen years in prison for not doing something.

ROBERT   [*Takes a swig.*] I didn't do anything.

SQUIRE   I know.

ROBERT   What do you know?

SQUIRE   I know you were there that night. At the park. I heard you and Kimberly.

ROBERT   You knew?

[*Beat.*]

Why didn't you say anything?

SQUIRE   Sometimes not doing something is far *better* than doing something. I knew you two were involved. I knew what would happen if everyone found out. I knew you made a horrible mistake. It wasn't for me to destroy your lives, and those of others, in desperation to save myself.

ROBERT   So you went to prison, knowing that you had two witnesses.

SQUIRE   Well, to be honest, I knew that even if I claimed you saw me at the park, they wouldn't have believed me. I didn't actually see you. I only heard your careless whispers. The mayor needed to punish somebody for his wife's murder, without delay. It was a futile situation.

ROBERT   It was wrong, and I should have done something. You shouldn't have gone to prison.

SQUIRE   There are all kinds of prisons, Mr. Harrington. You made your own prison and tortured yourself with guilty feelings.

ROBERT   It's funny, I sang some lyrics of "Careless Whisper" to Kimberly that night. There's another line.

[ROBERT *sings.*]

I'm never gonna dance again
Guilty feet have got no rhythm.

SQUIRE   Remember when you taught *The Scarlet Letter* in class? Don't brand yourself forever. Stop punishing yourself. Let me help you.

ROBERT   This isn't a chance encounter, is it Squire?

SQUIRE   No, sir, I've been looking for you for some time now. I heard what happened to you. You were my best teacher. You believed in me and encouraged me to pursue my dream.

ROBERT   You were my best student.

[*Beat.*]

I'm so sorry.

SQUIRE   Mr. Harrington, I forgave you years ago. Now you need to forgive yourself. I can help you.

ROBERT   [*Singing.*]
Sometimes I wish someone out there will find me.
'Til then I walk alone.

SQUIRE   I found you. You are not alone.

[*Beat.*]

I'm a social worker now, and I will help you. Together, Bob, we will change your address from the Boulevard of Broken Dreams.

[*Lights fade.*]

• • •

Journeys

Austin Peay

Austin Peay

Austin Peay has worked forty-two years in entertainment overseeing more than 150 plays and musicals and as a producer, production manager, and stage manager. Concurrent with this, Peay has been an educator for twenty years teaching English and drama at the high school and collegiate levels and served as an adjunct professor for Vanguard University of Southern California and Saddleback Community College. Peay has recently had a short play, *Just Make It Stop*, published in *New Voices Playwrights Annual Anthology of Short Plays 2014*. He has recently turned to writing short- and full-length plays. Austin earned his BA in drama from CSU, Fullerton; he has a graduate degree in English and master's degree in education from Cal Poly University, Pomona.

··· production history ···

Aliso Niguel High School, Aliso Viejo, California. March 5 and 6, 1999, One-Act Program.

> Directed by Austin Peay
>
> **MEGAN**   Megan Hutchison
>
> **DOUG**   Austin Peay

An NYC workshop lab September 28 and 29, 2013

> Directed by Jeramiah Peay
>
> **MEGAN**   Melanie Brook
>
> **DOUG**   Nicholas Fleming

Journeys was part of the New Voices Playwrights Theatre presentation Summer Voices 2014: Six One-Act Plays, held August 2, 9, 16, and 17, 2014, at the Stage Door Repertory Theatre in Anaheim, California.

characters

> **MEGAN**   a pretty eighteen-year-old girl. She is somewhat angry at life and a little bit cynical, which is a veneer for a gentle, vulnerable, and hurting young lady.
>
> **DOUG**   a man thirty-six to forty years old. Has lived hard, chasing life always somewhere over the horizon. He has had a rough time of it and has mellowed and grown wiser.

setting

Joe's Roadside Diner in small town USA. Joe's Diner also doubles as a bus stop.

time

Early summer evening around 7:30 p.m.

···

[Scene shift and music. Stage goes to black. Intro music plays. MEGAN *enters and sits. Stage lights come up. Intro music fades. Sound of bus stopping. Door opens and closes.*

At rise there is only one person, MEGAN, in the diner. She is drinking a Coke and is obviously a little bit nervous and agitated. She has with her a small suitcase and a backpack and is wearing a light jacket, a blouse, jeans, and sneakers. She is obviously ready to travel. After a few moments we hear a bus drive up and after a moment pull away. The diner door opens and another traveler enters. It is the man. While not shabby, he is dressed as a hardworking, blue-collar man and may have even slept in his clothes. He enters dragging a heavy backpack, walks over to the diner counter, and sits on a stool. After a few moments he reaches over and rings the bell. He gets up and looks around a bit, nods to the girl, who nods back, and again turns his back to the audience and sits at the counter. He rings the bell again and waits a moment and finally gets up, walks around the counter, reaches under the counter, pulls out a coffee cup and coffeepot, and pours. He sets the pot back down crosses around the counter and starts to sit down.]

MEGAN   How did you know where the coffee was?

DOUG   Some things never change.

MEGAN   What do you mean?

DOUG   Old Joe has kept the coffee there for one hundred years.

MEGAN   Yeah, but how did you know? I've never seen you around here before.

DOUG   Yeah, it's been awhile. About eighteen years or so but I used to live here.

  [*Crosses to her table.*]

  Mind if I sit?

MEGAN   [*Bitterly.*] It's a free country or so I'm told.

  [*He sits. There is an awkward pause.*]

  So you grew up here?

  [*He nods.*]

  Your mom and dad still here?

  [*He nods again.*]

  Why didn't you just go home then?

DOUG   Trying to find the courage to just pop in after all this time.

MEGAN   Why did you come back?

DOUG   The real question is, why did I leave?

MEGAN   That's the easy part.

DOUG   Going and coming.

[*He chuckles.*]

You know, it seems so easy but both propositions are pretty complicated. What makes you think going's the easy part?

MEGAN   Oh, I get why you left. Probably the same reason I'm leaving. Who wants to live in some two-bit tank town where all anyone wants to do is tell you how to live your life, butting in all the time where they're not wanted and they've got no right to be, talking behind your back.

DOUG   [*He chuckles again.*] Yeah, that's pretty much the same reason I left....And you know something? It's pretty much the same reason I'm coming back.

MEGAN   I don't get it. You're coming back because people are busybodies with nothing better to do than to harass the helpless and make someone else's life miserable just because theirs is?

DOUG   [*Chuckles again.*] You know when I left here I was just as angry as you are now. My family and everybody else in town thought I should marry the girl next door, settle down, and have the American average, two point something kids and live happily ever after.

MEGAN   Did you like her? The girl next door?

DOUG   [*Without hesitation.*] Oh yeah, I liked her all right.

MEGAN   Did you love her?

DOUG   [*After a pause, he looks away and finally turns back to her and says softly.*] Oh yeah, I loved her a lot and I think I love her more now than I did then.

MEGAN   Why didn't you marry her then?

DOUG   You know, kid, you ask a lot of questions for a stranger. Seems like you're a whole lot like everybody you been complaining about around here.

MEGAN Touché!

[*Winces as if in pain.*]

Ouch, that hurt. The truth is I never met anybody from anywhere else. Especially someone who used to live here and for some reason known only to God is coming back. You want me to shut up, alright just tell me to shut up and I will.

DOUG No, kid, that's all right. I don't mind.

[*Getting up to get more coffee.*]

You want a refill on your Coke?

MEGAN Sure. Thanks.

[*She hands him the empty glass. He crosses behind counter and refills the Coke and coffee, leaves money on the counter, smiles, and says as he crosses back to sit.*]

DOUG So go ahead and hit me with it. What was the question again, Miss Busybody?

MEGAN [*She grins at this.*] So why didn't you marry the girl next door?

DOUG I almost did. Everybody pushed hard enough and I finally asked her, she said yes, so we set the date. The closer it got to that date the more scared I got. I was so afraid if I got married that early in life I was going to miss out on things. I don't know what things but I think it was the not knowing that scared me so much. The closer that date got the more it began to feel like a ball and chain. It got bigger with every day that passed. I begin to think that real life was out there somewhere and like you I was afraid I was going to miss out by sticking around here in this little two-bit tank town.

MEGAN Well, what happened? What did you do?

DOUG After high school I'd gotten a job bagging groceries at Danny's Grocery Store. I think the day I quit was the longest day of my life up until then. I thought about leaving all day long and when five o'clock finally came I went home quietly, packed my bags, and left on the eight o'clock bus and never looked back.

MEGAN Until now.

DOUG Right—wrong. That's not really true. I guess I always looked back I was just too blockheaded to know it at the time.

MEGAN What you mean?

DOUG Every time I'd get lonely I'd think about my family; mom, dad, brother, sister, friends. Yeah, all the busybodies in this "little two-bit tank town"—The girl next door and two point something kids.

MEGAN Yeah, well, I don't think I'll be looking back like that. I've got no family except an overprotective mother who insists on meeting all of the few dates I've ever had and knowing exactly where I am all the time. She's put me on restrictions so many times that going to the DMV is a major outing. As for your two point something kids—not! You can have 'em—not for me! I want more out of life and I'm gonna get it out there somewhere!

DOUG Well, there's a lot out there, kid. Take it from this road-weary traveler, there is a whole lot out there.

[*He turns away lost in thought for a moment.*]

MEGAN Like what?—Hey!

[*She claps her hands.*]

DOUG What!

MEGAN Are you here or out there somewhere?

DOUG What? Oh, sorry my mind wandered for a moment. What was it you said?

MEGAN [*With a bit of attitude.*] I said, like what?

DOUG [*He's lost the thread of the conversation and is confused.*] Like what? What?

MEGAN [*Still a little bit of attitude but with a sigh of resignation.*] You said, "There's a whole lot out there," and I said, "Like what?" So what's out there?

DOUG You name it, kid. Anything the imagination can conceive of or money can buy. All kinds of places, people, towns, countries, and the deep blue sea. Yeah, believe me, there are definitely places to go, things to do, and people to see.

MEGAN Yeah, where did you go, what have you done?

DOUG It seems like I've been just about everywhere and there are still places to go. I've met all kinds of people and done all kinds of jobs, some of them a whole lot worse than bagging groceries but then you gotta eat. And there are still places to go, new people to see, and experiences to be had. I guess that never really ends. There's always something else but after a while they're all pretty much the same. That's when the loneliness sets in and the looking back comes a haunting.

MEGAN Yeah, maybe so but I still think I'd rather be lonely somewhere else.

DOUG What you mean? Why you think you'd rather be lonely somewhere else?

MEGAN I don't have a life here. The rare times when I'm out with my friends, I always have to be in earlier than anyone else. Sometimes Mom even calls and tells me it's time to come home.

[*Pantomiming the phone and in a mocking tone.*]

"It's time to come home, honey." It's so humiliating, I'm seventeen years old and I get a phone call from my mother telling me it's time to come home. My so-called friends wait till I'm gone and then giggle behind my back and make fun of me. I feel like I've been alone here all my life and I'm sick of it and I'm sick of this little two-bit tank town. A big city, that's where I want to live. I think I'd be happy in a big city with all those people and all those things to do.

DOUG What makes you think you'd be happier there with all those people and things to do?

MEGAN Mainly because I wouldn't have to put up with all these nosy, snotty, busybody, pushy people in this town. Everybody thinks they know more about my life than I do. You know how it is, you've lived here and you've lived in a big city, haven't you?

DOUG   I told you, kiddo, I've been just about everywhere—Los Angeles, New York, Paris, London, Rome, Istanbul, Hong Kong—you name it, I've probably spent time there, and you know what?

MEGAN   What?

DOUG   No matter where I went or where I was—and it didn't take long—I always wound up late at night feeling alone—sometimes in a city of millions of people and sometimes even in a little two-bit tank town like this one. I'd find myself looking back wondering what if…

MEGAN   I don't understand.

DOUG   I had no family there, no friends.

[*He chuckles a little bit.*]

No busybodies or pushy people to get mad at or be close friends with. No one I'd known for more than a few months, sometimes just a few hours.…

MEGAN   And then you'd think about your family.

DOUG   Yeah—

MEGAN   And your girl next door.

DOUG   Mostly the girl next door, mostly—yeah—the girl next door.…Sometimes I wish I'd…After eighteen years there is hardly a day goes by when I don't think about the girl next door—and the two point something kids I don't have.

[*He looks away to stage right to hide his emotion.*]

MEGAN   [*She looks down and finally stage left to hide her emotion.*] Well, I'm nobody's girl next door and neither is my mom, she doesn't exactly stir the hearts of men. She's never been married!

[*Turns toward him. Bitterly mocking finger quotes Miss Johnson.*]

"Miss Johnson"—the librarian's never been married.

[*He gives very quick look, then looks away and hesitantly turns back to her.*]

DOUG   Her last name—your last name is…?

MEGAN   Yeah.

DOUG   She never married?

MEGAN   [*She shakes her head no and says bitterly.*] Never.

DOUG   How old are you?

MEGAN   Seventeen.

DOUG   Seventeen! Then—

MEGAN   [*Interrupting again. Angry, her voice rising.*] I'm not too young, don't try to talk me out of leaving! My mom already lost that battle! You left! I want to go some of those places you went!

DOUG   But I came back!

MEGAN   That's your problem.

DOUG   [*Blinking back some tears.*] Yes, that's right. You're right. It is my problem, my mistakes. And I came back to try to solve some of those problems and correct those mistakes.

[*He pauses, looking at her for a moment, then says softly.*]

I hope I'm not too late. It's been a long, hard, obstinate road—I got to thinking of this "little tank town" like that old TV show where everybody knows your name—once you get past all the busybodying, gossiping, and everybody intruding into your life, everybody knows your name and you know there's —and they're your friends. Somewhere along the line I began to realize what looked like a ball and chain was really a taproot that gives nourishment and purpose to life. Looking at you I can tell you something else, I already know I should've stuck it out the first time.

MEGAN   Well, good for you. There's not gonna be a second time around for me. I'd have gone with you eighteen years ago if I'd been alive then.

[*Sound of a bus driving up and stopping. She looks toward the door for a moment, then back at him.*]

Eighteen years?

DOUG   [*He has difficulty holding back tears and can only whisper.*] Eighteen years…and…

[*A horn honks.*]

MEGAN [*She is confused, emotional, upset, and finally.*] Then…no—no. Sorry, mister, I gotta go.

[*She rises, grabs her bags, and crosses toward the door.*]

DOUG Wait!

[*He holds out his hand to her. She pauses and looks back at him.*]

MEGAN [*The horn honks again. She considers seriously for the first time that this stranger might be her father, can't wrap her head around it ,and finally.*] No, no…I'm sorry, I gotta go.…

[*She turns and starts toward the door again.*]

DOUG I'd sure like it if you go with me to visit your mom.

MEGAN [*After a pause turns to him.*] After all these years, huh?

DOUG Yeah, and every year and every day in between.

MEGAN [*She stops, pauses, and slowly turns back to him blinking back tears.*] If you've been gone…?

DOUG [*He can barely whisper now.*] Eighteen—long—years…

MEGAN [*Trying hard to hold back tears.*] Then—you're…?????

[*She shakes her head, unable to believe it might be true. He nods. The horn honks again.*]

No!

[*She turns to leave.*]

DOUG [*He is pleading now, barely audible.* MEGAN *freezes with her back to him.*]

There'll always be another bus—honey.…

[*She turns toward* DOUG. *He opens his arms and steps toward her; she drops her bags and does the same. They hug as the bus is heard driving away. The lights fade to black.*]

• • •

Variations on a Composition in Blue

Anne V. Grob

Anne V. Grob

Playwright Anne V. Grob, originally from New York, resides in Southern California. She studied playwriting and enjoyed staged readings of her works at South Coast Repertory's Playwriting Conservatory. Her plays have been produced in NYC's Greenwich Village Players Theatre SPF, Only in New York, with *Hemingway at the Larchmont* voted best of festival, week two, in June 2014. *The Planting Moon* was a semi-finalist in Little Black Dress Ink's National Festival of New Works, and *Variations on a Composition in Blue* had its debut production in New Voices Summer Voices 2014. *How to Have a Kosher Christmas* debuted in the New Voices Holiday Show, December 2014. Anne Grob is an active member of New Voices Playwrights Theatre.

···production history···

Variations on a Composition in Blue was produced in August 2014 as part of the New Voices Summer Voices' production of six one-act plays. It was directed by Geoffrey Gread.

LISA   Megan Tice

ED   Arturo Jones as Ed

characters

LISA   A young woman in her mid-twenties, art student

ED   A slightly older man in his thirties, artist and art professor

LISA and **ED** years later

LOUDSPEAKER VOICE-OVER

···

scene 1

[*At rise, we are in the Museum of Modern Art in NYC. LISA stands in front of Monet's painting of water lilies. She studies the painting intently. She is not aware that ED watches her from the doorway.*]

ED   Squint.

LISA   Pardon?

ED   You should squint when you view this painting.

LISA   Why?

ED   Trust me.

LISA   But I don't know you.

ED   Trust me anyway. Go ahead. Squint.

[LISA *squints.*]

LISA   Uh-huh.

ED   Take a few steps back.

LISA   Why?

ED   Just do it.

> [*She takes a few steps back.*]

Now take a few steps closer.

LISA   Make up your mind.

[*She walks forward two steps.*]

ED   Closer.

[*She takes two more steps.*]

LISA   Oh, wow. Now I see. Yes, you're right. It's…it's stunning.

[*A long pause.* ED *and* LISA *stare quietly at the painting. Suddenly,* ED *breaks the silence.*]

ED   You're a student, right? At NYU? And you're studying, let me see, art history, and you're here on a pre-assignment from your professor for the class, Modern Movements in Contemporary Art, which begins tomorrow at 9 a.m.

LISA   Now wait a minute. Have you been…?

ED   Let me introduce myself. I'm Ed Rousseau.

LISA   The artist?

ED   Guilty as charged. And I'm also your professor, the same one who gave you that assignment. And you are—

> [*He leans in closer and studies her college I.D.*]

Elise Bloom.

LISA   I prefer Lisa.

ED   So, Elise, have you seen the Rothko yet?

> [LISA *shakes her head "no."*]

Well, then you're not finished. Come with me.

LISA   The truth is, I needed to leave. I've got a—

ED   A date? Believe me, no mere mortal can measure up to what's in store for you on the other side of this wall.

LISA Not that it's any of your—

[ED *takes* LISA *by the arm and leads her running toward the gallery labeled Abstract Expressionism. They both stop short as they enter the space, then slowly approach Rothko's painting. It is a large canvas composed of the same blues as the Monet, with subtle bands of pink and orange toward the top.*]

Oh my.

ED Shhh. Don't talk.

[ED *leans in toward* LISA. *She doesn't respond, but she does not move away either. They linger as they view the painting.*]

LISA I think I could stand here forever.

ED You are.

LISA Is it okay to talk now?

ED If that's what you want to do.

LISA There's so much to know.

ED And what is it you want to know?

LISA I, I don't…I mean, I think—

ED Don't think, just be here, in this space, with this magnificent painting. And me. Now tell me, how do you feel standing here with me right now?

LISA Well I, I don't know. I'm confused.

ED Try. Describe where you are, what you see, what you feel.

LISA I'm standing on the precipice, and there are these gates.

[ED *slowly positions himself behind* LISA, *leans closer to her, and speaks softly.*]

ED And?

LISA And I'm not sure. I'm not sure what they're asking of me.

ED The gates, are they opened or closed?

LISA There's something, something ominous about them, like a warning, that's telling me—

ED   Proceed with caution.

LISA   Yes, and it's exciting and frightening at the same time.

ED   Don't rush it. Let yourself fall, slowly.

LISA   And I want to enter, I have to enter, and yet something is holding me back.

ED   Trust your first impulse.

LISA   You've been here before?

ED   Yes.

LISA   Alone?

ED   Is that important?

LISA   Funny, I feel alone right now, just in this moment, I'm feeling quite alone.

[LISA *becomes aware of* ED's *advancement toward her. She moves away.*]

ED   Am I making you nervous? Sorry, I don't mean to. But we had a moment back there. Just then, when we entered the space of the painting. We had a moment.

[ED *offers his hand to* LISA. *She ignores the gesture and folds her arms in front of her.*]

LISA   No. No, there was no moment. I was just…no.

LOUDSPEAKER VOICE-OVER   Attention, visitors. The galleries will be closing in ten minutes.

LISA   We should leave now, before we get locked in here.

ED   Wait. Don't go, not yet. There's something I want to show you. There's a third piece. It's not complete…you have to see all three pieces together.

[*A bell. Stop action.*]

LISA   Is that how it happened?

scene 2

[LISA *and* ED *return to their opening marks.* LISA *stands in front of Monet's painting of water lilies, unaware that* ED *watches her from the doorway.*]

ED Squint.

LISA Pardon?

ED You know you have to squint when you view the Monet.

LISA You're...you're Ed Rousseau, aren't you?

ED Guilty as charged.

LISA I'm in your class, at NYU, Modern Movements in Contemporary Art! I can't believe this. To find you here. And I was just doing research for your class. I can't believe this!

ED You mean you're not following me?

LISA Well, no, why would you think that?

ED I thought I saw you, in the other gallery, looking at the light installation.

LISA I came here for the essay, the assignment you gave. See?

[LISA *takes out a piece of paper and reads from it.*]

"Compare two pieces of modern art, one from the Impressionism Era and one from Abstract Expressionism. Write a three-page essay establishing the roots of the latter in the former, with respect to aesthetics and formal properties."

ED I wrote that? I should be shot at dawn.

LISA What?

ED Do you really think art should be experienced in such an academic way?

LISA Well, it's your course. I signed up for it because I wanted to study with you.

ED Then this is your lucky day, because here I am and I'm available for a private lesson.

LISA   All right, sure. Where do we start?

ED   Right here. But you have to trust me, and do everything I tell you.

[LISA *nods.*]

Good. Now close your eyes.

[*He covers her eyes with his hands and guides her up close to the Monet.*]

Now when I tell you to open your eyes, do it slowly and squint. Stay with it as long as you can. Don't move a muscle, don't speak, just take it all in with your eyes. Ready?

LISA   Ready.

ED   Okay, open.

[*He removes his hands from her eyes. There is a long pause as* LISA *and* ED *look at the painting.* ED *places his hands over her eyes again and guides her away.*]

Keep your eyes closed and come with me.

[ED *guides her from the room to a nearby gallery. He stops her in front of the blue painting by Rothko.*]

Okay, open your eyes, slowly.

LISA   Oh my.

ED   Shhh. Don't talk.

[*There is a long pause as* LISA *and* ED *look at the painting.*]

LOUDSPEAKER VOICE-OVER   Attention, visitors. The galleries will be closing in ten minutes.

LISA   I think I get it now, the link between the two paintings. But in the textbook it says—

ED   Forget everything you've read in that book. This is your source, this museum. Come here often, use your skills of observation, that's how to study modern art. The book breaks it all down into *isms*, movements. Forget that, just focus on the genius of the artists.

LISA   Like what you said about Cezanne? That without him there could never have been a Picasso? You lectured about it last week, something about the Post Impressionists laying the groundwork for future movements which would culminate in the revolution of Cubism.

ED I said that?

LISA Yes, yes. That's precisely what you said, word for word. I wrote it down. And I think you're absolutely right. I saw it today, when I was looking at Picasso's painting.

ED Which one?

LISA Well, I, uh, I think it was—

ED You're lying.

LISA Excuse me?

ED You didn't see Picasso's painting. In fact, you haven't been anywhere in this museum except here, and in one other gallery.

LISA Well, I—

ED I saw you here yesterday and the day before. I saw you in the Blue Room, my Blue Room, looking at my light installation. You were checking me out, weren't you?

LISA Can you blame me? You do have quite a reputation.

ED Is that what you're curious about then, my reputation?

LISA As an artist, yes.

ED What else then?

LISA Well, to be honest, some of the women in class are a bit afraid of you. *Some* of them are.

ED And you?

LISA You don't scare me. Want to know what really bothers me about you?

ED No.

LISA I just don't get it. I don't get your art.

ED Come with me.

[*He reaches for her arm.*]

LISA   But we can't…I mean…they're closing!

ED   Don't worry. I have connections here. Worst-case scenario, we get locked inside together.

[LISA *appears frozen, stares at* ED. *He takes her by the arm and guides her out of the gallery and toward another room from which a deep blue light emanates.*]

Remember, you have to do everything I tell you. Do you trust me?

[*A bell. Stop action.*]

And what happened…later?

scene 3

[LISA *and* ED *return to their opening marks and look at each other momentarily. They switch places so that* ED *stands in front of Monet's painting of water lilies and* LISA *watches him from the doorway.*]

LISA   Squint.

ED   What? Oh, Lisa.

LISA   Hello, Ed.

ED   How long have you been standing there?

LISA   Just a few minutes. Did I disturb you? You seemed deep in thought.

ED   I'm glad you came.

LISA   Why did you want me to meet you here?

ED   This has always been our place.

LISA   Especially after a fight. This became our DMZ. I remember.

ED   I guess I'm still shell-shocked from last week. Papers? You serve me papers?

LISA   It's not working, Ed. We both know that. We've been over and over this. Can't we just quit now before we end up hating each other?

ED   I don't hate you, not yet.

LISA You know, it just wasn't good anymore. Maybe it never really was.

ED That I will never agree to. Granted, we grew apart. And the fights…we damaged each other.

LISA Beyond repair.

ED Beyond repair.

LISA Ed, I can't—

ED Don't stand there and tell me…don't do that. Don't…you can't just rewrite history.

LISA What do you want from me?

ED It all started here, you know.

LISA Please, don't do this.

ED This is where it happened. This is where we—

LISA No. No, it wasn't here. It was upstairs, we went upstairs, and…You wanted to show me another painting. A large canvas. I think it was… was it the Pollock? Yes! You were excited about the Pollock. You wanted to show me *Lavender Mist*.

ED I hate Pollock. You must have come here with someone else.

LISA No, no, don't you remember? You said the colors in it reminded you of the Monet. You said it was color, it was all about color. Trust me. That's how it happened. C'mon, let's look for it.

[*She takes him by the arm and leads him to another gallery. They enter. LISA sees the Jackson Pollock painting and points to it as she approaches. ED breaks away from her, walking slowly toward a large blue canvas on the opposite wall.*]

There it is! Wait, no. It couldn't be. Ed? Ed?

[*She looks for* ED, *then notices him staring at the blue painting. She slowly approaches.*]

Oh, of course, the Rothk—

ED Shhh. Don't talk.

[*They both stare at the painting for what seems like an eternity.*]

LOUDSPEAKER VOICE-OVER   Attention, visitors. The galleries will be closing in five minutes.

LISA   Why are you doing this to me?

ED   What exactly am I doing to you?

LISA   You're making me feel…I can't, I just can't do this. Let's go.

ED   Wait. There's one more. Remember? We have to see the light installation.

LISA   You mean *your* light installation. You know, you can't seduce me with your art anymore. I'm not that same college kid who fell prey to your brilliance and charm.

ED   I know, you're immune to me now. You've made that perfectly clear. Please just come and look at it with me. For old times' sake? Besides, there's a new addition I want you to see. I thought of you when I made it.

[*They exit the gallery together and enter a nearby room. It is devoid of art and light.*]

Looks like we're too late, damn!

LISA   What happened? Was it removed?

ED   It better not had been. I was just here the other day.

[*He looks around as if searching for something.*]

LISA   It's kind of eerie, you know, like there are ghosts lurking about.

ED   They're our ghosts. We died here. We were born here and we died here. Hang on a sec. I know what to do. Close your eyes and wait here.

[ED *walks over to a circuit panel and throws on several light switches. The room floods with a blue light that emanates from a series of large light fixtures in the shape of arches.*]

Okay, open your eyes.

[ED *stands in the middle of the room and watches as* LISA *walks slowly around the perimeter of the structure. She pauses to read the wall text.*]

LISA   "Für Elise?"

[ED *nods yes.*]

Oh, Ed.

ED   Come. Let me take you through the tunnel.

[*He takes her hand and leads her beneath the arched light fixtures. As they emerge from the other side,* LISA *is shaking and* ED *draws her closer toward him.*]

LOUDSPEAKER VOICE-OVER   Attention, visitors. The museum is now closed. Please make your way to the main exit.

LISA   Ed, I…I can't. I can't leave.

ED   I know. I know.

• • •

Let Rise

I. B. Hopkins

I. B. Hopkins

I. B. Hopkins is a playwright and librettist from Gainesville, Georgia. His work has been seen at the Horizon Theater as a selectee for the New South Playwrights' Festival, at the International Thespian PlayWorks Festival, at which he has been three times recognized, and at the Lucille Lortel Theater for the Young Playwrights, Inc., National Conference, and at the Irondale Center with the National Theatre for Student Artists. He is also the founding artistic director of the North-East Georgia Stage Artists' Guild. He has authored a dozen plays and five musical libretti (with composer/collaborator Harry N. Haines), which have appeared in *Dramatics* magazine and anthologies published by Samuel French, Inc., and the Athens Playwrights' Press.

···production history···

Let Rise was workshopped and premiered at the Opera to Okra: The Conference on Southern Culture on April 18, 2014, at Converse College in Spartanburg, South Carolina.

Director: Boone J. Hopkins

Dramaturge: Chandra Owenby Hopkins

ROSEMARY   Tessa Russell

EVA   Anushka Senanayake

CURRY   Ashly Sutherland

Everlasting Bread

1 quart milk, scalded and cooled

1 cup melted lard [or substitute]

1 cake compressed yeast, softened in

½ cup water

2 teaspoons baking powder

1 teaspoon sugar

5 teaspoons salt

½ cup sugar

Flour to make a soft sponge

Let rise until full of gas bubbles, add flour to make a stiff dough, knead thoroughly and put in refrigerator. It will keep well for four or five days and must be kept cold.

From this foundation can be made many kinds of bread and rolls, by rolling and shaping dough in desired shape, let rise in warm place until light and bake. For coffee cake for breakfast, roll out at night, leaving it in refrigerator overnight, and in the morning it will be ready for the coating of butter, sugar, and cinnamon in the oven.

This dough is a great time-saver, especially when preparing for guests. Rolls will rise in about one hour. A six-quart covered kettle is needed to keep this dough in.

Dry yeast may be used. One cake.

—*Mrs. Dull's* Southern Cooking, 1928

characters

ROSEMARY MUNDY   Forties, suburban homemaker

EVA MANZANA CARR   Thirties, Rosemary's brother's wife, Bolivian American

CURRY MUNDY   Rosemary's daughter, nineteen, freshman at the University of Georgia

setting

A comfortable kitchen in a suburb of Atlanta. Just before 7 a.m. Easter morning in our time.

Later—a church pew.

Note: The physical act of mixing and shaping the dough as above should continue throughout the action of the play. It should never interfere with the action, instead underscoring the dialogue.

• • •

[*At rise: It's early, and the Mundy house is not yet stirring. April's lavender dawn peaks in through the window over the kitchen sink. ROSEMARY MUNDY, determined, has already begun assembling ingredients for her task. She wears a purple terrycloth robe, sings under her breath.*]

ROSEMARY   "Praise with Elation, praise every morning…God's re-creation of the first day…Blackbird has spoken like the first day…."

[EVA MANZANA CARR *has been standing at the door. It's not clear for how long.* ROSEMARY *notices.* EVA *wears yoga pants and a soft magenta hoodie, tennis shoes.*]

EVA   Oh.

ROSEMARY   [*Trying.*] Good morning.

EVA   Oh, sorry. Did I startle you?

ROSEMARY   What? Oh, no. No! I just didn't know you were there is all. What are…What are you doing up so early?

EVA   Oh, I went for a jog around the neighborhood.

ROSEMARY   Already? Goodness, you musta gotten up with the chickens. And anyway, I figured you'd all be sleepin' to the last this morning after last night.

EVA   You should have played with us!

ROSEMARY   No.

EVA   Yes!

ROSEMARY   No. No, I knew I needed to get on up anyhow. We're doing the full spread for Easter dinner.

EVA   But just for a bit you could have stayed! It's the…the Battle of the Sexes….The men versus the women. We needed you to make it even, fair. Of course, Curry and me, we trumped them, the boys, anyway.

ROSEMARY   You know, I have just never really cared for those kinds of games.

EVA   You know how Cliff is if he is losing.

ROSEMARY   Besides, I was exhausted. I don't know how you have the energy to get up and go for a run this morning.

EVA   I never did sleep.

ROSEMARY   You never even slept?! Were you not comfortable? Did you get cold?

EVA   No, no. I just could not.

ROSEMARY   Oh, no?

EVA   Cliff—you know Cliff—was dead asleep the minute we laid down. Like that. But I could not close my eyes. I read most of the night.

ROSEMARY   Just…*read*?

EVA   I haven't done that since I was a teenager!

ROSEMARY   Listen to you….

[*Beat.*]

EVA   What are you stirring up?

ROSEMARY   [*A little off-kilter.*] I—? Oh, the dough. Rolls we're having later.

EVA   Yummy.…

ROSEMARY   I fix them like my—like Cliff's and my mama used to.

EVA   She must have been a very good cook. Cliff is always telling me to "fix" a meatloaf or pancakes or a cobbler like Merriam did….

ROSEMARY   She knew how to keep him comin' around the house.

[EVA *pours a cup of coffee.* ROSEMARY *continues mixing ingredients, surprised that* EVA *is settling in.*]

EVA Let me help with that.

ROSEMARY Oh, no. No, don't worry about it. I've got it.

EVA Just thought you might like—

ROSEMARY I'm sure you need to go ahead and get ready. I didn't at all mean for you to get cooped up in here getting diner together.

EVA Like you?

ROSEMARY You've probably got a million better things to do than sit here and watch me cook.

EVA [*Edging over into* ROSEMARY*'s space, trying to take the bowl.*] Let me help...!

ROSEMARY Oh, all right. The celery could use choppin'. I don't mind doing it myself.

EVA I can handle it.

ROSEMARY There now.

[*The two set about to their tasks. It is quiet but for the roll and slap of their utensils at work. An uneasy rhythm sets in.* EVA *breaks it.*]

EVA What is the celery for?

ROSEMARY That? That's for the potato salad, and I do want to go ahead and chop the onion as well.
[*Peering over* EVA*'s work.*]
Oh.

EVA ...

ROSEMARY It's just—the celery has to be in smaller chunks, real small.
[*Shows her.*]
Diced. See, Jesse won't even touch it if they're all chunked up like that....

EVA Yes, yes. Do you want me to start the potatoes?

ROSEMARY   No, no, no. I can do that just the moment I set this bread.

EVA   You do enough! Why not let me finish this? You can go get ready.

ROSEMARY   I have it under control—

[EVA *moves again to take the dough.*]

EVA   I'm a fast learner....

ROSEMARY   [*Wrenching it back.*] Would you—just let me—finish it!

[EVA's *coffee mug jostles, spills.* CURRY *has been watching from the door for it's not clear how long. Long enough. She wears exercise garb; she seems to be counting something.*]

CURRY   Hey?

ROSEMARY   Curry, sweetie. What are you doing up?

CURRY   I thought Eva and I were going for a run....

EVA   Oh, I am so sorry, Curry! I completely forgot. I just came back.

CURRY   It's no big deal. I can go by myself.

ROSEMARY   [*Her mind somewhere else.*] As long as you're not late getting ready for church.

CURRY   I know how long it takes to run around the neighborhood. I used to go, like, every morning.

EVA   I should have waited for you. I got lost down the wrong road. I could not remember which one we were on....I had to ask an old man walking his shiatsu if he knew you. I think I nearly gave him a heart attack!

ROSEMARY   Imagine that.

CURRY   You should have waited.

EVA   I should go back and check on Mr. Shiatsu!

[*They laugh.*]

ROSEMARY   [*Bearing into the work.*] You'd better go on, Curry, if you're going to make it back in time. I'm sorry about the bathroom situation, but since we only have the two it looks like we'll have to take shifts.

And I want everyone ready to go by ten—not nearly ready, not just waking up. All kinds of people show up on Easter, and we don't want to have to sit in the overflow room again....

EVA Overflow room?

ROSEMARY They just project the preacher onto a screen in a room down the hall. It's the same thing, really. I just would rather us be in the sanctuary. Is Jesse up?

CURRY I don't think so.

ROSEMARY Can you go make sure he gets out of bed—and stays out. He's gotten to where he'll act like he's getting up, but then he just crawls back in.

CURRY Yeah. Fine.

ROSEMARY I'll have to go get your father up after I get this dough to where it can set while we're gone.

EVA Rosemary, I have an idea.

ROSEMARY I'm sorry?

EVA Why don't you all go on to church, and I can stay here and get to work on lunch?

[*Beat.*]

ROSEMARY [*"No."*] That's fine. We're fine.

EVA I'm sure Cliff will want to go, but I'm feeling rather tired, too.

ROSEMARY Well, you did stay up half the night....

CURRY Mom.

ROSEMARY That's very sweet of you to offer, Eva, but I have dinner completely under control. The ham is done; it just needs to be heated up again and set out. And everything else I can whip up after we get back from church. Besides, this dough needs to set awhile anyway. C'mon, you can go with us.

EVA Oh, I wouldn't want to seem out of place. I always mess up at Baptist church.

CURRY So you're just going to hang out here?

EVA I think so. That way I can be "fixing" the lunch. You're too nice, Rosemary. I insist you take a break.

ROSEMARY [*Firm.*] This is my break, my family is here.

CURRY Mom, I think I might stay here, too. With Eva.

ROSEMARY No. You're going. We didn't spend all day at Lenox looking for that plum-color dress for you to not wear it.…You're going.

CURRY Okay, but that's not even what we were looking for.

ROSEMARY You know I don't ever mind going shopping with you. I just wish—

CURRY What I needed was something for semiformal.

ROSEMARY I just wish you could think things through just a little bit beforehand.

CURRY How was I supposed to know they wouldn't have anything?

EVA We should all go sometime!

CURRY I can wear it some other time.

ROSEMARY Do you remember when we used to go every year and buy you an Easter dress?

CURRY Yeah, when I was little.

[*Beat.*]

And anyway, Mom, you already said literally everyone is going to be there. We won't even get to talk to people.

ROSEMARY That's not quite the point of going to church, Curry.

EVA You'd better listen to your mama.

ROSEMARY And go ahead and wake up Jesse.

CURRY Mom, I'm not going. Okay?

ROSEMARY Curry.

CURRY I don't want to go.

ROSEMARY   Come back here. What's wrong?

CURRY   I just—I don't want to go.

ROSEMARY   Why not?

CURRY   It's just going to be those same people asking the same questions What do you think about college? How do you like living in Athens? How're classes?

ROSEMARY   What's wrong with that?

CURRY   It's boring!

ROSEMARY   You are just like your daddy. If you'd just take the time to talk to people—ask them about themselves— you wouldn't feel like you didn't have anything to say.…

CURRY   I'm sick of it.

ROSEMARY   You're going to church.

CURRY   But if I stay here, I can help Eva with lunch.

EVA   Curry, I want to see this dress! Go and put it on for me. Just like a model.…

[EVA *gives a huge wink to* ROSEMARY.]

CURRY   Look, Mom. If I stay here, then that gives Dad something to talk to people about! It's really helping him out. Otherwise it's just all of us standing around—awkward—while you dart around to everybody.

ROSEMARY   Y'know, come to think of it, sweet'eart, I'm not sure you do have time to go running.

CURRY   No, I— I have time.

EVA   And it's so chilly out this morning!

ROSEMARY   You'd better hurry on. I'm just tellin' you now the minute Jessie and your daddy and Uncle Cliff get up, the whole house'll be in chaos.

CURRY   Mom, you're not listen—

ROSEMARY   No, Curry. You're not listening to me. I said you're coming with us to church, and that's done—

EVA   And you will look so pretty in that dress—

ROSEMARY   It's Easter, and church is not optional.

CURRY   It's been a really long week, and I need to finish some projects and things for class before I head back....

ROSEMARY   It can wait. You have all afternoon. You had all day yesterday, you didn't seem to want to stay home to do it then.

CURRY   I'm just supposed to stay shut up in the house every time I'm home?

ROSEMARY   I thought you said you'd help me with baking the pies last night.

CURRY   I'm only really here for one night.

ROSEMARY   You used to love to.

CURRY   [*Done.*] Sorry.

ROSEMARY   I'm not even asking for that. Just an hour or two. Go to church, come home, have Easter dinner with your family.

CURRY   You're not being fair.

ROSEMARY   Go get dressed.

[*Long Beat.*]

I'm going to wake your brother up. Be ready to leave by eight.

[ROSEMARY *exits, leaves* CURRY *and* EVA *with a gap.*]

CURRY   Did you see that? Do you see the way she treats me? That's exactly what I was talking about.

EVA   I know. I know.

CURRY   I swear, she thinks I'm still like fourteen.

EVA   She's your mother. To her, you are always going to be her baby— that is how she will treat you.

CURRY   But I'm not! I—I don't see what the big deal about whether I go with them to church is anyway. It's like she needs to prove to every Baptist in this town that I haven't turned to sin, lost my religion!

EVA   A mama worries.

CURRY   [*Half a laugh.*] Actually, it's kind of like what Ms. Perle—do you know Perle Cavey who owns The Deli downtown?—anyway after I told her I was going to UGA she got all serious and looked down her glasses at me and said, "You know God doesn't count anything against you that you do in that town."

EVA   Maybe she's right.

CURRY   She gave me a free sandwich.

EVA   You sound like me. Maybe you don't know this, but I was a bit of a devil when I was your age....

CURRY   Oh, yeah?

EVA   I never cared a wit before, but now that I am married, away from my family, I try to see them whenever I can.

CURRY   That's different, though.

EVA   How?

CURRY   I don't know....Didn't you say your family is really spread out?

EVA   Yes. We were never close—

CURRY   And you ran away from home, right?

EVA   Run away? No...I was seventeen. I barely knew what that meant.

CURRY   Okay....

EVA   Really!... Curry, you really think your mama is not good to you?

CURRY   No, of course she is—Just—Tell me about when you ran away.

EVA   Well, first I did not run away. It was more of a very fast walk. And I had to leave my mama's house or I would have needed to be carried away in a straitjacket! Two older sisters still there, one younger. And no sign that any was going to be leaving anytime soon. But I knew I was.

CURRY   So…you just left?

EVA   You want me to tell you it was the middle of the night—a new moon. Creeping down the stairs, nudging at the front door. No. Really, I was just out with my friends one afternoon when Ruby Louis drives past. She's in this cobalt blue Durango. She's got her nails painted hot pink, and I can barely hear over the music what she's saying to me when she stops.

CURRY   ….

EVA   And she's yelling at me, and I think she's totally lost it at this point. Who goes down the street screaming in a blue Durango?! Anyway, I hear her, and she is telling me she just left broke up with her boyfriend—Michael? Danny?—and wanted to leave town forever. I had just had a fight with my mama, and it sounded like a good idea at the time.

CURRY   You just took off with her?

EVA   I never said I was the smartest seventeen-year-old! Maybe there is such a thing…but anyway I'm telling you now you got to ease up on Rosemary.

CURRY   But you saw her! She's basically trying to start something.

EVA   You don't really think that.

CURRY   You want to fill the position? We're hiring.

EVA   Ah, no! Arguing with that woman is like being between a hard rock and a hard place.

CURRY   Exactly.

EVA   Don't get me wrong, I love your mother.…

CURRY   *But?* C'mon, you wanted to say. . . "but…"

EVA   But, but. No but! She is a very sweet lady.
   [*Checking over her shoulder.*]
   As long as she has her way. That's it. That's all I'm saying.

CURRY   I knew it! I knew she'd made you feel that way, too! That's why you're not going to church, isn't it?

EVA   No.

CURRY   Steer clear of all the grand parade....

EVA   I am staying put so that I can finish preparing lunch for everyone. I think she will appreciate that when she lets herself.

CURRY   To avoid Mom.

EVA   To show her that I can take care of Cliff.

CURRY   [*Scoffing.*] Okay...Exactly how much taking care of does Uncle Cliff need?

EVA   He's stubborn. That's not the same as self-sufficient. And that's not the point.

CURRY   What is then?

EVA   I know—I know she doesn't really think this, but sometimes it feels like—Sometimes she treats me like I am some two-bit floozy that Cliff picked up on the street!

CURRY   But didn't you two meet...

EVA   In the rehab, yes! It's nothing like the street.

CURRY   [*Slowly.*] Did you ever think maybe that's why she treats you like that?

EVA   Because I'm not from the street?

CURRY   No, I mean because you two met in rehab....

EVA   It's a possibility.

CURRY   Yeah.

EVA   You're changing the subject. Your mama—

CURRY   My mama thinks that if you aren't sitting in a Baptist church every Sunday morning, then you might as well be hell-bound cross-eyed. Look, how long are you going to let her make you feel bad about this? You and Uncle Cliff love each other, right?

EVA   Yes. Of course.

CURRY   So, if you met in rehab, then isn't it kind of the best place you could have been? Kind of. It's perfect! You both walk in raging alcoholics, and you walk out engaged. You got your lives back on track....

EVA   That's not exactly how it happened....

CURRY   How then?

EVA   It's not simple. It's not some dopey love-at-first-sight. It was dumb. I was just sitting alone, eating my little dinner—alone—when I hear this voice behind me ask if he could buy me a drink.

CURRY   That's Uncle Cliff.

EVA   I wanted to laugh and cry and slap him. But I just told him, "Sure."

CURRY   No witty comeback?

EVA   It worked, didn't it? Same as it did when he asked me to marry him three months later. What is that look for?

CURRY   You're wrong. It is dopey.

EVA   [*Turning away.*] Ah, no.

CURRY   Uh, yes! But you see what I mean, you and Uncle Cliff getting married is a beautiful thing! And Mom can't stand that it doesn't fit her perfect 8" x 12", so she's on a crusade to make you miserable.

EVA   Everybody needs a little time to adjust.

CURRY   Three years?

EVA   Some people need a lot.

CURRY   Well, it's not right, and I'm going to let her know it.

EVA   Please, Currita, don't aggravate her anymore. Today's a special day—a holiday! Can't you just put a grin on the bear for today?

CURRY   No! This is a protest. I'm not going to church until she stops tyrannizing this family.

[*But* ROSEMARY *has already re-entered. She has been standing at the doorway long enough. Still in her bedclothes, she holds a bottle of Absolut Vodka erect in one hand.*]

EVA   Rosemary, tell me what it is I can do while you're all gone…!

ROSEMARY   Would you give us a moment, please, Eva?

EVA   Yes, yes.

[*But* EVA *doesn't go anywhere.*]

ROSEMARY   Or stay here. That's fine, too.

CURRY   I didn't mean—Mom, I didn't mean…What I said—

ROSEMARY   [*Bottle brandishing.*] Explain.

CURRY   What is…? Did you go through my stuff?

ROSEMARY   Start explaining. Now.

CURRY   Please don't freak out.

ROSEMARY   I really thought that we raised you better than this. You go runnin' around like some sort of wild girl, like you don't have any kind of family at all. Is this how you carry on at school? Curry? I need to know.

CURRY   Listen, I'm sorry.

ROSEMARY   That's it?

CURRY   That's it.

ROSEMARY   No, you look at me and tell me what is goin' on here.

CURRY   I'm just going to head on back.

[CURRY *starts to leave.*]

ROSEMARY   Back? To school?! Uh-uh. Not until you talk to me first.

CURRY   What do you want me to say, Mom? Just tell me what I need to say to you, and I will. Yes, it's a bottle of vodka! Yes, it's alkey-hol! Can you just stop making everything out to be the end of the world?

[*Long beat. Long everything.*]

EVA   Curry, I think you need to apologize to your mama.

ROSEMARY   Are you still here?

EVA Excuse me?

ROSEMARY This is really a private family matter, Eva. I'm trying to have a conversation with my daughter.

EVA And I am trying to help!

ROSEMARY Good! Advice from our very own, in-house booze queen.…

CURRY Mom!

ROSEMARY I'm sorry! I'm sorry if I just can't understand. I'm supposed to let a lush lecture my daughter.

CURRY I don't need lecturing!

ROSEMARY I should pretend that I didn't find this in your room? Walk down here, cook some eggs, and go on like nothing happened?

CURRY Well, you could start by treating me like I'm an adult.

ROSEMARY Is that what you are now? Adults don't sneak around with bottles of vodka.

CURRY Yeah, 'cause you never drink alone in the basement.

EVA I am no lush! No booze queen! No leftover part!

ROSEMARY Please, this doesn't concern you.…

EVA How are you going to talk to your daughter, then? How long ago were you in college?

ROSEMARY What difference does that make? I know how it was. I went to those parties. I saw plenty.

EVA Ah, yes! Cliff has told me all about you and the party scene.

ROSEMARY So I should have followed his lead then?

EVA I'm not saying—

ROSEMARY Follow the crowd then, friends, big-time career connections, alcohol poisoning…

EVA It's not black and white—

ROSEMARY Ruined marriage…

EVA Lisa never loved Cliff!

ROSEMARY Rehab. And now you.

CURRY You're not being fair.

ROSEMARY Curry, you're going upstairs right now. You're going to go put on that dress that isn't exactly appropriate for Easter service and cost too much, but you're going to put it on anyway. You're going to get ready. You're not going to do that cat thing with your eyeliner. Then you're going to walk back down stairs, smile, take pictures, and go to church. And we're not going to discuss this anymore. Not today.

EVA That's healthy.

ROSEMARY No more.

EVA Yes more! You're stuck with me. Once you mix up a family, it doesn't unmix!

ROSEMARY It makes sense. Cliff has lived his whole life to make me miserable. Why shouldn't his wives, too?

EVA Are you going to keep up with that when we have a baby?

CURRY Are you?

EVA We are trying.

ROSEMARY I bet.

EVA You don't approve?

ROSEMARY You can do what you want to. Nobody's going to stop you.

CURRY Do you ever listen to what you say?

ROSEMARY It's fine. It's fine, Eva. I'm very happy for the both of you. I hope you…I hope it works out.

CURRY It's just eating you up inside….

ROSEMARY What are you still doin' here?

CURRY Do you remember how Grandma used to get every year at the holidays?

ROSEMARY   What?

CURRY   You know, like Christmas, Thanksgiving?

ROSEMARY   How she would get?

CURRY   Oh, c'mon! She turned into a dragon every year.

ROSEMARY   [*More to* EVA.] That's not true.

CURRY   Seriously? Mom, she would sit in the dining room—alone—drinking black coffee while we opened presents. You had to put her name on presents so we didn't feel like Grandma didn't love us.

ROSEMARY   Love you? Of course she loved you.

CURRY   Right.

ROSEMARY   She just didn't love Christmas.

EVA   Cliff said she hated it....

ROSEMARY   She might have slipped down to the basement once or twice.

EVA   Okay, we'll see what they say about you when you start picking up the dog mess with the stockings....

ROSEMARY   She never—

CURRY   She did. And what I'm trying to say is that it doesn't matter. It doesn't. It doesn't matter if I go to church or wear that dress or anything like that. Grandma hated Christmas, but she loved us.

ROSEMARY   I don't know what happened to this family.

EVA   Your family changes. You change, too.

ROSEMARY   We used to all be really close, you know?

EVA   We are all here now.

CURRY   That's not what she means.

EVA   What then? What do you want, Rosemary?

CURRY   Who knows?

EVA   Then I don't feel bad....There's nothing we can do....

CURRY   This is all you, Mom.

ROSEMARY   It used to be that everyone could *unplug* long enough to come together at the holidays. Now, you're right, Mamma didn't much care for Christmas. But she loved Easter. That was her day. Yes. The lilacs putting out and chill finally wearing off. God knows how many years we went out to Mamma's house, sat around that big oak table, and had our Easter. Ham, potato salad, and always—always—homemade bread from scratch. Her mama's recipe. Even after Cliffie had moved out west, after the children came, after everything, we could all still fit around that table, eat those rolls, and feel like a family. See now I don't really know what's happened. I know Mamma's gone. That's fine. She was ill; it was a blessin', really. I know we sold their house. What were we gonna do with it? I know the table's sittin' in storage on the other side of town now—maybe somebody'll need it one of these days. But dammit, we're all at my house now. We have a table to sit around, and I'm making the bread.

EVA   No one is arguing with you. But maybe if you gave people a little room to—

ROSEMARY   And the last thing I needed was Chiquita Banana sashaying in here to tell me what's what.

CURRY   Mom!

ROSEMARY   What?!

CURRY   How can you say that?

EVA   [*Eyes limply fixed on* ROSEMARY.] It's fine, Curry. It's fine.

ROSEMARY   I didn't mean that....

EVA   That I what? That I'm not you're color? Eek, Bolivian.

CURRY   Mom, that's way out of line.

ROSEMARY   You don't get to talk to me like that. We still need to discuss—

[*Pauses looking for words, finally indicates bottle.*]

What I found in your room. And—

[*Checks time on the stove.*]

You have got to go get ready for church!

CURRY   Will you just stop?! I'm not going. And you need to apologize to Eva.

EVA   She will not.

ROSEMARY   I didn't mean it like that.

EVA   I don't fit your picture with the farmhouse and the table and the rolls. I understand there are no tortillas on your Easter table.

ROSEMARY   [*Trying to laugh.*] I'm not a racist! I swear....

EVA   I'm going to make sure Cliff is awake. I'll see how he's feeling, if we wants to go to the Baptist church with you.

[*She goes to the door, before exiting.*]

I know how they love to save the sinners.

[*Exit EVA.*]

[*Beat.*]

CURRY   I can't believe you.

ROSEMARY   You know I didn't mean anything by it.

CURRY   I don't know why I'm surprised....

ROSEMARY   Look at me I know you don't want to, but for me— please—come with us to church. It would mean so much to me.

CURRY   Mom, I have never tried to hurt you. I don't think you get that sometimes.

ROSEMARY   And I have done everything, everything since the day you were born for you.

CURRY   You gotta let me do it myself, though.

ROSEMARY   I'm not going to watch you drink your life away like—

CURRY   Ohmygod.

ROSEMARY   I can't watch you do it.

CURRY I'm not doing anything! Can we just—not?

[CURRY *backs away to the door. As she goes....*]

ROSEMARY Curry. Curry! Are you coming to church, honey? Curry?

[*She is gone, though.*]

[ROSEMARY *is alone. She fidgets with the rest of the items around the kitchen, cleans, pours herself another cup of coffee. She covers with plastic and places the dough in the refrigerator. ROSEMARY exits through the doorway. Split stage: ROSEMARY sits alone on a church pew. Eyes forward. After a moment, she stands and begins to sing.*]

ROSEMARY [*Sings.*]
Morning has broken, like the first morning.
Blackbird has spoken, like the first bird.
Praise for the singing, praise for the morning,
Praise for them springing fresh from the Word.

[*While* ROSEMARY *continues to sing the hymn,* CURRY—*too alone, alone too— creeps back into the kitchen. She paws around at a few items before finding the dough covered in the refrigerator. She removes it, setting it on the counter. She kneads it.*]

Sweet the rain's new fall, sunlight from heaven.
Like the first dewfall, on the first grass.
Praise for the sweetness of the wet garden,
Sprung in completeness where His feet pass.

Mine is the sunlight, mine is the morning.
Born of the one light Eden saw play.
Praise with elation, praise every morning;
God's re-creation of the new day.

[CURRY *is also rising by this time.*]

Morning has broken, like the first morning.
Blackbird has spoken, like the first bird.
Praise for the singing, praise for the morning,
Praise for them springing fresh from the Word.

[CURRY *has risen.*]

• • •

Goodnight Lovin' Trail

John Patrick Bray

John Patrick Bray

John Patrick Bray (PhD, MFA) has written plays under grants from the National Endowment for the Arts and the Acadiana Center for the Arts (Louisiana), and he has earned commissions from theater troupes in downtown NYC and South Louisiana. A number of his plays have been published by Next Stage Press and Indie Theatre Now, as well as in Applause, and Smith and Kraus anthologies. Bray is a resident writer with the Rising Sun Performance Company (Off-Off-Broadway), and he is a member of the Dramatists' Guild of America. Bray is a lecturer of dramatic writing at the University of Georgia. Visit: johnpatrickbray.webs.com.

···production history···

An earlier version of *Goodnight Lovin' Trail* was produced in July 2001 as part of the Shandaken Playfair at the Shandaken Playhouse in Shandaken, New York. The production was directed by Gregory Bray and featured R. A. Stanley and Violet Snow.

On February 12, 2014, the Rising Sun Performance Company produced the most recent version of *Goodnight Lovin' Trail* at the Kraine Theatre in NYC to raise money for the Nicholas Mevoli Memorial Fund. (Mevoli had played Mr. Coffee and Cigarettes in repertory with Rising Sun. He passed away attempting a free-diving record in November 2013.) The production was directed by Akia and featured the following cast members:

LEE   Christina Germaine

MR. COFFEE AND CIGARETTES   Ryan Duse Dusek

characters

LEE   Thirties. A waitress trying to get by. Wears a standard waitress uniform, complete with apron (helps with various props); like a Mama Kangaroo.

MR. COFFEE AND CIGARETTES   A drifter, age uncertain (30–50). He has a youthful energy, but is held back by the grip of alcohol. Wears a red-neck tuxedo, and a hat, slouch hat, fedora, Skoal tobacco cap; any hat, really.

setting

Andy's Piggy Diner and Truck Stop, West Texas, near the mythic "Goodnight Loving Trail," Not too long ago.

Note: The author did not compose music for the song. He has left it up to the imagination of the actor (or the actor and director in collaboration) and this has yielded some amazing results. Think about the characters, the world of story, and have a great time! For any questions regarding the lyrics (i.e., if you need to cut a syllable or two to make it fit your preferred meter) please contact the author. He's happy to help out.

···

scene 1

[*A truck stop diner in West Texas. Some greasy spoon you'd expect to find at the cross-roads. This is Americana forgotten. The Southwest as imagined by Edward Hopper. On the back wall, there is painting of the ocean. There is a jukebox. Sad tables, lonely chairs.* LEE, *a waitress, is on the pay phone.*]

LEE No, Austin, don't you talk to me like that. You want a switchin' when I get home? Huh? You tell Mr. Johnson, if he calls back to call me here. Never you mind what I'm sellin.'

[MR. COFFEE AND CIGARETTES, *hereafter referred to as* COFFEE, *enters with a start.*]

COFFEE Did you see it?

LEE See what?

[LEE *slams the phone down and jumps in front of the counter.* COFFEE *moves a chair roughly and looks under a table.*]

COFFEE Did you see it?!

LEE See what? Get a hold of yourself!

COFFEE Well, I was in here before, and I think I left something valuable—

LEE What? Like a diamond?

[*She crouches down on the floor near him.*]

COFFEE My guitar!

LEE A guitar?

[*She walks away and returns to the counter.*]

COFFEE Yessum. A big Goddamn guitar. I got to drinking earlier, and I know I had to have left it here.

LEE I haven't seen any guitar.

COFFEE You sure?

LEE I'd tell you if I'd seen one!

[*Beat.*]

When were you here?

COFFEE I don't remember.

LEE You don't remember?

COFFEE No.

LEE Hours ago? Days? Weeks? Months?

COFFEE Hours ago. It must have been before sunset.

LEE Were you with anybody else?

COFFEE I was drinking by myself.

LEE Where?

COFFEE Well, just outside. I usually keep a bottle with me in case I need a nip. And I got to feeling kind of lonely, and all by myself, so I went ahead and downed more than half the bottle.

LEE That wasn't too smart, was it?

COFFEE No, I reckon it wasn't. But then, I stumble in here, I remember, with Della, Della I call her, and, and the rest is just blank. I ended up down the road a piece with my sack weighing heavy, and me breathing in a face full of sand.

LEE You sure you brought "Della" in here?

COFFEE I wouldn't have left her outside. I don't think I would have.

[*Beat.*]

But maybe.

LEE I'm just saying it might be possible.

COFFEE Shit. I'm destroyed. That's not fair. I mean, after all that I went through to…I'm like a, a conductor without a train. I'm a wave of the ocean hung out to dry.

[*He walks towards the door.*]

I gotta get into town.

[*He burps and grabs his stomach and leans.*]

Nope, I gotta sit.

LEE You ain't pukin' in here.

COFFEE If I'm still, nothing will happen.

[*He poses, still.* LEE *helps him to a seat near the counter.*]

Man, I'm feelin' green.

LEE Drinking and pukin' go hand in hand.

[LEE *pours a cup of coffee and brings it to* COFFEE.]

Here. Have a cup.

[COFFEE *bends over to reach into his pocket.* LEE *reacts.*]

Oh, no, it's on the house.

[*He nods, and sits back. His face is awash with tears.*]

Come on, what's with all the tears, ain't she just a guitar?

[*She places the coffee down in front of him.*]

COFFEE No, you see, Della's pretty rare. She's called a National Style O. Came out in the twenties. Real old, see? It has an aluminum cone behind the strings. Causes her to resonate like a bitch in heat.

[LEE *rolls her eyes and returns to the counter.*]

Beyond that, it's got this dull, bellyache kinda echo in there. Sadness. It's the only thing I know that matches my kinda voice. Scratchy, like sandpaper. You got a match?

[LEE *hands him a book of matches from near the cash register.*]

Thanks. I'm sorry about cussin' such, ma'am.

LEE Ain't like I never heard it before.

[*He starts striking unsuccessfully.*]

COFFEE She was sandblasted and painted something beautiful once. There's no mistaking it if you see it. It's kinda, um, of a sea green, like that painting! I always imagined when I played, that I'd be out there, on that sand, right near the ocean. The ocean would call, and my National O, sweet Della, with her coyote bellow would call back for me. And me and the ocean would just sit there, talking. Just talking.

LEE Well, if I happen to find a tropical guitar, I'll be sure to look for a drunken man in denim.

COFFEE A lot of that around here?

LEE Except for the guitar part. And the ocean.

[*Tries striking another match. LEE continues diner business, such as filling salt shakers, etc.*]

COFFEE I've actually never been to the ocean. Not yet. I've always been afraid of the water. I was heading out there now, figure I'd stare my fears right in the eye.

LEE Better late than never, I guess.

COFFEE I would love to see Hawaii.

LEE You plan on walking on the water?

COFFEE Well…no, but…

[*Indicates painting.*]

you see, that's where I imagine this beachfront to be. Nothing that beautiful can exist on the mainland, not even our beaches.

LEE That's for sure.

COFFEE Yeah? You go to the ocean a lot?

LEE Used to. All the time. Me and my old man would take the little ones to the Gulf. Then when my sister-in-law got her place in National City, we'd head out west to visit her. We'd lay out on towels that we got from the hotel, and watch the gulls eat the baby turtles coming out of the sand. Life after death, you know? Something's gotta die so something else can live.

COFFEE I hear ya. Well, I guess I'll walk up into town.

[COFFEE *starts to stand.*]

LEE Your stomach can handle it?

COFFEE Yeah. Got a book of matches?

[*She starts to hand him a lighter.*]

LEE What's wrong with the book I just gave you?

COFFEE The sandpaper is rubbed down clean.

LEE   Frankly, mister, you look like you could strike a match on your cheek.

COFFEE   Feels that way.

LEE   Here, take my lighter.

COFFEE   I'm fine with matches. The way I see it, lighters are these like big ol' institutions. They create fire with a click, and floom! With matches, you strike, strike, maybe, damn, go to the next, strike, strike, there you go. Striking out like that builds character. And with lighters being anywhere from a sixty-nine cents to a whole dollar fifty, I say stick with the little guy.

[*He notices something. A matchbook under one of the tables.*]

LEE   What is it?

[*He picks up the matches.*]

COFFEE   My matches.

LEE   Your matches?

COFFEE   These—these are *my matches*! Yes, sir! Ha! I was in here!

[*Beat.*]

LEE   *I* never doubted you were.

COFFEE   No, but see, look, you see this blue thread here?

[*He holds up the matches by the piece of thread, and it dangles in front of them.*]

LEE   Yeah.

COFFEE   I keep these matches tied off of the E-string tuner, so I always know where they are. I'm terrible with pockets. That means Della was in here!

[*He pauses.*]

Ma'am, I hate to ask you this, but is your husband of a, well, musical nature?

LEE   I'm not sure I like where this conversation is going.

COFFEE   Well, is he?

LEE   The only thing he's suited for playing is a harp.

COFFEE   I'm sorry.

LEE   Yeah, three years now. I guess you could say that his heart exploded.

COFFEE   Exploded?

LEE   Yeah. Gave out on him completely.

COFFEE   I'm sorry to hear that.

LEE   Mmmm.

COFFEE   I don't imagine your children play—

[*She glares at him.*]

Well, maybe it's behind the counter.

[*He walks towards the counter.*]

You have a lost and found here?

[*She blocks it off.*]

LEE   There's nothing back here but some coffeepots cracked from the heat.

[*He starts to move around her; she blocks him off again.*]

LEE   Do I look like I'm sporting shades, a little white cane, a tin cup?

COFFEE   No, ma'am.

LEE   And if the manager comes in and sees you behind this counter, you know what happens to me?

COFFEE   I guess you would see it....

[COFFEE *looks at the matches in his hand. He looks at a defiant* LEE. *He pauses.*]

LEE   There is one place in town I know of.

COFFEE   Yeah?

LEE   Antique store. Run by a guy named Johnson.

COFFEE   No kiddin'! It's gotta be closed by now.

LEE   You could at least look in the window, see if she's there!

COFFEE   Of course! And if she is, oh, man, I don't know what I'll do. Do you know him?

LEE   Not really.

COFFEE   Shit. Pardon.

[*He rubs his stomach a bit as he speaks.*]

There's gotta be some way to convince him that she's mine, just in case she's in there.

LEE   Here!

[*She tosses him antacid.*]

For your stomach.

COFFEE   Thanks!

[*He exits. LEE watches him. She takes a deep breath and picks up the pay phone again. She smacks it, as opposed to putting a dime in, then dials.*]

LEE   Austin, I know I raised you to answer a phone better. Don't you take that tone. Did Mr. Johnson call back? Yeah, well tell him to forget about it. No, I got nothing to sell him. Yeah.

[*Shocked look.*]

I'll be home someday, and when I do…don't you hang up on me! I'll whip your little…hello? Hello?

[*She slams the phone and looks out the window. She pulls down the blinds. She flips over the closed sign. She goes to the offstage area and picks up the guitar. She emerges into sight for a moment and looks around. She goes offstage again, into the kitchen. She returns, takes a look around, smacks the jukebox, and a jazz tune begins. She removes her apron, and exits upstage. Lights change.*]

scene 2

[*The song changes. Another jazz number. LEE enters from the back with an unlit cigarette. She crosses to a stool at the counter and picks up her lighter. She goes to light her cigarette but doesn't. She puts the lighter down. She picks up a book of matches, strikes a match, and lights her cigarette. She picks up another match, and strikes it, and puts it out. She repeats this several times, lost in thought. She stands up, ready to leave.*]

She goes to the door and unlocks it. She takes one last look around and sees that she has not dumped the coffeepots on the counter. She reacts. She takes one of the coffeepots and exits to the kitchen. COFFEE enters and sits on a stool. He is no longer in a drunken stupor. LEE enters and is shocked to see him.]

LEE   That was quick.

COFFEE   Didn't make it. Guess it's further than I thought.

LEE   Well, there's always tomorrow.

COFFEE   No. If someone picked her up, she could be in a thousand different places. Especially by tomorrow.

LEE   True.

COFFEE   But that's the part I'm having trouble with, ma'am. I can't remember seeing anyone.

LEE   Kind of hard seeing anybody when you're "face down with a mouthful of sand."

[COFFEE *doesn't respond.*]

Come on, mister. There are other guitars.

COFFEE   Not like this one.

LEE   I see.

[*She picks up her keys from behind the counter.*]

Stranger, I want to go home.

COFFEE   Isn't this place all night?

LEE   Not tonight. I'm having problems with my boy.

COFFEE   Ah.

LEE   So—

COFFEE   You been striking out?

LEE   Excuse me?

[COFFEE *walks over and picks up one of the matches off of the counter.*]

COFFEE   These yours? Don't you use a lighter?

LEE I'd really like to go –

COFFEE Sticking with the little guy! See what I mean? Shit, you and I aren't so different after all.

LEE Good night, stranger.

[*She motions to the door.*]

COFFEE If I could just have a quick cup, before going.

LEE Look, I really need to—

COFFEE Just to wake me up, and then I'm gone. A faded page of history.

[*She considers.*]

LEE Okay, but this one you have to pay for. Making me stay out all hours.

COFFEE I'll get ya, don't worry.

LEE Right.

[*He pulls out a cigarette and a match.*]

COFFEE You know why it's so important for me to get to the ocean?

LEE So you can take a bath?

COFFEE I'm visiting my mama.

LEE She a mermaid?

COFFEE She was staying in Northern California. Right on the water. "The view is nice," she says, "come visit." I meant to, but I never liked traveling. When Daddy died, she left Texas to be close to her brother. Then when he passed on, she moved into the retirement home. So, a month ago, I get the news. Mama died sitting at the beach, peaceful as Heaven. With her ukulele on her lap. She played ukulele, if you can believe it. Used to sing me lullabies when I was a kid. I just figured it was my turn, that's all. Go down to the beach sing something for her.

[*Beat.*]

LEE That's something else.

COFFEE What is?

LEE Well, a man who wants to play guitar just for his mama.

COFFEE What do you want to play it for?

[*Beat.*]

LEE I don't play.

COFFEE No?

LEE But I used to see myself…well…singing.

COFFEE Really?

LEE Sure. I could see myself…oh, never mind.

COFFEE No, let's hear it. You could see yourself what?

LEE Naw, it's silly.

COFFEE Silly? Come on, I'm about to strike a match on my cheek.

LEE Oh. Well, I guess. I used to imagine myself, when I was a kid…you really want to hear this?

[*He nods. She thinks about it. She might as well play along.*]

I guess I could see myself as…some New York City jazz singer. You know what I mean?

[COFFEE *shakes his head.*]

COFFEE Never been out that far.

LEE I see myself as this black woman, if you can believe it, all dressed in glitter, and twinkling under the lights. Oh, this is silly.

COFFEE No, no, go on.

LEE I see all these people in suits. Tuxedoes. Some kind of, you know, one night only event. Everybody is sweating, but nobody's taking their tux jackets off. And then I appear onstage. And when I open my mouth, the sound I produce echoes from my very soul. Every note bends and folds, like a wave of the ocean. I sing them so sweet high, and down and low, that it makes you feel like the whole world is gonna burst around you. And that's where I am. Right in the middle of this great tide that's about to break. And the applause comes down like rain on a tin roof, just in time for the spotlight to go out.

COFFEE   I could play at the bandstand for you. With Della strummin' gently behind you.

LEE   Different kind of music.

COFFEE   My mother didn't raise no dummies, this old dog can learn a new trick.

LEE   But you can't play Della, she's gone.

COFFEE   How come you're so certain?

LEE   You said it yourself, she could be anywhere.

COFFEE   No. Only one place, really.

LEE   You want to check behind the counter here, be my guest?

[LEE *steps aside.* COFFEE *considers.*]

COFFEE   No.

LEE   So, where is she then?

COFFEE   Anything that is lost usually wants to be found. She'll find her way back to me.

LEE   Cocky, ain't ya?

COFFEE   Just a little.

LEE   Well, Mr. Coffee and Cigarettes at 2 a.m.—

COFFEE   Just Coffee and Cigarettes. Mr. Coffee and Cigarettes was my daddy.

LEE   I'm fixin' to close. And unless you want to live in here—

COFFEE   I don't blame you for taking her.

[*Beat.* LEE *freezes.*]

Now, I've been more than patient, ma'am, but let's get down to it. Johnson's in town is closed. Why would you be sending me to the window of a closed antique store in a town five miles away? That I had to walk to?

LEE   I was trying to help.

COFFEE   It can't be easy to pawn off a guitar when the only place in the world that seems open is glowing around us, right here.

LEE   You've taught me a thing or two about trying to help a stranger.

COFFEE   Well, it seems like you have a few more life lessons to learn, if you're gonna—

LEE   Life lessons? Does marrying the wrong man count? Having just enough for rent, but not the heat? Or water? Do you know anything about shoes? It's time for size ten, because the size sevens of last year have just about bust off a boy's feet. So, don't tell me—

COFFEE   That doesn't make it right to—!

[*Takes a breath.*]

Okay, look…I came by Della in a pawnshop window. And you know the shape of the guitar. Doesn't look like others. It's like the big brother of what Mama used to play for me. The shop was run by a fellow known as Tall Glass. We called him that on account of his height. He has a big hole in the center of him where humanity used to live. He'd kick around his old tied-up greyhound just to get his frustrations out.

LEE   Sometimes it's better to kick a dog!

COFFEE   And he wouldn't sell me the guitar—

LEE   I wouldn't have sold it to you, either!

COFFEE   [*Getting heated again.*] Despite my pleading, and trying to turn in an old watch and chain from my uncle Wink?

LEE   Not for all the coffee in Guatemala!

COFFEE   So, one night, I look in the window of the shop, and give it a good elbow, like you would see in the pictures. That was it. I eloped with her! I probably have a warrant on my ass! Look, I still have the scars on my arm!

LEE   Some scars run deeper.

COFFEE   Deeper?! Like what?

[*She doesn't answer. He gets closer.*]

Like what?

[*Again, she doesn't answer. She's fighting back from saying anything.*]

I'm trying to level with you, and this is what I'm getting. Look, I'm sorry you don't have two nickels to rub together, I'm sorry you're raising a child by yourself, and I'm sorry you don't have a man in your life to help, but the way you've been acting, stealing guitars and shit as a means of getting by, I don't blame him for checking out!

LEE   [*Almost interrupting.*] He didn't check out—I killed him!

[*Beat.*]

COFFEE   What?

LEE   I said what I said.

[*Beat.*]

COFFEE   Uh…we talking literally?

[COFFEE *is uncertain. He looks as if he's itching' for the door.*]

LEE   Yes, sir. I was never gonna tell no one, but *you*, going on and on about the ocean and shit, and scars—!

COFFEE   Well, I didn't mean to make you feel so bad, ma'am—

LEE   Feel so bad? He fuckin' got it! He hit the children, see. He hit them hard. When Austin was five years old, just five, he walks over and strikes him so hard upside the head, Austin ends up saying nothing for three whole years. Each second, I'm waiting. I know he'll come around, I know it. Then the old man starts hitting baby Sarah. And I can't take it. I ask my son on a rainy night in June what to do, what to do, and he stares at me. Others might say that he isn't there, but I can see him screaming in his eyes, "Stop him, Mommy. Do what you can, and stop him." So I do. He's out on the porch, back from hunting. Of course he didn't catch nothing. He sets down his shotgun for a moment, and in that moment, I snatch it up. He doesn't hear me, not at first. I'm not sure if I would really have gone through with it, but he spins around, screaming. It startles me. And that was it. His heart exploded. I even buried him, I...I...oh, Lord. And when I'm done, done, patting down the last of the dirt, crying why, and spitting on the ground, my boy Austin comes up behind me, quiet as a mouse and whispers. "What have you done, Mommy?" What have I done?

[*Pause.* COFFEE *isn't sure how to respond.*]

COFFEE Life after death.

LEE No, no. I got no money. I got no man to help support us. What can I do but work? It's been three years, and Austin's getting a mean streak in him, now that he's talking. How can I make sure he don't become his daddy? How?

COFFEE I reckon I don't know, ma'am.

LEE You must think I'm something else, to kill my own man, and tell some ol' drifter. No one knows about it, but you.

COFFEE It's not my job to judge, ma'am. It's my job to tell a story.

[LEE *pauses for a moment and considers what he has said. With their eyes still in contact, she backs up into the kitchen and retrieves the guitar. She hands it to him.*]

Della! Son of a bitch. I knew you had to be hiding her. Pardon for the suspicion on my part.

LEE Well, I know she's old. I figured I'd sell her to some antique... Johnson's...or...or some shit. Get some cash. I've been busy looking up different...It might help me get out of my situation, or just give me enough, just to buy...you gonna tell the cops?

COFFEE No, ma'am. Don't forget, I didn't exactly get Della by honest means, either.

LEE Look, I know I was doing you wrong.

COFFEE Yeah, but it was for the right reasons.

LEE You can believe it was.

[COFFEE *smiles. He looks at* LEE, *looks at Della. He begins to exit.*]

Wait!

[*He stops.*]

If...if your job is telling stories...do you think...could you tell mine?

[COFFEE *stops for a moment. He looks at her and smiles. He pulls a stool up and sets Della on his knee. He takes out his matches on the string and hangs them on one of the tuners. He starts strumming a melody.*]

COFFEE   [*Singing.*]
Night was cold, rain came down
Built a fire in a one gun town
The ol' man was swearin', hit the kid again
You put them in the prison, once they're out of their pen

You got two dead ends and you still gotta choose
You got two dead ends and you still gotta choose
You walk the whole Goodnight Lovin' Trail
With nothing more to lose
You walk the whole Goodnight Lovin' Trail
And you're singing the blues

He's back from hunting, set down his gun
Went chasin' rabbits, but he didn't catch one
He says he loves you, 'swhy he beats you to death
And so you pick the gun up, and you hold your breath
You got two dead ends and you still gotta choose

LEE and **COFFEE**
You got two dead ends and you still gotta choose
You walk the whole Goodnight Lovin' Trail
With nothing more to lose
You walk the whole Goodnight Lovin' Trail

LEE
And you got the wrong sized shoes

[LEE *steps forward. A spot comes up on her.* COFFEE *is behind her. He gradually fades upstage as she sings. There is only the one light on her towards the end. She can hear gentle applause rising.*]

You got two dead ends and you still gotta choose
You got two dead ends and you still gotta choose

You walk the whole Goodnight Lovin' Trail
With nothing more to lose
You walk the whole Goodnight Lovin' Trail
And you got the wrong sized shoes.

[*She bows to the applause. She turns around as if to introduce* COFFEE, *but he is no longer there. Lights return to normal. The guitar is set by the counter. She goes upstage and looks out the door for him. She returns to the guitar and picks it up. She has a moment, as a song such as Lucinda Williams' "Drunken Angel" starts to play. Lights fade.*]

• • •

Fractaland

A Farce in Infinite Pieces

Andrea Sloan Pink

Andrea Sloan Pink

Andrea Sloan Pink writes for theater and film. She wrote and produced *The Best and Brightest*, a televised film festival of early works by American film directors. Her first play, *The Physiology of Solar Flares*, received a full production in the Francis Ford Coppola One-Act Festival at UCLA. Her *Hollywood Trilogy* of plays includes *Les Hollywood Hills*, *Warner Bros.*, and *The Golden Age*. Her other plays include *Origami*, *Ode to Provence*, and *Light*. She received her BA and MFA in screenwriting from UCLA School of Film and Television and a Juris Doctorate from UCLA School of Law. She is an award-winning poet, playwright, and essayist and is currently producing a music album featuring artists from around the globe.

··· production history ···

Fractaland received a staged reading as a part of the Discoveries: New Horizons triple bill at the Newport Theater Arts Center on July 12, 2014. It was directed by Richard Stein, member of the Society of Directors and Choreographers, and was produced by Eric Eberwein of Orange County Playwrights Alliance.

cast

MEMPHIS   Paul Freeman

GREEK CHORUS   Sarah Zen Hoist, Jessica Lamprinos, Jill Cary Martin

BOB   Patrick Brien

FRAME   Paul Gillette

RAY GIRVAN   Dave Barton

BENOIT MANDELBROT   Richard Stein

characters

MEMPHIS   A middle-aged man dressed in the simple clothing of a furniture store clerk from the Pacific Northwest.

GREEK CHORUS   Three women. They should either be very similar-looking, or be very distinct, with unusual bodies and strange faces.

BOB   A man in his fifties dressed as a stereotypical professor with a tweed jacket with suede elbow patches, glasses, dorky shoes.

FRAME   A sixty-year-old, owlish man with a round face and a beard. He dresses in a dark turtle neck and dark slacks with a professorial jacket thrown over it.

RAY GIRVAN   A man in his fifties who dresses like an engineer, button-down shirt, glasses.

BENOIT MANDELBROT   A man in his late sixties who dresses like an elegant Central European gentleman, portly, with a silk tie.

setting

A black box stage.

time

The present.

Note: House music should be fractal instrumental music or Jonathan Couton's "Mandelbrot Set." Light projections of gaskets and Mandelbrot sets may be used before the opening of the play.

• • •

[*A black box set.* MEMPHIS *is at center stage. The* GREEK CHORUS *is on a raised platform at stage left. The lines of the* GREEK CHORUS *may be read in unison, or distributed according to their characters, as determined by the director.*]

MEMPHIS   So, I was hit on the side of the head. I wish I could say it was something like a baseball on opening day. But it wasn't. Just a dumb car crash.

GREEK CHORUS   A dumb car crash. Aren't all car crashes dumb?

MEMPHIS   When I woke up, I saw everything different. Differently. Different. With a difference. There were arcs of lights coming off the car. Arcs, like geometric patterns, emanating from the sun.

CHORUS   The sun. The sun. The sun.

MEMPHIS   I'd never been a good student, see? In fact, I was pretty average in all ways. I grew my sideburns long. I drank beer. I sold cars. I loved to work out. I loved to party. On Saturday nights, I looked to go out and get in trouble. That's right, it was trouble.

CHORUS   Not the car crash?

MEMPHIS   No. Trouble. I remember now. I'd walked out of the bar. It was a Karaoke club in Tacoma. It was still light. These losers—then I was down. One of them kicked me in the head. They kicked me while I was down. And kicked me. I had nothing to steal. They finally took my jacket, cheap leather. I'd paid ninety-nine bucks for it. How could I forget? That kick to the head changed my life—forever.

CHORUS   How could you have forgotten? You forgot in the past. If you forget, you are currently forgetting.

MEMPHIS   I forgot. How could I have forgotten? It was a trauma. Trauma to the head. That's what they called it. Emergency room. They stitched me up. But the side of my head.

CHORUS   The corpus callosum. You suffered damage.

MEMPHIS   Yeah, right, damage. And you know, I would see a beam of light, and I started—after a week or so, drawing, because it was so overwhelming. I tried to explain it to my mother. She just looked at me like I was daft. So I drew it down. So she could see it. And she said, "That looks right fine."

CHORUS   But that wasn't all.

MEMPHIS   That wasn't all. You'd think it'd be good—to see all this beauty. But it wasn't. It came with a dark side, too. The light. See, the light had dark in it. I was seeing the light all the time. In everything I looked at. So I got some Hefty bags and taped them to the windows. All the windows. So I could get some rest. And I had to wash my hands all the time. My fingers became chapped and red. And then they bled. I used anti-bacterial soap, the kind from a pump, because a soap bar, you know, it's dirty.

CHORUS   Dirty, dirty, dirty.

MEMPHIS   I wasn't all right. No. I can see that now. But at the time, it's what I had to do, you know? Like a compulsion. No. A compulsion. I was absolutely compulsed to do it.

CHORUS   Compulsion. Emulsion. Repulsion.

MEMPHIS   I became obsessed with numbers. I dream about it. There's not a moment I can't see it. I can't turn it off.

CHORUS   Turn out the light. Turn out the light.

MEMPHIS   Right, so it turned out these things I was seeing, there's a name for them. Fractals. It's the patterns underlying everything in the universe. Eventually, I went to the school near me, the junior college, and there was this guy there, Mr. Can. He teaches math. And he helped me understand. He showed me some books, geometry. And I showed him my pictures. Before I left, he sent an e-mail, to a professor of his. This guy was at Yale.

CHORUS   Yale! Yale! Yale!

MEMPHIS   The guy's name was Michael Frame. Frame, like in a picture. My name is Memphis Choufleur. I work at furniture store in Tacoma, Washington.

[BOB *enters.*]

BOB   My name is Bob Schipke. I am a retired professor of combinatorics, a branch of math that explores finite or countable discrete structures. I became interested in Udo of Aachen. Udo is a thirteenth-century German Benedictine monk who devised many important mathematical structures. I took a vacation to Bavaria specifically so that I could visit the Aachen Cathedral, the burial place of Charlemagne, and the monastery where Udo did his work. Little was known about Udo. I was deeply interested in learning more about him. It wasn't long after I arrived that I began looking at a tiny nativity scene that was part of the illuminated manuscript of the thirteenth-century carol, *O froehliche Weihnacht*. There, in the background of this page, I see something that looks like the Mandelbrot set. "Holy Mother of God," I think to myself. It's as if I'm seeing Bill Gates's face in the background of the Sistine chapel.

CHORUS   The Mandelbrot set! The Mandelbrot set!

BOB   It wasn't until 1976 that Benoit Mandelbrot, an IBM researcher, identified the most famous fractal, which was later named after him: the Mandelbrot set. We all assumed that it was only because of the advent of super-fast computers that were capable of the repeated calculations that he was able to discover it. These are mathematical objects that have the property of infinite detail. The most famous representation of these mathematical objects to this day is still known as the Mandelbrot set. So, here was Udo, working with the most rudimentary tools, pen and ink and the human mind, and yet he had made the same discovery a full seven centuries before Mandelbrot.

CHORUS   How did Udo discover the Mandelbrot set?

BOB   Udo was doing this mathematical work for one simple reason: He was trying to calculate who would gain entry to heaven. You see, he believed that a person's soul was made of two parts: the "profanus," or profane, and the "animi," or spiritual. These two halves of the soul were represented by ordered pairs of numbers. He spent hours working with these numbered pairs to develop an algorithm. The wavering between good and evil was like a frequency that he could chart. His algorithm functioned as a divination system that could determine who would get into heaven and who would go to hell. A system for divining the eternal future!

CHORUS   I want to go to heaven! I want to go to hell!

BOB   Unfortunately, Udo gave up just when he was on the brink of success.

[CHORUS *wails*.]

BOB   What happened was, he finally convinced the abbot to give him help in his mathematical work. This was supplied in the form of Thelonius, a young aide. The schism between Udo and Thelonius was nearly instant. Udo had always understood Mandelbrot to be a symbol of God. Thelonius, on the other hand, was convinced that it was the Devil. Thelonius believed that numbers that flew from infinity were souls escaped from heaven that were drawn into the gravitational pull of Earth and sucked into the pit of hell. Udo's concept of predetermining salvation was deeply heretical. Thus, his writings were hidden by the Church for centuries.

CHORUS   Lost! The divination is hidden!

BOB   Udo and Thelonius came to fisticuffs in the refectory. Thelonius told the abbot about the nature of Udo's work. Udo's concept of predetermining salvation was deeply heretical. The abott sent Udo's written work to the archives with the instructions that it be hidden for centuries. The abott threatened to excommunicate him from the church. On the final page of his *Codex Udophus*, Udo wrote, "I have seen into a realm of heavenly complexity, and my heart is heavy that the door is now closed."

[*Silence. Lights fade for a moment of silence, then rise as* RAY *enters*.]

RAY   My name is Ray Girvan. I am a technical writer living in the United Kingdom. My wife is a playwright. On April Fools' Day in 1999, I posted an article on the Internet called "The Mandelbrot Monk." In it, I wrote about a discovery of some early work by a monk named Udo that suggested the Mandelbrot set was independently discovered centuries ago. I wrote that the discovery was made by a retired mathematician, a fictional Harvard professor I named Bob Schipke.

[*To* BOB.]

BOB Schipke does not exist! To lend credibility to my hoax, I aligned Udo's fantastic discoveries with several other real discoveries of the time. I ended my post, "With sincere thanks to the late Bob Schipke for allowing me to reproduce his work." My story was so influential that it was picked up as part of a course at Yale taught by a brilliant professor, Michael Frame. My invention of Bob Schipke is my most famous work to date.

CHORUS You can find Bob Schipke in the Museum of Hoaxes. Bob Schipke is a fiction.

BOB I may be fictional, but does that make me unbelievable? Am I not worthy of believing? Sometimes fictions contain more truthier truths than truth. Let me tell you about combinatorics. As I said, it's a branch of math that studies finite or countable discrete structures. Finite. Knowable.

CHORUS I love something that is finite and knowable.

BOB One of the interesting things about combinatorics is how it can be applied to language. If you think about it, each word is a sequence of symbols that forms a finite set. The alphabet, like math, is a symbolic language. And language itself can be viewed as a set of finite sets. The English alphabet is also a finite set of twenty-six letters. The first book on the application of combinatorics to words was written by M. Lothaire. Actually, M. Lothaire was not a person at all but a group of more than a dozen mathematicians that decided to adopt that persona for the purpose of authoring the book collectively. Were they not, too, a finite set? Were they not also a fiction? Many of them were students of the French mathematician Marcel-Paul Schützenberger, who first began to apply combinatorics to language. We are given to thinking about irreducible words and square-free words. We are given the concept of the empty word, which is a word with a symbol length of zero.

CHORUS   Empty word. Empty word.

BOB   A book is a sequence of typographical symbols. This play began as a sequence of typographical symbols. It is now a sequence of typographical symbols converted into a sequence of sound frequencies. Thinking about how words can be represented mathematically led to the development of codes, coding, and the development of computer languages.

MEMPHIS   Language is a system of words. Words are a frame for this story. The Frame for this story, the story I'm trying to tell, is Michael Frame. Michael Frame of Yale. It's a Framed story see, a story within a story, a story with a Michael Frame.

[FRAME *enters walking stiffly with a cane.*]

FRAME   "My name is Inigo Montoya. Prepare to die."

[FRAME *thrusts his cane in the air.*]

I don't know why every time I speak, this is how it begins.

CHORUS   Prepare to die! Prepare to die! It's a reference to William Goldman's book, *The Princess Bride*, the book, which contained himself as a character, telling about a book that was, in fact, not a book. The book was made into a film. The film was—. It was a gasket.

FRAME   Can we move on? I have something to say. Nothing is measurable.

CHORUS   Is love measurable? How much do you love me? What is the number? Infinity? No. Infinity plus one.

FRAME   Measurement depends upon the frame of measurement. The Frame. What I mean to say is—here, let me give you an example: If you set out to measure a coastline, and you measure it in kilometers, you get one measurement. If, instead, you measure it in millimeters, you get a vastly different number because you pick up more of squiggles, wrinkles, and crinkles. There is no one measurement. It is unknowable. The more you try to measure it, the longer it gets.

CHORUS   Measurement eludes us. The more closely we try to measure reality, the farther the truth gets.

FRAME   What is a fractal? A fractal is a geometric figure, each part of which has the same characteristics as the whole. We say they are self-similar. Gaskets are an important example of fractals. The Sierpinski Triangle is a gasket. It's an equilateral triangle subdivided into smaller equilateral triangles. No matter how big you make it, no matter how small you make it, the pattern repeats again and again. Let me explain the rule of gaskets: Shrink by half, move over, repeat again and again. That's the gasket rule. Here's a little ditty that I like:

Big gaskets are made of little gaskets,
The bits into which we slice 'em
And little gaskets are made of lesser gaskets
And so ad infinitum.

CHORUS   [*Singing.*]
Are we only gaskets? Are we only gaskets?
A tisket, a tasket,
A green and yellow gasket.
I brought a fractal to my mom
and on the way I lost it.

FRAME   The truth about fractals is that we can see how tiny changes grow into huge effects. The ultimate question is, do fractals have predictive qualities? Isn't that what we want to know, our own destinies? Girvan wasn't so far off the mark when he suggested Udo used fractals to predict who would go to heaven and hell.

RAY   In fact, I knew that fractals were often used for predictive modeling, for everything from hydraulics to stock market analysis.

BOB   Is it possible that our destiny could be predicted by applying simple mathematical rules?

MEMPHIS   I'd like to know my destiny. Will I ever get out of the furniture store? Wouldn't it be ironic, if the kick to the head, the very thing that changed me, ended up bringing my work enough recognition that I could get out from behind the counter?

BOB   If I am a fiction, can my destiny be predicted by mathematical rules?

FRAME   It's true that fractals might make a perfect predictive model. The problem is, inevitable uncertainties in our knowledge of the initial conditions grow to overwhelm long-term prediction. Fractals are a fascinating body of knowledge, but they are also a metaphor, a way of looking at the world.

MEMPHIS   I see the world in fractals.

FRAME   Art discovered self-similarity before math did. Cezanne said, "Everything in Nature can be viewed in terms of cones, cylinders, and spheres." But, actually, Cezanne was wrong. The boundary of the Mandelbrot set contains infinitely many copies of the Mandelbrot set. In fact, as close as you look to any boundary point, you will find infinitely many little Mandelbrots. The boundary is so "fuzzy" that it is two-dimensional. At the boundary, it is crinkly. Also, the boundary is filled with points where a little bit of the Mandelbrot set looks like a little bit of the Julia set at that point. The Mandelbrot set and the Julia set—it even sounds poetic!

CHORUS   Poetic. Poetic? Poetic!

FRAME   In meteorological terms, the flapping of the butterfly's wings does not cause the tornado in Oklahoma, rather, its selects the tornado in Oklahoma from amongst many possible outcomes. There is tension between prediction and the selection of possible outcomes. The inevitable uncertainties in our knowledge of the initial conditions grow to overwhelm long-term prediction. Each snowflake is formed by the chaotic movement of water molecules. It is a unique product of the turbulence of clouds and atoms. Each snowflake tells the story of its journey through the storm, if only we knew how to read it.

MEMPHIS   If I knew how to read my story—.

FRAME   The frustration is that this is just a story, someone else's story. The Mandelbrot set is a mathematical set of points that creates a fractal two-dimensional shape. But to me, Mandelbrot is a human, a mentor, a friend.

CHORUS   [*Improvisational singing.*] This research was supported by the National Science Foundation under Grant No. 0203203.

[BENOIT MANDELBROT *enters.*]

MANDELBROT   I am Benoit Mandelbrot. My mother was a doctor. The fact that she was a doctor led me to have a peculiar education. She was afraid of epidemics, so she wouldn't send me to school. Instead, she asked my aunt's husband to tutor me at his home for first and second grade. He hated rote education. As a result, he wouldn't teach me even the alphabet and multiplication tables. His emphasis was on training my memory and on teaching me creatively and independently. So instead of accumulating facts, I spent my time reading, examining maps, with all their branching tributaries, playing hours of chess, and opening my eyes to all the detail of reality. When I was eleven, we left Poland for France as economic refugees. My mother was a dental surgeon and my father worked in the *schemata* trade. My father had an uncle in France, the mathematician, Szolem Mandelbrojt, and it was toward him that we headed.

    In high school, whenever the teacher was talking about a geometric problem, I always heard another voice inside my head, one that made the problem more elegant, or symmetrical. I would aesthetically complete it, sometimes by projection, sometimes by inversion. After a few transformations, everything became more harmonious. I felt, in a way, it was cheating because I could impose familiar shapes, then fill in the algebra later. I was simply translating algebra back into geometry, solving it visually, then translating it back again. In France, we lived in constant fear. We knew if someone reported us, we would be sent to our deaths. This happened to a close family friend from Pairs, Zina Morhange, who was also a doctor. Another physician denounced her, simply to get rid of the competition. We escaped detection. Who knows why? I had a dream of finding order where everyone else saw a lawless mess. My uncle, Szolem, mocked my romantic dream. He died believing I had squandered my intellectual gifts.

CHORUS   You squandered your intellectual gifts. Squander. Squander. You took them on a wander!

MANDELBROT   I pursued roughness. I returned to Mother Earth for inspiration. The world is not fundamentally mild and simple.

CHORUS   Because of the roughness, the roughness.

MANDELBROT   Roughness is how I got to France. Roughness is how I got to America. Life, from moment to moment, is nothing but roughness. We spend so much time on smoothness: Creating the appearance of smoothness, smoothing things out, un-ruffling our feathers. The very word ruffling means to disorder or disarrange! Roughness is more real than smoothness. Is there anything that is truly smooth?

CHORUS   Smoothness is a lie. Smoothness is a fiction.

MANDELBROT   All those hours of my childhood, lying on the floor, looking at maps, as a young man, I kept wondering: How long is the coast of Britain? The answer, I was surprised to discover, depends on how closely I looked. On a map, an island may appear smooth, but when you zoom in, the map reveals jagged edges that add up to a longer coast. Zooming in further will reveal even more coastline. The length of the coastline is, in a sense, infinite.

CHORUS   The length becomes infinite!

MANDELBROT   The existence of my uncle, Szolem, saved us in more ways than one. My uncle was a professor of mathematics. One day, he said to me, "Why don't you solve this problem? It was a construction by Julia and Fatou. If you can solve it, it will make your whole career," he said. I tried for years, but nothing. Nothing! It wasn't until much later, when I was at IBM, and we were starting to work with super-fast machines, that I decided to apply the computer to this old problem. What came out was—sheer beauty.

CHORUS   The beauty. You have never seen such beauty.

MANDELBROT   As an adult, I started to apply my ideas to financial markets. At first, no one wanted to listen to me. They had their charts! Their averages! So they can make a chart with the biggest five discontinuities taken out. Here, look at this! It looks beautiful, right? Yes, discontinuities are a nuisance! Acts of God! You can't control them, so—. In many studies of price, they set them aside, take them out. Just random, stupid acts. Discontinuities are the music! They are the meat! The five Acts of God are as important as everything else. It is not the discontinuities we should put aside. If you master these, you master price! You master the universe! You can master the little noise as well as you can, but it's not important. Life is in the discontinuities!

CHORUS   Life is in the discontinuities. But I want it to be smooth!

MANDELBROT   For two years in the 1940s, I went to Cal Tech where I ended up getting my masters. Can you imagine what that was like, Cal Tech in the forties? I heard Richard Tolman's late lectures on thermodynamics. That started the second chapter of my life in which I studied something new: Turbulence. Turbulence is a flow regime characterized by chaotic property changes. Can you imagine the metaphorical implications of turbulence? There can be no true explanation of turbulence. As humans, we have the desire to tame turbulence. "This is your captain speaking. This is your seat belt warning."

CHORUS   Hold on for turbulence!

MANDELBROT   When we look at turbulent systems, are we just naming structures in order to feel more in control of what we truly have no control over? Are we merely charting chaos? Turbulence brings wild variability and randomness. *If you are looking for growth, seek turbulence.*

FRAME   In life, we often want to get rid of turbulence. We want to be safe, to keep our seat belts on. You can think of the heartbeat as a kind of turbulence. If the line is flat, you're dead.

CHORUS   Flat, flat, flat: you're dead!

[*Soprano solo.*]

Natural death is as it were a haven and rest to us after long navigation. And the noble soul is like a good mariner; for he, when he draws near the port, lowers his sails, and enters it softly with feeble steerage (81. Dante, Convito IV. 28).

MANDELBROT   A maverick's research requires slow and gradual buildup and maturation. You must be adaptable and open to change. Mavericks are punished. Should they be tolerated?

All civilizations know that even the best intentioned, best designed rule, if applied absolutely, will lead to disastrous results. Society finds unplanned diversity to be intolerable. Society crushes malcontents and troublemakers as a serious threat to the status quo. Who is Society? It is all of us. For its own welfare, society must let some people opt out. Labeling, rebuking, crushing mavericks does nothing to improve society. A good sprinkling of diversity is indispensable to humanity. Mavericks create a kind of humanistic turbulence. Sometimes forward motion requires violent action.

FRAME   Diversity is the basis of evolution.

BOB   Schutzenberger challenged Darwin's theory of evolution by suggesting that the probability of random mutations consistently gives negative results.

FRAME   To spread human action, sometimes a small push may cause the intensifying spread of an idea or behavior. Progress must contain setbacks and net change over time. Punctuated progress is the only kind of progress we are able to perceive.

MANDELBROT   We build by iteration.

FRAME   Shrink by half, move over, and repeat, again and again: The gasket rule.

MANDELBROT   It is in the arrangement of grains of sand; in the distribution of galaxies.

BOB   A fractal is a story about how it grows. This play is a story about how it grows. The scenes are gaskets. Repeat again and again.

MANDELBROT   Science has a narrative component.

FRAME   Infinite complexity can be described by simple rules.

MANDELBROT   What I want to talk about is the roughness. In 2010, I was diagnosed with pancreatic cancer. I moved into a hospice in

Cambridge, Massachusetts. Six weeks later, I was dead. Is death not the ultimate form of human turbulence?

MEMPHIS   I sell my pictures on the Internet. I would like to stop working in the furniture store. If there was a God, I would no longer be working in the furniture store.

FRAME   [*To* RAY GIRVAN.] Girvan was a liar. But that didn't mean that his work didn't have value. In fact, it brought attention to Mandelbrot. Of course, the persistence of his fiction, and the lack of its detection, confuses the facts for the origination of fractal theory. It makes it fuzzy, Adds noise into the signal. But is it untrue that fractals existed in the time of the fictional monk? Is it untrue that humans used fractals prior to the observation of the mathematical objects by Mandelbrot? Is it untrue that humans incorporated fractals into physical structures since the beginning of man? Is it not true that our very DNA encodes fractal instructions for growth: repeat, repeat, repeat?

MANDELBROT   If you look at my life, if you take the beginning in Paris and the end at Yale, I have had a conventional career. But it was not a straight line between the beginning and the end. It was a very crooked line. I see the trajectory of my own life in the rough outlines of the clouds.

[*Movement gradually begins to increase to convey a sense of unstable electrons and chaotic action, building to a loud climax to end.*]

RAY   [*To* BOB.] My invention of Bob Schipke is my most famous work to date.

BOB   I am only an invention. Are we all only our own invention?

FRAME   What is the difference between fictions and lies?

MEMPHIS   Some people call me an idiot savant. I am not an idiot, or a savant. I am just an average guy.

FRAME   Fictions tell us deep things about the world.

MEMPHIS   It was a discontinuity. I was just some random guy. And then they kicked me. Is this not a form of turbulence?

FRAME   [*To* MANDELBROT.] Science has a narrative component.

MANDELBROT   [*To* FRAME.] I am a storyteller.

BOB   [*To* GIRVAN.] I am only a story.

RAY   [*To* BOB.] My invention has an echo.

MEMPHIS   [*To* FRAME.] My drawings are echoes of the underlying geometry of nature.

FRAME   [*To* MEMPHIS.] The set is a mathematical echo.

MEMPHIS   [*To* FRAME.] The work persists.

FRAME   The work persists.

RAY   The work persists.

BOB   The work persists.

MANDELBROT   The work persists.

CHORUS   [*Increasing in speed and volume.*] The work persists. The work persists. The work persists.

ALL   [*Building to a crescendo.*] The work persists. The work persists. The work persists.

MANDELBROT   The work persists!

[*Cut to black.*]

• • •

Right Sensation

Rich Orloff

Rich Orloff

Rich Orloff is the one of the most popular unknown playwrights in the country. *The New York Times* called his comedy *Big Boys* "rip-roaringly funny" and named *Funny as a Crutch* a Critic's Pick. His documentary-style play *Chatting with the Tea Party*, based on interviews with leaders of Tea Party groups around the country, was named a finalist for the 2014 Woodward/Newman New Play Award. Other full-length plays range from the documentary-style *Vietnam 101: The War on Campus* (thirty productions around the country) to the comedy revue *Romantic Fools* (sixty productions around the world). Orloff's eighty short plays have received over 1,200 productions on six continents (and a staged reading in Antarctica). With the publication of *Right Sensation*, his short comedies have been published seven times in the annual *Best American Short Plays* anthology series. Learn more about Rich's plays at: www.richorloff.com.

··· production history ···

Right Sensation was originally produced by the WorkShop Theatre Company, New York City, in their annual short play festival. The cast included Tracy Newirth and David Walters. The production was directed by Holli Harms.

    Right Sensation was subsequently produced at the WorkShop as part of Rich Orloff's *Couples*, a collection of short plays with two-character casts. That production featured Jacqueline Raposo and Michael Anderson, under the direction of Paula D'Alessandris.

place

Paula's bedroom.

time

Evening.

characters

    PAULA   Thirties–forties
    STEWART   Thirties–forties

• • •

[*At rise:* PAULA *and* STEWART *are in* PAULA's *bedroom, kissing with enthusiasm. They're horny and attracted to each other, but not yet comfortable and confident with each other. They're both dressed and have not yet reached the bed.*]

PAULA   You kiss really well.

STEWART   Thanks. You, too.

PAULA   And I'm not just saying that because I'm drunk.

STEWART   Me, neither.

PAULA   I'm not that drunk.

STEWART   I'm as drunk or as not drunk as you want me to be.

[*He puts his hand up her blouse. She moves it away from her breasts, and so he slides it to the back of her blouse. They continue to kiss.*]

PAULA I don't normally do this.

STEWART Me, neither.

PAULA I've never done this.

STEWART I'm willing to have done this or not done this, whichever you prefer.

[*She moves his hand away from her bra strap. They continue kissing, and his hand moves to the bra strap again.*]

PAULA Please don't.

STEWART Okay.

[*Their kissing becomes more passionate.* STEWART *puts a hand on her bra strap and quickly unsnaps it.* PAULA *recoils, grabbing her blouse so her bra stays on.*]

PAULA I said no, you bastard!

[PAULA *runs into her bathroom and slams the door.* STEWART *is a bit stunned. He approaches the door.*]

STEWART Look, I'm, I'm, I'm sorry, I—I didn't mean to, it's just—when my hand gets in the vicinity…I can't tell you how proud I was when I mastered the skill…I'm, I'm really sorry.…Patty, are you okay?

PAULA [*Offstage. Not okay*] I'm fine, and my name's Paula.

STEWART Will you come out—Paula…please?

PAULA Why should I?

STEWART 'Cause, 'cause I'd like to see you.

PAULA Why?

STEWART Because, because you're nice, and, and you're really sexy, and you have a great smile.

PAULA What if I didn't have teeth?

STEWART You'd still be sexy.

PAULA Why?

STEWART Well, you have beautiful eyes.

PAULA What if I didn't have eyes?

STEWART You'd still be sexy.

PAULA Why?

STEWART You have a great neck.

PAULA What if I didn't have a neck?

STEWART Is this a puzzle? Because I suck at puzzles. You want to torture me? Lock me in a room with a crossword puzzle.

[PAULA *enters.*]

PAULA What if I only had one breast?

STEWART I see two…don't I?

PAULA I had a mastectomy.

STEWART Oh…Oh, well, you know, that's okay, no, I mean it's not o—I mean, whatever…So you had cancer?

PAULA No, my right breast just got in the way during archery.

STEWART I'm sorry, I was—

PAULA No, no, that's—

STEWART They look fine. From here.

PAULA I had an implant.

[*A long silence.*]

If you want to go…

STEWART No, I, I, I just can't think of anything to say that doesn't make me sound like a jerk. Which I'm not, I swear, I'm not, it's just not always readily apparent.

PAULA You don't seem like a jerk.

STEWART Yeah, well, the night is young. How long ago did—

PAULA Uhhhhhwhile ago.

STEWART Am I your—

PAULA Uh-huh.

STEWART How much did you have to drink to—

PAULA I didn't count.

STEWART Well, I'm honored you chose me.

PAULA You should be.

STEWART You know, you really don't have to be self-conscious, I mean, I've seen implants before.

PAULA You have?

STEWART Sure. Plenty of times.

PAULA Plenty of times?

STEWART After my divorce, I, uh, I, uh, I kind of went through a, a strip joint phase—which I'm *way* over—

PAULA Uh-huh.

STEWART Anyway, so, like, shifting subjects, like, I know this must be traumatic but, well, like, what's the big deal?

PAULA What's the—!

STEWART I just mean, lots of people have fake parts these days. Like hip replacements, or fake knees, or hair plugs. Most people are not 100 percent there—if you know what I mean.

PAULA It's just not the same as it was. It's like replacing, ummm—

STEWART A Lexus with a Honda?

PAULA No!

STEWART [*Defensive.*] Sorry. Just trying to empathize.

PAULA It's like replacing an orange, with a wax orange.

STEWART Better than a wax prune.

[*Off her glare.*]

You know, you don't cheer up easily.

PAULA How would you like it if you had surgery and woke up with a wax testicle?

STEWART My trousers would be more comfortable. Look, I'm sorry about your, your misfortune and everything, but you still got one good one, don't you?...Was that a stupid thing to say?

PAULA For a human being, yes. For a guy, not necessarily.

STEWART Look, I don't know what you—I just want to—I, I, I've had some moles removed....Not that I'm equating.

PAULA I probably shouldn't have—

STEWART No, no, you did the—

PAULA It's just that, it was my favorite one.

STEWART You had a favorite breast?

PAULA Yes, I did.

STEWART Why?

PAULA It was rounder and, and perkier.

STEWART And your other one?

PAULA It's, it's—none of your business.

STEWART Fine.

PAULA I just liked my right one better.

STEWART Okay.

PAULA Women often prefer one over the other.

STEWART Do you have a favorite ear? Do you prefer one nostril?

PAULA Do you have a favorite testicle?

STEWART I just thank God I have two....Oh, shit, I mean, I'd thank God if I had one also.

PAULA Probably not with the same gusto.

STEWART I'm just grateful I'm not a eunuch...most days.

PAULA Look, Steven, I just—

STEWART Stewart.

PAULA It has no nipple.

STEWART I think nipples are highly overrated.

PAULA You do?

STEWART Well, starting now.

PAULA Look, *Stewart*, I really liked kissing you—

STEWART Same here.

PAULA It's, you see, when I had my mastectomy, well, I thought if I had an implant, you see the doctors warned me, because of where my cancer was located, they—they had to take the nerves out with the breast. So there's not just no nipple, there's no sensation there. None.

STEWART Nothing?

PAULA You can touch it and lick it and put pins in it, and it feels…nothing.

STEWART Oh.

PAULA I, I wasn't going to say anything, but, but then I thought, what if he starts sucking on it, and I don't respond, and he'll think—

STEWART It's okay.

PAULA I mean, it's there, but don't waste your time on it.

STEWART Does it affect your balance?

PAULA What?

STEWART Like, you told me you like to swim. Does it affect your stroke?

PAULA They don't weigh that much.

STEWART Well, I've never weighed one.

PAULA Look—

STEWART Guys have a lot of fixations about breasts, but weighing them is not one of them.

PAULA And what fixations *do* you have about breasts?

STEWART Well, you know, the normal ones.

PAULA Do you prefer them big or small?

STEWART I've never been with a breast that's either too big *or* too small.

PAULA Never?

STEWART Mostly I'm just glad when they're…available.

PAULA Well, one of mine isn't really available.

STEWART That's—you know, you never asked how *many* I prefer.

PAULA How many do you prefer?

STEWART Five. So you're four short; live with it.

PAULA [*Not amused.*] Thanks.

STEWART Listen. I can see why this would be hard for you and why you had to get sloshed and all that—

PAULA I wasn't sloshed.

STEWART It's just—I don't care if your right boob is made of plastic, Formica, recycled linoleum, used tires, or filled vacuum cleaner bags. I like you. I find you attractive. I would like to fondle any and all of you. If you like me, you're welcome to do the same. If you don't like me, fine. But if you *do* like me, and you don't—enjoy me because you're afraid, well, well, well, like, now we're talking loss.

[*A moment, then.*]

This is about as articulate as I ever get, so don't expect better.

PAULA What if, what if you touch it and go "ugh"?

STEWART Then I'm a real loser.

PAULA What if, what if you like it better than my real one?

STEWART Then, then you can write a thank-you note to your surgeon.

PAULA What if, what if after all this, I give in and you decide I'm a lousy lover?

STEWART   I'm not that picky.

PAULA   And what if I decide *you're* a lousy lover?

STEWART   I'll add you to the list.

PAULA   What if, what if, what if we find out we really like each other?

[*A long beat.*]

STEWART   Well, that sobered me up. How about you?

PAULA   It's like I just drank a double espresso.

STEWART   If, um, we don't have to—

PAULA   You know, about a month after the operation, I, uh, I decided—I—how to put this delicately—

STEWART   I'll be more turned on if you don't.

PAULA   I decided it was, it was time to "own" my sexuality again.

STEWART   Before that were you just renting?

PAULA   So one night I took a warm bath, with bubbles, and candles, and a glass of sherry, and I relaxed. And I came into my bedroom, and I lit some more candles, scented candles, and I got into bed, and I began to caress myself. Slowly. Delicately. Skillfully. But, but every time I touched my right breast, it was, it was as if, instead of candles, someone was shining a thousand harsh, cold fluorescent lights on me. And, and I tried to, to close my eyes and get into it again, but every, every time I touched…the lights went through my eyelids.

STEWART   [*Warmly.*] Hey…

PAULA   [*Near tears by now.*] And if I focused on not touching my right breast, the lights they still—

STEWART   It's okay.

PAULA   *No, it's not.*

STEWART   Of course not, but, but—look, I haven't had the light thing—

PAULA   Then don't—

STEWART With me it's noise. Nights when all I want to do is be with a woman, you know—I don't mean sex. I don't mean not sex, I just mean—be with her, you know? And then the noise starts. And nothing I do adjusts the volume. And soon I'm with the noise more than with the woman.

PAULA And what do you do when that happens?

STEWART I do what any guy would do. I beat myself up.

PAULA And what if I, what if I do something like that while you're here?

STEWART I dunno…I'll, I'll try to dim the lights for you.

[*A Beat.*]

PAULA I got new sheets. Do you like 'em?

STEWART I can't tell from this far away.

[*They move to the bed.*]

PAULA If we could just kiss and not—

STEWART Whatever.

[*They resume kissing.* STEWART *doesn't know what to do with his hands. Eventually he just sticks his arms out to his sides.*]

PAULA Oh, hell…Give me your hand.

[PAULA *takes one of* STEWART*'s hands and places it on her right breast. Tears well up in her eyes.*]

STEWART I thought you said it had no sensation.

PAULA Shhh.

[*She leaves his hand there and just absorbs for a moment. Then they kiss again. It's slower now and more intimate. The lights fade.*]

• • •

Ski Lift

Chris Holbrook

Chris Holbrook

Chris Holbrook is the author of two full-length plays, *Les Fantômes* (2012) and, more recently, *Doorman* (2014). His short plays include *Fountain of Youth* (Wimbledon Attic Theatre) and *Ski Lift*, a winner of Theatre Oxford's (Oxford, MS) and Longwood University's (Farmwood, VA) 2014 short play contests. When he is not writing, he produces and directs documentaries, in addition to serving as the director of Rough Cuts, an organization in San Francisco that supports documentary filmmakers (www.sfroughcuts.com).

··· production history ···

Ski Lift was first produced on April 24, 2014, at Longwood University (Farmwood, Virginia) with the following cast:

RALPHE   Kenneth R. Hopkins

EGBERT   Jimmy Mello

It was subsequently performed the same year, October 16–19, at Theatre Oxford (Oxford, Mississippi) as part of their 2014 Ten-Minute Play Festival, with the following cast:

RALPHE   Greg Earnest

EGBERT   William Chandler

characters

RALPHE

EGBERT

···

[*A ski lift at a swank ski resort.* RALPHE, *Londoner, tall, contoured, wearing the full ski regalia, waits for the ski lift.*]

[EGBERT *is* RALPHE'*s opposite, straight out of a lost twenty-something "Mumblecore" film. Slouched over. Glasses. Wearing a jacket better suited for golf in May.*]

[*But the real striking thing about* EGBERT *is that he doesn't have any skis—or poles or boots. The lift arrives and sweeps them up. As they go up,* RALPHE *looks around and admires the view.*]

[EGBERT, *meanwhile, pulls out a pen and a piece of paper and begins writing.*]

RALPHE   Hell of a view.

[EGBERT *continues to write.*]

I said, hell of a view.

EGBERT   It's a mountain.

RALPHE   It's not just a mountain. This is one of the pearls of the Alps. And the fifth highest in France. Is this your first run?

EGBERT   I suppose.

RALPHE   Fourth one for me. Was here at 9 a.m., as always. Nothing like the mountain when it hasn't been touched all night. Snow like a virgin on her wedding night. You can hear the gasp of the mountain, while you admire the danger in her curves, the beauty of her face.

EGBERT   [*Still writing furiously.*] Do you mind? I'm busy here.

RALPHE   Doing what?

EGBERT   What does it look like?

RALPHE   Taking notes on the beauty. Good man. The mountain inspires me too. I get all my best ideas when I'm looking at her, but I rarely have the foresight to get out the pen and paper and start writing.

EGBERT   This isn't about the mountain.

RALPHE   A love letter?

EGBERT   No.

RALPHE   A lonesome ode to a paradise lost?

EGBERT   If you must know, it's a suicide note.

RALPHE   You don't say?

EGBERT   Isn't it obvious? Do I look like a skier?

RALPHE   Not an orthodox one, I admit. But those are the ones you have to fear. Remember Toni Sailer, that Austrian scoundrel? Picked up three golds in Cortina D'Ampezzo like he was shopping for bread.

EGBERT   Or poles.

RALPHE   Who needs poles? Andrea Lawrence won a gold in '52 without them.

EGBERT   I don't even have any skis!

RALPHE   A point well taken. But neither did Sondre Norheim. A little before your time, I admit. nineteenth century, Norwegian. Jumped all the time without them.

EGBERT   You're not understanding what I'm saying.

RALPHE   You're saying, you're a real ski bird.

EGBERT   I'm saying, I'm jumping.

RALPHE   Jumping?

EGBERT   Head first.

RALPHE   You devil, you.

EGBERT   I'm serious.

RALPHE   A bit cheeky, I admit, but I can see you're the type. All the same, don't you think it's a bit dangerous? Especially with this being your first run and all.

EGBERT   That's the point.

RALPHE   What's the point?

EGBERT   I'll die.

[*Silence.* RALPHE, *unperturbed, continues to admire the mountain.*]

RALPHE   [*Indicating the letter.*] Mind if I have a look?

EGBERT   I do, in fact.

RALPHE   Just a peek.

EGBERT   Why?

RALPHE   I could help. With the note, I mean. I know I'm just an amateur, with my skis and poles. You're the pro. But, now and then, I've been known to go *hors de piste*.

EGBERT   *Hors de* what?

RALPHE   Off the trail. Where you're not supposed to go. Right for the trees and the cliffs and the impossible thrill.

   [*Confiding.*]

   Put differently, I've been in your shoes.

EGBERT   You have?

RALPHE   Often, in fact.

EGBERT   That's hard to believe.

RALPHE   Trust me, I know you've got to think these things through. And if you jump now, no one will be impressed. It just snowed last night, and you'll land like a quail feather on a bed of pillows.

EGBERT   What should I do?

RALPHE   You want a hard landing?

EGBERT   Very.

RALPHE   Wait until we get over that ridge. Then you'll slam into those diamonds of rock and they'll pierce through you like hot butter on a crusty biscuit.

EGBERT   You're serious?

RALPHE   Deadly. And in the meantime, you can have me take a look at the letter. We'll tweak it a bit, and then when you jump, I'll make sure it gets into the right hands.

[EGBERT, *hesitating, hands it over.*]

[RALPHE *reading the letter out loud.*]

"Honey, could you cancel my subscription to the *Economist*? And I forgot to tell you that Juanita is coming on Tuesday instead of Wednesday. Can you make sure the house isn't a mess?"

[*To* EGBERT.]

Who's Juanita?

EGBERT   My maid.

RALPHE   You've got to clean up for the maid?

EGBERT   Don't ask.

RALPHE   [*Continuing to read.*] "Feel free to use my MetroCard. It's in the top shelf of the living room bureau on the right-hand side. It's good for another two months. Gotta go. Sorry about everything. Bye. Egbert."

[*Back to* EGBERT.]

That's it? "Sorry about everything. Bye. Egbert"

EGBERT   Well, like I said, I don't have much time.

RALPHE   You want me to disseminate *this*?

EGBERT   No, don't disseminate it. Just make sure my family gets it.

RALPHE   Okay, we'll start with the family. Good thinking. But at the same time, with this kind of letter, you've got to reach for more. Live up to the moment. Evoke the spirit of our times. And, if you're good, capture the scream of the soul in free fall. You game?

EGBERT   I don't know.

RALPHE   Listen, Egbert. If you want to make a splash with this, we've got work to do.

EGBERT   Work?

RALPHE   Yes. And we've got about one minute left before we're over those razor-sharp spirals. First step, we've got to acknowledge history. You're not the first to pull the plug, you realize?

EGBERT   I guess.

RALPHE   Kurt Cobain. He didn't talk about magazine subscriptions. He said that he rather "burn out than fade away." The gentleman acknowledged history, you see. Found a seat in an empty pew and gave it up to the master fiddler, Neil Young. Who are you referencing? The cleaning lady?

EGBERT   I'm not—

RALPHE   Or Stefan Zweig. He said his beloved homeland was "gripped with madness." He was doing it for the future of his country. What's your cause? To save money on the metro?

EGBERT   Who is Stefan Zweig?

RALPHE   Or Virginia Woolf. You've heard of her, I assume. She said she had "never been happier" than when she was with her husband. Who do you love? Where is your sense of family, history, literature, the edge of the abyss, the fragility of humanity....

EGBERT   How do you know so much about this?

RALPHE   Oh, I've written a few suicide notes in my time. Nothing I'd present to the Queen, mind you....

EGBERT   You've written suicide notes?

RALPHE   Sure. I'm no expert. But I know you've got to work at it, not just scribble a shopping list on a ski lift. I've been working on my current one for at least two months.

EGBERT   Your current one?

RALPHE   Sure. Posted it this morning.

EGBERT   To who?

RALPHE   Oh, with these things, you can't trust anybody. Sent it registered mail to my mother, wife, the children.

EGBERT   You sent the note to your children? That's horrible. How can you just send a letter like that and have them open it?

RALPHE   You think it's better if they wait until the newspaper publishes it? You really have no appreciation of the tradition.

EGBERT   Are you saying…

RALPHE   I'm telling you.

EGBERT   What?

RALPHE   This is it, Egbert.

EGBERT   But…but…this…is ridiculous. We can't jump at the same time.

RALPHE   [*Thinking hard.*] Tell you what. You go and then I'll do it on the next lift.

EGBERT   What?

RALPHE   You heard me. You go and then I'll take the next lift.

EGBERT   Suppose you change your mind?

RALPHE   What will you care, you'll be dead.

EGBERT   No, no. You go and then I'll go on the next lift.

RALPHE   Ah, very gallant of you, Egbert. But just so I understand, you're saying you'll let me go first and that I should commit suicide now?

EGBERT I didn't say it like—

RALPHE You don't trust me, is that it?

EGBERT No, I just…

RALPHE Or you want to create a distraction, so no one will try to stop you when you do it.

EGBERT Maybe…but…

RALPHE Good thinking. Maybe you do know what you're doing here. Okay. Here we go.

[RALPHE *begins to remove his clothes.*]

EGBERT What are you doing?

RALPHE Taking off my clothes. No use wasting them.

EGBERT What am I going to do with them?

RALPHE Give them to some poor chap on the way down. Or looks like you could use some them. Don't want to die from frostbite before you take the plunge.

EGBERT But how can I get down? I don't even have any skis.

RALPHE [*Lifting the bar of the lift.*] That's why I'm giving you mine. Well, it's been a real pleasure.

[*About to jump.*]

See you on the other side!

EGBERT Wait!!!

RALPHE Sorry?

EGBERT I've got something to say.

RALPHE Step on it, Egbert. We've only got thirty more seconds of deadly peaks.

EGBERT Like I was saying, I've got experience too.

RALPHE We all have experience. It's called age.

EGBERT But I know how beautiful life can be. Especially with age.

RALPHE   Don't lecture me about beauty. Why do you think I'm jumping here, on the most beautiful mountain on the planet?

EGBERT   I don't know.

RALPHE   Why do any of us want to do this?

EGBERT   Because we have doubts. Because we lose our way.

RALPHE   Egbert, please.

EGBERT   Because we've taken too many wrong turns. Because we didn't fulfill our dreams.

RALPHE   This really isn't the moment....

EGBERT   Or maybe we can't face the realization that our minds and bodies aren't what they used to be; and that our hopes for the future are just shadows lost in the early morning sun of younger generations.

RALPHE   Egbert, that's enough!

EGBERT   You think you're so special because you want to do this? You're not. You said it. We all think like this. Some more than others. But in the end, these thoughts visit all of us, and what matters is how you fight against them rather than how you give in!

RALPHE   Goddamn it, you made me miss the peaks!

EGBERT   I'm sorry.

RALPHE   Now, I'm going to have to ski down the mountain and start this all over again.

EGBERT   I didn't mean to—

RALPHE   This is already my fourth run today. I told you that.

EGBERT   I know.

RALPHE   With you, I thought I had a real shot. Finally, someone else on his way to the other side. But what do I get? A total amateur. A pre-debutant. Give me those bloody polls back!

[RALPHE *begins to put on his clothes.*]

EGBERT   Why are you smiling?

RALPHE   No reason.

EGBERT   You seem very happy.

RALPHE   It's a beautiful day.

EGBERT   But you were about to commit suicide!

RALPHE   That was then. Now we're going to ski down one of the most beautiful mountains in the world.

EGBERT   You weren't planning to jump, were you?

[*Looks.*]

RALPHE   It's a hell of a view, Egbert.

EGBERT   Yeah. Hell of a view.

[*Blackout.*]

• • •

A Long Trip

Dan McGeehan

Dan McGeehan

Dan McGeehan is an artist/actor/author. As an artist, his illustrations have appeared in countless international publications, magazines, children's books, and ads. As an actor, after attending Philadelphia's Arden Theatre training program, he has performed in and/or directed over one hundred productions in regional theaters across the country. As an author, he has penned a number of children's shows and short scripts that have won awards at several playwriting festivals in the U.S.

···production history···

A Long Trip premiered at the Third Annual Heller Shorts Festival, presented by Heller Theatre (Tulsa, OK), August 2012, and was directed by Miriam Mills. Cast: The Man, Older—George Nelson; The Woman, Older—Rita M. Boyle; The Man, Younger—Bryce Davis; The Woman, Younger—Hannah Westlund. It received the Best of Festival Award.

Subsequently, it has been produced at the following venues:

The Fourth Lab-Works 15-Minute Play Festival, presented by Valley Repertory Company (Enfield, CT), February 2013, directed by Dorrie Mitchell. It received the First Place Drama Award.

The First Annual Judith Karman Hospice Short Play Festival (Stillwater, OK), March 2013, directed by Valerie Thrasher.

The Nineteenth Annual New York City 15-Minute Play Festival, presented by Turnip Theatre Company in association with American Globe Theatre (NYC), April 2013, directed by Erick Devine.

The First Annual Phoenix Stage Company's One-Act Festival, presented by Phoenix Stage Company (Naugatuck, CT), May 2013, directed by Agnes Dann. It received the First Place Award.

The Second Annual Method & Madness Festival, presented by Denton Community Theatre (Denton, TX), June 2013, directed by Robert Ize. It received the First Place Award and Audience Favorite Award.

The Second Annual Summer Reading Series, presented by the Core Artist Ensemble (NYC, NY), July 2013, directed by Michael Padden.

The Fifth Annual Minnesota Shorts Play Festival (Mankato, MN), September 2013, directed by Cynthia Uhrich. It received the Second Place Award.

The Fourth Annual Landmark Festival, presented by Prologue Theatre Company (Chicago, IL), October 2013, directed by Rebecca Willett.

The Seventeenth Annual Paw Paw One-Acts Festival (Paw Paw, MI), February 2014, directed by Jane Starr. It received the First Place Award and People's Choice Award.

The Starting Point Festival hosted by Duel Theatrics (St. Paul, MN), March 2014, directed by Amelia Kritzer.

The Twenty-Second Annual Nantucket Short Play Festival (Nantucket, MA), March 2014, directed by Ursula Austin. It received the Second Place Award.

Boston Play Café (Boston, MA), July 2014, directed by the author.

And as of this writing, it is scheduled for production at

The 2014 BolderLife Festival (Denver, CO), October 2014. Encompass Productions (London, UK), spring 2015.

characters

THE MAN, OLDER   He is sixty+ years old, dressed comfortably.

THE WOMAN, OLDER She is sixty+ years old, dressed in a housecoat or robe.

THE MAN, YOUNGER   He is the same man, but in his late teens or early twenties.

THE WOMAN, YOUNGER She is the same woman, but in her late teens or early twenties.

setting

At home. Two chairs.

time

The present.

synopsis

An elderly man tries to connect with his wife one last time before he completely loses her to dementia. In an attempt to reawaken the bond they have held for so long, he tells her of the moment they fell in love.

• • •

[*Daytime. Inside the house somewhere. The stage is empty save for two plain wooden chairs upon which sit* THE MAN, OLDER, *and* THE WOMAN, OLDER. *Both are in their sixties. He is gently focused on her, softly rubbing one of her hands. She is vague, confused, struggling to focus her thoughts, and does not look at him.*]

THE WOMAN, OLDER   I—I just don't remember....

THE MAN, OLDER   Anything at all?

THE WOMAN, OLDER   Why do you keep asking? What do you want?

THE MAN, OLDER   That night. What did you do after you left? I want to know. Did you laugh or sing or…what? I always wanted to ask. Maybe I waited too long.…

THE WOMAN, OLDER   That night?

THE MAN, OLDER   Yes.

THE WOMAN, OLDER   [*She tries to think.*] Was it…warm?

THE MAN, OLDER   [*Gently.*] No, it was chilly.

THE WOMAN, OLDER   Oh.

[*Pause.*]

It was March, then. Right?

THE MAN, OLDER   No, it was June.

THE WOMAN, OLDER   Oh, I see.

[*Her brow furrows.*]

It's not usually chilly in June, is it?

THE MAN, OLDER   No, not usually. But it was at night, so…

THE WOMAN, OLDER   Oh…I see.

[*Struggling.*]

I just…I just don't…

THE MAN, OLDER   It was an early summer night. I didn't know you really but I had seen you before. Many times.

THE WOMAN, OLDER   At the school?

THE MAN, OLDER   Yes, many times…from across the room.

THE WOMAN, OLDER   And the church?

THE MAN, OLDER   Yes, yes…but from across the room.

THE WOMAN, OLDER   Always across the room?

THE MAN, OLDER   Well, I was so shy and you were so…

THE WOMAN, OLDER   And that night? That night in June?

THE MAN, OLDER   Well, it was at the church. School was out and the church was holding a dance, and I...

THE WOMAN, OLDER   Oh no, now I know you're wrong. My mother never let me dance. I was raised right....

THE MAN, OLDER   That's right. That's right. You didn't dance.

THE WOMAN, OLDER   I don't dance. You said it was a dance.

THE MAN, OLDER   Yes, but I didn't say *you* danced. You were volunteering....

THE WOMAN, OLDER   Oh!

THE MAN, OLDER   You served the punch. You know, ladling the punch into the paper cups.

THE WOMAN, OLDER   Oh! That's different. I was not allowed to dance.

[*Pause.*]

Did you dance?

THE MAN, OLDER   Oh, no, no. I—I couldn't....

THE WOMAN, OLDER   Was there someone you wanted to dance with?

THE MAN, OLDER   [*He looks at her hands, then up to her face. Quietly.*] Yes there was.

THE WOMAN, OLDER   Oh, that's right, you were shy. I guess you were too shy.

THE MAN, OLDER   [*Almost imperceptibly.*] Yes.

THE WOMAN, OLDER   So what did you do?

THE MAN, OLDER   I stood and watched. From across the room.

THE WOMAN, OLDER   That doesn't sound like you had a very good evening.

THE MAN, OLDER   Oh, but I did. Standing there doing nothing was the best thing I could have done.

THE WOMAN, OLDER   Oh, I don't see how that could be....

THE MAN, OLDER   Yes. You see, you had to leave the dance early. The next day you were going on a long trip. It was dark out and you didn't want to walk home alone. You wanted someone to walk with you. But everyone was having such a great time that you didn't want to spoil their fun. You needed to find someone who wasn't doing anything....

THE WOMAN, OLDER   Oh! Did I?

THE MAN, OLDER   Yes, you found me. I walked you home.

THE WOMAN, OLDER   Oh, how nice.

[THE MAN, YOUNGER, *and* THE WOMAN, YOUNGER, *enter. They are in their late teens or early twenties, and are casually dressed. They mime a conversation.* THE WOMAN, OLDER, *watches them. They are in her mind;* THE MAN, OLDER, *doesn't see them.*]

THE MAN, OLDER   Normally, I was so tongue-tied around girls, but you were different. There was something warm...

THE MAN, YOUNGER   ...inviting...

THE MAN, OLDER   ...and comforting about you. I found it easy to open up to you...

THE MAN, YOUNGER   ...to talk and not feel foolish or blush.

THE WOMAN, OLDER   What did we talk about....

THE WOMAN, YOUNGER   ... anything?

THE WOMAN, OLDER   ...all that time?

THE MAN, OLDER   Anything...

THE MAN, YOUNGER   ...and everything.

THE WOMAN, YOUNGER   Of school?

THE MAN, YOUNGER   Gym class and volleyball. Lunch and study hall. Of Mr. Robinson and the funny way he talked. Mrs. Deery and her odd hair color.

THE WOMAN, YOUNGER   Of church?

THE MAN, YOUNGER   The squeaky organ and the dirty vestibule. The Reverend Manning and his old mother. The smells, the brand-new hymnals, and the broken doorknobs.

THE MAN, OLDER   We talked and talked. All the way to your house…

THE MAN, YOUNGER   . . . still talking.

THE WOMAN, YOUNGER   Not stopping.

THE MAN, OLDER   It was wonderful.

THE WOMAN, OLDER   [*She stands and crosses to the younger couple.*] Was I pretty?

THE MAN, OLDER   Oh my, yes!

THE WOMAN, OLDER   Was I smart? Did I—Did I remember things then?

THE MAN, OLDER   [*He stands and crosses to her.*] The smartest in the class!

THE WOMAN, OLDER   Oh, I wish I could remember.…

THE MAN, OLDER   That night I could barely keep up with you. You had so much to say and I loved every second.…

THE WOMAN, YOUNGER   Look, it's a little chilly out. Would you… would you like to step into the house? We can keep talking there and be warm.

THE MAN, YOUNGER   Well…I—I…Okay.…

[*The younger couple cross to the chairs and sit. They mime a conversation.*]

THE WOMAN, OLDER   We went inside?

THE MAN, OLDER   Inside your house. *This* house, back before we bought it from your parents. We sat in *those* chairs. And talked and talked. To think that just a short time before that we barely knew each other at the dance and…

THE WOMAN, OLDER   Oh no. That can't be right. My mother never let me dance. I was not allowed to dance.

THE MAN, OLDER   But you were allowed to sit, right?

THE WOMAN, OLDER   Oh, yes…yes….

THE MAN, OLDER   Well, that night we sat so close we almost touched. And we talked.

THE WOMAN, OLDER   About what?

THE MAN, OLDER   It doesn't matter.…What matters is we talked. We talked for hours. Then suddenly I looked up at the clock—

THE MAN, YOUNGER   [*Alarmed.*] Holy crap! It's 3 a.m.!

THE WOMAN, YOUNGER   Oh! I got to go in a couple of hours!

THE MAN, YOUNGER   I…Well, *somebody* better leave! Might as well be *me*, it's your house!

THE MAN, OLDER   What a stupid thing to say.

THE WOMAN, OLDER   I like it.

[*She puts her hand on his arm.*]

THE MAN, YOUNGER   I didn't mean to…I…Oh, I'm sorry.…

THE WOMAN, YOUNGER   It's okay. It's okay.

THE MAN, OLDER   And so I said—

THE MAN, YOUNGER   Well, I gotta go.

THE MAN, OLDER   So I stood up to go.

   [THE MAN, YOUNGER, *does.*]

   But then you—

THE WOMAN, OLDER   Stood up?

   [THE WOMAN, YOUNGER, *does.*]

   And…

[THE WOMAN, YOUNGER, *pointedly moves in close to* THE MAN, YOUNGER.]

THE WOMAN, YOUNGER   I'm going on a long trip. You'll wait for me, won't you?

THE MAN, YOUNGER   [*Gulping.*] Of course. I'll be right here.

THE WOMAN, YOUNGER [*Closer.*] You have my phone number, don't you?

THE MAN, YOUNGER Y-yeah....

THE WOMAN, YOUNGER [*Even closer.*] You'll call me, won't you?

THE MAN, YOUNGER Well, yeah...

THE MAN, OLDER Well, then you leaned in.

[THE WOMAN, YOUNGER, *does, lifting her head and closing her eyes.*]

Well, I didn't know what to do, so I grabbed you by the shoulders to stop you.

[THE MAN, YOUNGER *does.*]

But then I thought—

THE MAN, YOUNGER [*In a gentle panic.*] Oh, geez! I touched her! Now I gotta do something!

THE MAN, OLDER I didn't know what it was but I was pretty sure I didn't want to do it. But I leaned in...and kissed you on the forehead.

[THE MAN, YOUNGER, *does.*]

And I said—

THE MAN, YOUNGER Well, I gotta go.

[THE MAN, YOUNGER, *tries to exit, but* THE WOMAN, YOUNGER, *gets there first and blocks his exit.*]

THE WOMAN, YOUNGER [*Standing close.*] I—I just want to know if you had a good time this evening.

THE MAN, YOUNGER I had a great time.

THE WOMAN, YOUNGER [*Closer.*] Really?

THE MAN, YOUNGER Well, yeah....

THE WOMAN, YOUNGER [*Even closer.*] So did I.

[*She leans into him.*]

THE MAN, OLDER And you leaned into me again! So I cupped your face in my hand. And kissed you...on the cheek. And then I said—

THE MAN, YOUNGER Well, I gotta go.

THE MAN, OLDER So I stepped outside and then…

THE WOMAN, OLDER [*She touches his arm.*] Shh.

[THE MAN, OLDER, *looks at her as she watches as* THE MAN, YOUNGER, *attempts to leave.*]

THE WOMAN, YOUNGER Hey!

[THE MAN, YOUNGER, *turns to her, she grabs his collar, and pulls him into a long, dynamic, volcanic kiss.*]

THE WOMAN, OLDER Oh my!

THE MAN, OLDER My first kiss. And yours.

THE WOMAN, OLDER Oh my!

THE MAN, OLDER We exploded apart.

[*The young couple separates, panting, staring at each other.*]

THE WOMAN, OLDER Our hands?

THE MAN, OLDER Burning like an electric shock ran through them.

THE WOMAN, OLDER Our lungs?

THE MAN, OLDER Gasping for air.

THE WOMAN, OLDER Our eyes?

THE MAN, OLDER Staring at each other like two big sets of dinner plates.

THE WOMAN, OLDER [*Catching her breath.*] And then?

THE MAN, OLDER And then you said to me—

THE WOMAN, YOUNGER, and **THE WOMAN, OLDER** Well, I gotta go.

THE MAN, OLDER And you went inside the house.

[THE WOMAN, YOUNGER, *moves to the opposite side of the stage, then turns her back to the audience.* THE MAN, YOUNGER, *turns out and closes his eyes.*]

THE WOMAN, OLDER [*Confused. Vaguely.*] I—I have to sit.

[THE WOMAN, OLDER, *moves to the chair.*]

THE MAN, OLDER [*Pressing the issue.*] So what did you do?

THE WOMAN, OLDER [Sitting.] When?

THE MAN, OLDER [*He crosses to her.*] When you went inside that night. I asked you earlier about it. What did you do?

THE WOMAN, OLDER I—I…

THE MAN, OLDER Did you laugh? Sing? Did you yell? Cry in your pillow? What? What did you do at that moment? Your first kiss. *Our* first kiss. How did you react?

THE WOMAN, OLDER I—I…

THE MAN, OLDER Please…think. Please. I want to know.

THE WOMAN, OLDER [*Upset, a little confused.*] I—I…I'm so sorry. I don't remember it at all. I don't remember any of it.

[THE MAN, OLDER *sits dejected. A pause.*]

What…did you do?

THE MAN, OLDER I stood there and did nothing.

THE WOMAN, OLDER I don't…I don't understand.…

THE MAN, OLDER I did nothing.

[*He looks out, fondly.*]

I stood there with all my senses cut off from the world. It was the middle of the night and there was nothing to see. No one was awake, so there was no noise to hear. I had nothing to eat, nothing to smell. The only sense left to me was touch.

[THE MAN, OLDER, *crosses and stands next to* THE MAN, YOUNGER.]

I felt the cool summer early-morning air. I felt it all around me, wrapping my entire body. I felt it seep through my clothing and touch my skin. I was cold from head to toe except for one small spot of warmth—

THE MAN, YOUNGER, and **THE MAN, OLDER** [*They raise their arms and lightly touch their lips simultaneously.*] Right here.

THE MAN, OLDER   I didn't move. I didn't want anything to take away my focus on that spot. I knew it would fade away and I wanted to feel every second of it while it was still there. It was as if there was no one or nothing else in the world that mattered but that warmth around my lips. That moment was mine! I owned it! I was alive and I lived in and for that one moment! I didn't think of anything else! No school, no church, no dance. Nothing else in life. No years past, or all those years to come. No graduation, no jobs, no marriage, no children, no moving, no retiring, no slowing down.

[*He turns to look at her.*]

No sickness. No Alzheimer's. No dementia. No…

[*He covers his eyes, cries.*]

Oh God! Please! Don't leave me! Don't leave me!

[THE MAN, OLDER, *staggers back to his chair and crumples.*]

I don't know what I'll do without you. Oh God. Please.

[*He cries.*]

[THE WOMAN, OLDER, *looks at him for the first time and an obvious change occurs: a certain clearness and focus comes to her eyes, face, and voice. She gently touches him.*]

THE WOMAN, OLDER   [*Quietly.*] Hey. I know you. You're my boy.

THE MAN, OLDER   [*Looking up.*] I'm an old man.

THE WOMAN, OLDER   No, I'd know those eyes anywhere. You're that nice boy who walked me home. You gave me my first kiss. You're the only man I ever loved.

THE MAN, OLDER   [*Simply.*] Hi.

THE WOMAN, OLDER   Hi.

[*She envelops him comfortingly. A moment, then.*]

Do you remember that night we first kissed? I always wanted to know. What did you do after I left?

THE MAN, OLDER   I turned and floated home.

[THE MAN, YOUNGER, *exits in a warm fog.* THE MAN, OLDER, *sits up and looks at* THE WOMAN, OLDER.]

And you? Do you remember?

THE WOMAN, OLDER   I did too. In my own way.

[THE WOMAN, YOUNGER, *turns around, looks around to see if anyone is watching, then begins to gently dance in circles. Her face in joy.*]

THE MAN, OLDER   I'm so glad.

[THE WOMAN, YOUNGER, *dances off. It's quiet for a moment as the older couple holds hands and look at each other. They get serious.*]

I missed you.

THE WOMAN, OLDER   I missed you, too.

[*Pause. Pointedly.*]

I'm going on a long trip.

THE MAN, OLDER   I know. But you'll be back, won't you?

THE WOMAN, OLDER   I don't know. I hope so.

[*Pause.*]

You'll wait for me, won't you?

THE MAN, OLDER   Of course. I'll be right here.

[THE WOMAN, OLDER, *stands and gently tugs his collar.*]

THE WOMAN, OLDER   Live this moment for me, will you?

[*He stands. They look at each other for a moment.*]

When you remember our first kiss for what it is, remember this one for what it might be.

[*They fold into each other and kiss, gently but firmly. When they separate, she mouths the words "I love you," and he mouths back, "I love you, too." THE MAN, OLDER, closes his eyes, turns out. He gently touches his lips, then stands there in the same pose THE MAN, YOUNGER, held moments—and years—before. He doesn't notice that THE WOMAN, OLDER, falters. The clearness falls away from her eyes and face. The fog of dementia returns. She spreads her arms out and slowly, gently dances in small circles.*]

[*The lights slowly fade to black.*]

• • •

Actor

Joe Maruzzo

Joe Maruzzo

Joe Maruzzo is a professional actor appearing in theater, film, and television since 1980. Some of his credits include the series *Unsub*, produced by Stephen J. Cannell, *Law and Order*, *CSI Miami*, *The Sopranos*, *Bluebloods*, *NYPD Blue*, and many more. He just appeared onstage opposite Ellen Burstyn in Anton Chekhov's *The Cherry Orchard*. As a young actor, he studied with the great Kim Stanley, Stella Adler, and Uta Hagen. He's a lifetime member of the Actors Studio. As an actor, he would watch endless scenes from great writers in class and would find himself in cafes writing dialogue in speckled notebooks constantly. Basically he would write what he was going through and what he imagined others were going through. Finally he wrote his first play, *Bricklayer's Poet*, then another full-length called *Red Roses*, and another called *Leftovers*, and a couple of screenplays. He lives in Manhattan and continues to write and act.

···production history···

Actor had a September 2008 staged reading at the Actors Studio in Los Angeles, directed by Peter Flood, with Keven Kelly as John, Beege Barlette as Rosalie, and Maria Cardona as Amber.

···

characters

> **AMBER**
>
> **ROSALIE WEINSTEIN**
>
> **ACTRESS**
>
> **JOHN**

scene

ABC Television Casting. Nineteenth floor.

It's a small waiting area with a coffee table and small couch mixed with four or five chairs.

[*An elevator rings and a man wearing a long coat, sunglasses, and the* New York Times *in his hand enters. He looks around, goes down the hall, comes back, goes to the desk, and looks at a list of actors as a frazzled* ACTRESS *escorted by* ROSALIE WEINSTEIN, *head of ABC casting, and her assistant,* AMBER, *head towards the elevator. The man leaps into an empty room peeking out at the elevator.*]

AMBER   Why don't I leave a couple of tickets at the box office just in case…!

ROSALIE   How long is it running?

[ROSALIE *presses the elevator button for her.*]

ACTRESS   Just this weekend. But hopefully we'll extend…!

> [*The elevator door opens, and the* ACTRESS *steps in but holds the door open with her body.*]
>
> They're all young writers.

[*Elevator buzzes.*]

I'm in the first two pieces, so you can leave right afterwards…!

[*The elevator buzzes again.*]

ROSALIE   Go now…!

[*As door closes.*]

ACTRESS   No pressure either way!

[*She is gone.* ROSALIE *turns and heads back to her office followed by* AMBER.]

AMBER   Ronnie Lyons called, Jonathan Tyler's stuck in a cab midtown, some explosion or something.

ROSALIE   Reschedule for Monday before noon. Go home.

[ROSALIE *disappears down the hall as* AMBER *quickly heads to her desk and dials.*]

AMBER   [*Into phone.*] Hey, Tim, it's Amber. Oh, Jesus, me too! Rosalie wants to reschedule Jonathan Monday morning between 10 and 12. You got it. And enjoy that martini! Oh believe me, I will! Bye…!

[*The man comes out and slowly heads towards her.*]

Oh my God! You scared me!

JOHN   Sorry.

[*She gets up.*]

AMBER   May I help you?

JOHN   Would you like to help me?

AMBER   I'm sorry, and you are?

JOHN   Marlon. I'm an actor.

[*She looks at list.*]

AMBER   And you're here for!?

JOHN   What's your name?

AMBER   Excuse me!?

JOHN   What do they call you!?

AMBER   I'm sorry, but we only see actors through agent submissions.

[*He reaches in his coat pocket and motions pointing a gun from it.*]

JOHN   What is your sorry-ass name!?

AMBER   Amber.

JOHN   And what is it you do here, Amber…?

AMBER   I'm Rosalie's assistant.

JOHN   Listen, Amber, would you do me a favor? I want you and I to walk to an empty room, and do not think of attracting attention amongst your *pee*-ons, because if you do, I'll shoot you, then myself, and we'll be a match made in heaven! Go!

[*They walk stage left into an imaginary room. He pulls out a chair and sits her down.*]

This is what happens when you work for a monster!

[*He takes a bottle and cloth from his coat pocket and wets the cloth.*]

This will not harm you. I give you my word. I did extensive research!

AMBER   Please don't hurt me.

JOHN   All it will do is allow you sweet dreams for say an hour or so, and then you'll wake up to your fucking self…! Okay!?

[*A slight struggle ensues.*]

AMBER   No….

[*He puts the cloth over her mouth.*]

JOHN   Just…

AMBER   Let me…Ouhhhh…

[*He checks her heartbeat, looks at her, listens again, adjusts her comfortably in the chair, feels her cheek, looks at his watch, and heads down the hall as…*]

[*Lights up on ROSALIE sitting behind a large glass desk texting on her Blackberry. JOHN enters quickly.*]

JOHN   Hi…!

[ROSALIE *looks up.*]

ROSALIE   May I help you...?

JOHN   Would you like to help me...?

[*He shuts the door behind him.*]

Actually I wanted to tell you, you do amazing work! Your TV shows are very classy! First rate in fact! That last one you did about the woman who gets bit by a snake, then turns into one!? Wow! And what casting! Mike Piazza as the hero love interest!? Boy, can he act! Ever watch a tree!?

[*He takes his hat and shades off, revealing himself. A moment. She reaches for the desk phone, but he intercedes and slams it down. He reaches in his coat pocket again and points at her like a gangster with a gun.*]

I will put a bullet in your head and go to prison for the rest of my life because after what you have done to me, I'm in a prison as it is! You got that! DO YOU!?

[*A beat.*]

It's gotta be like twenty-something years or so that we first met. Just a starry-eyed actor, I was.

[*She doesn't answer.*]

I WAS JUST A STARRY-EYED LAD WHEN I FIRST GAZED UPON YOUR PRESENCE. ISN'T THAT CORRECT!?

ROSALIE   That is correct.

JOHN   How old are you, if you don't mind me asking?

ROSALIE   How old am I?

JOHN   Echo chamber! Echo chamber! How old are you?

ROSALIE   I'm in my late fifties.

JOHN   You think you'd have compassion for the younger! I'm forty-four. Look pretty good for forty-four, wouldn't you say? I mean, I'm not that ugly, am I!? Am I ugly to you!? Is my nose too fat!? My eyes too deep!? Are my teeth not white enough!? Am I a washed-up broken-down actor!?

[*A beat.*]

You're a Capricorn, aren't you?

[*She doesn't answer.*]

Your sign!? Your astrological sign!?

ROSALIE   I am a Capricorn.

JOHN   You got that Capricorn nose. But you're a fierce Capricorn!
Ruthless! Bitter! Would you say you fall under those adjectives?

ROSALIE   I don't find this the least bit.

JOHN   Just answer the question, you monster of a Richard the Third
monster! Do you identify with that part of yourself that is mean and
cruel and venomous?

ROSALIE   No.

JOHN   WELL, LOOK WHO'S HER OWN BEST FRIEND! Where
were you born? Upper West Side, Upper East Side?

ROSALIE   Brooklyn.

JOHN   Hey! Me too! What part?

ROSALIE   Flatbush.

JOHN   I was born right down the street a bit in Canarsie! Maybe we're
related! But that's impossible because you're a Jew and I'm a guinea!
Unless we got mixed in the crossfire of the old country there! I
wouldn't mind having some of that Jewish fervent literary cut throat
mixed in with my street-smart guinea ass!

[*Her Blackberry plays a Barbra Streisand love song. She looks at him.*]

Go on! But you insinuate anything in the wrong direction, your brain
will be splattered all over that picturesque window and we will make
the morning's *Post*! How's that for dialogue!? A little Preston Sturges!?
Maybe I can get a writing job. Answer it!

ROSALIE   [*Into phone.*] Hi, Bob.

JOHN   [*Muttering to self.*] I've only written four plays, all produced with
major audience appeal!

ROSALIE   [*Into phone.*] No. We test Marsoni at ten.

JOHN   Marsoni? As in Rocko Marsoni?

ROSALIE   [*Into phone.*] Tony Rossi is at one.

JOHN   Tell him you'll call him back.

ROSALIE   [*Into phone.*] Bob...

JOHN   Tell him you'll call him back!

ROSALIE   [*Into phone.*] Bob! I gotta go! Call me in half an hour. My stomach's gonna explode. You want me to spell it out!? Terrible!

[*She clicks off.*]

JOHN   You're bringing in Tony Rossi and Rocco Marsoni!? You know who those guys are!?

ROSALIE   They are actors, who have been submitted by their agent.

JOHN   No! They are mobsters who have just gotten out of prison for racketeering is who they are! They're all over Court TV! MOBSTERS TURNED ACTOR! "Wanna be an actor!? Go to mobster college on Mulberry Street! Learn technique!" I assume you're reading them for the *Capone* series!? That big mega talked about show that's going to surpass *The Sopranos*! And you're also an executive producer on that show, is that not correct?

ROSALIE   I'm one of the executives, that's right.

JOHN   And what role are you testing them for? WHAT ROLE MIGHT YOU BE TESTING THESE ACTORS FOR!?

ROSALIE   The Lucky Luciano role.

JOHN   Which is one of the leads, is it not?

ROSALIE   It's a decent-sized role.

JOHN   It's the second lead, is what it is!

[*He takes out a crumpled piece of paper from the "breakdowns" and reads.*]

"Lucky Luciano, Italian, early forties, dark brooding intensity, an underlying rage, actor should have strong presence, looking for an unknown!" What am I?

ROSALIE What are you?

JOHN I'm dark! I'm Italian! And I'm in a fucking rage! And after twenty-eight years in this business, I'm still pretty much unknown! And guess what, my first acting job was in the sixth grade, guess who I played!

ROSALIE Who?

JOHN Al Capone! Threw my hat out into the audience! And did you know I was nominated for an Outer Circle Critic's nomination, for Best Actor in a Dramatic Role!? Guess what I played when I was nominated? Guess what type I played!?

ROSALIE Tell me.

JOHN JOEY DAMARCO, MOBSTER IN DRAG! Got shot onstage, blood coming through the walls, wore a dress, had every agent in town with their pens hanging out of their mouths, so tell me, am I not right for the Lucky Luciano role, YES OR NO!?

ROSALIE There are other people involved. The director has a definitive…

JOHN The director has a definitive bullshit! Because the director and I spoke last night at the HBO Christmas party! You were there! Stuffing your face with coleslaw surrounded by all your little actors feeding upon you! Richard and I spoke at length last night because Richard and I are friends who have worked together on various TV schlopp over the years! We worked on *The Equalizing*. You remember that show, don't you!? I did three of them!

[*She gives him a look.*]

I'm just a little bit curious here, Rosie, have you ever seen me on any of the other forty or fifty television episodes I've done over the years!? *NYPD Blue*; *Murder, She Wrote*; *Special Victims Unit*; *21 Jump Street*; *Law and Order*; *Murder, She Wrote*! *Star Trek*!

ROSALIE I think I recently saw you on a *Law and Order*.

JOHN You think!? Which one? I did three of them.

ROSALIE I think you where mopping the floor in prison.

JOHN   Freddie the inmate, little scene, got good feedback from that scene. What did you think?

ROSALIE   It was late. I was channel-surfing.

JOHN   So I guess you just surfed right over me because I'm just a nobody actor trying to make his insurance so I can get my teeth fixed and say, "Look, Ma, I'm on ABC tonight playing the drug dealer who rapes that little girl, then gets killed by her mother in that amazing car chase!" So there you were last night, all chummy with your coleslaw, and Richard was telling me about a certain role he thought I was right for, he said he mentioned to you twice, not once, but twice, that I, John Marane, would be perfect for the Lucky Luciano role, and you replied, this is what he told me you said, "Don't ever mention that actor's name to me again, what he has done to me, no actor has ever done!" Did you say that!?

ROSALIE   Not in those exact words.

JOHN   Something along those lines?

ROSALIE   Something to that affect, yes.

JOHN   Great! So I'm about to approach you after hearing this, but I take a deep breath and think of the Dali Lama instead and head for the nearest bar! But fate has a funny way of working to the heart of things. Don't you think fate has a funny way of working to the heart of things!? LISTEN TO THE WAY FATE GOT ME HERE TODAY! I'm in my apartment this morning, sipping my coffee, lighting my incense, talking to Unemployment, you know, actory stuff! The phone rings, it's my angry manager, Anrdew Tautambaum! Andrew says, "Have I got a story for you! What in the hell have you done to Rosalie Weinstein?!" THERE YOU WERE AGAIN! I WAS TRYING TO GET RID OF YOU BUT THERE YOU WERE! You see, Andrew was having a drink last night with his cousin, Lynn Crest, you know Lynn, don't you? Of course you do! Head of CBS Casting! And Lynn was telling Andrew about this *casting convention* she attended a couple of years ago at the Waldorf Astoria! Ring a bell!? It must ring a bell because Lynn said you're the president of that convention! You see, Lynn said you were all sitting around the bar afterwards, sipping your margaritas, and my name came up! Popular guy, I must be! You see, Lynn told Andrew that when you heard my name, you flew off your stool like a woman possessed and went on a tirade about how, quote unquote, "I'm a desperate actor!? That the camera doesn't like me! How I frighten people! That I'm a charlatan!? That I DO DRUGS!?" And you said this in front of everyone! Roberta Tillman, that other fucking midget witch! Anthony Amato, the freak with the hunched back who should be brought up on charges! Cindy Coin, Julie Taylor at CBS, Debbie Johnson, who does all of De Niro's and Scorcese's films! Janice Ross, Samantha Chambers…and a whole bunch of independent casting! I'M THINKING! "WHAT!? WHAT HAVE I DONE TO THIS WOMAN!?" Is it my hair!? Do I remind you of you!? Your fucking father!? BUT NOW IT ALL MAKES SENSE TO ME! EVER SINCE THAT FUCKING CONVENTION, MY CAREER HAS STOPPED STONE DEAD! I CANT GET ARRESTED! NO ONE WILL SEE ME! SAG JUST TERMINATED ME AND I GOTTA WAIT TABLES AGAIN AT FORTY-SIX!

[*A long beat.*]

ROSALIE Are you through?

[*He points the gun at her.*]

JOHN I should do it. I should shoot you in the stomach and watch you bleed to death! See what it feels like to die slowly…!

ROSALIE You walk out that door, I give you my word, I'll forget this ever happened and that will be the end of it.

JOHN The cops'll be at my doorstep before I get on the subway!

[*A long beat.*]

ROSALIE You want to talk? Let's talk. Let's have a chat, shall we!

JOHN Don't get too cute with your schmooze!

ROSALIE Let's talk about the way fate brought you here today. The first time I met you was at the Gulf and Western building, you remember when that was?

JOHN …around 1980.…

ROSALIE   May of '79. I was casting theater back then. You remember what you read for?

JOHN   *Grease!*

ROSALIE   Very good. You were supposed to prepare two standard ballads, you remember what you sang?

JOHN   Ah…

AMBER   "Happy Birthday."

JOHN   Oh yeah, right, right.

AMBER   Do you remember what you said in front of everyone as you were leaving the room?

[*A beat.*]

Quote unquote, because I have the memory of a dinosaur, "I don't know why my agent is sending me on all these John Travolta–type parts, he's a pretty boy and I'm not!"

JOHN   Yeah, so, I'm a character actor, what's wrong with that?!

ROSALIE   Let's cut to, say, around five years later, you came in for a little play I was casting with Al Pacino.

JOHN   *American Buffalo.* They loved me…!

ROSALIE   …Do you know why you didn't get that part in *American Buffalo?*

JOHN   The feedback was they thought Pacino and I shared similar qualities, they wanted to go lighter in skin color or something.

ROSALIE   You frightened the director by waiting outside his building with a hypodermic needle!

JOHN   The character in the play was a junkie! It was a prop! The director and I had breakfast and talked all morning!

ROSALIE   He thought you were nuts!

JOHN   Well, isn't it ironic that the guy who really got the part wound up dead for real in some hotel from a heroin overdose! I told the director I'm the best guy for the part and that my uncle Charlie in real life was a junkie and I had a passion to play the part! What's nuts about that!?

ROSALIE Did you not also tell him that you had reoccurring dreams, and in those dreams, Al Pacino was your dead uncle!?

JOHN Yeah, so?

ROSALIE And that Pacino comes to your bedside, and you hold each other and cry into the night!?

JOHN I did dream that!

ROSALIE Pacino thought you were insane!

JOHN Oh, Al thought I was insane, did he!? Pacino would never say that! He knows what artists go through!

[*She looks right at him for a beat.*]

ROSALIE How old are you, John?

JOHN How old am I?

ROSALIE Echo chamber! Echo chamber! How old are you?

JOHN I told you, forty-four.

ROSALIE You live in the city?

JOHN Yeah.

ROSALIE Where in the city?

JOHN 43rd and Tenth.

ROSALIE Hell's Kitchen.

JOHN That's right.

ROSALIE Nice apartment?

JOHN I like it.

ROSALIE One bedroom?

JOHN Like an L-shaped studio.

ROSALIE Live alone?

JOHN   Why, you wanna go on a date!?

ROSALIE   What have you done professionally in, say, the last three years?

JOHN   I don't think that's any of your business.

ROSALIE   Oh, but it is my business! Here you are in my office with a gun telling me you want to play Lucky Luciano! That you want to be in my television show at ABC Television! Have you made 30,000? 25? 20? What jobs have you gotten? Let's talk jobs!

JOHN   I took some time off…! I'm writing! I did a soap. What the fuck difference does it make!?

ROSALIE   So basically, in, say, the past three years, you've had maybe one or two paying jobs as an actor?

JOHN   That's right!

ROSALIE   Maybe I'm trying to help you! Maybe my fit at the Waldorf was for a reason! Maybe I've brought you in five or six times over the years and you've sabotaged yourself in every audition!

JOHN   Oh, here comes the sabotage onslaught!

ROSALIE   I'm not alone on this!

JOHN   Oh, you're not, huh?

ROSALIE   Everyone concurs! You're a problemed actor, John!

JOHN   Oh, I got problems, huh!?

ROSALIE   You can smell the desperation a mile away!

JOHN   Alright, chill out now!

ROSALIE   Are you broken, John!? YOU WANT THE TRUTH!? Yes, I, Rosalie Weinstein, knocked you to hell in front of the New York casting world! And yes! I did tell Richard Crane I'd never see you for another role as long as I live!

JOHN   Which isn't going to be too long!

ROSALIE   Because it's my right!

JOHN   Oh, it's your right, huh!?

ROSALIE   People talk! We communicate! We get things off our chest! Which brings me to the *pièce de résistance*. The last audition I brought you in on, two winters ago....

JOHN   The *Pineapple* pilot?

ROSALIE   A week before the convention. Now listen to the way fate brought you here!

JOHN   Is that it!?

ROSALIE   I hadn't seen you in years! I bring you in on a pilot your agent fought to get you in on! We had to cast the part that day!

JOHN   Yeah, and...?

ROSALIE   Producers waiting for your tape. You walk in and tell me you'd rather not read for the role!? That you can't connect to the rhythms of the script!?

JOHN   I couldn't! I explained that to you! We had a talk! You smiled and said it was okay and we came back here because you wanted to have a chat! "Let's have a chat," you said.

ROSALIE   Are you not aware of what you said to me in the course of that chat!? DO ACTORS THINK BEFORE THEY OPEN THEIR MOUTHS!?

JOHN   What did I say?

ROSALIE   I asked how you were doing?

JOHN   Yeah.

ROSALIE   What Los Angeles was like for you?

JOHN   Ah-huh.

ROSALIE   What brought you back to New York?

JOHN   Yeah!? And...?

ROSALIE   You told me you left Los Angeles because you were going through a breakup with an older woman....

JOHN   Debbie Flynn, that's right!

ROSALIE   . . . How you would cry on your acupuncturist's table for hours in the Valley!

JOHN   That happened!

ROSALIE   How you stalked her!

JOHN   I didn't stalk her!

ROSALIE   Did you not say to me you stood outside her bedroom window on Thanksgiving night because you where sad!?

JOHN   I was confiding in you!

ROSALIE   That you had to slide down her chimney and hide under her Mercedes because her son was pulling up the driveway!?

JOHN   I thought we were having a heart to heart!

ROSALIE   You are here for employment! To represent a major network!

JOHN   You squirming monster! What's safe!? Nothing's safe!

ROSALIE   And then you had the stupidity to tell me that you're tired of bad TV!?

JOHN   I am!

ROSALIE   What am I!?

JOHN   You tell me! Beast or human!? Chemical or mineral!

ROSALIE   I am the head of ABC Casting for twenty-five years!

JOHN   Wowy-wowy!

ROSALIE   I take home over a million a year.

JOHN   Big deal!

ROSALIE   I own an apartment overlooking the park.

JOHN   Maybe we can spend Christmas together and watch the snowflakes fall!

ROSALIE   A home on the Jersey Shore.

JOHN   Do a little skinny dipping.

ROSALIE   I have stock in this company!

JOHN   Is it true you sleep with two pigs, I heard!?

ROSALIE   You sat here, pontificating about how this older woman was the daughter of Errol Flynn....

JOHN   She is Errol Flynn's daughter!

ROSALIE   [*Imitates him.*] "Me and Sean Penn did this! George Clooney and me play basketball at the YMCA!" And this was the *pièce de résistance!* The cream that closed the deal! How you and Al Pacino were in the men's room at the Actor's Studio, reciting Shakespeare back and forth to one another while he was taking a leak and you were in the stall!

JOHN   That happened!

ROSALIE   [*She gets up.*] Don't you get it!?

JOHN   Why don't you tell me!

ROSALIE   All your grandiosity is a desperate plea to hide the self-loathing that reeks from your pores!

JOHN   Sit down!

ROSALIE   You're a loser! A name dropper!

JOHN   Sit the fuck down, I said!

ROSALIE   People don't trust you! You're not healthy! There's three kinds of actors on this fucking planet! Those that never make it but continually demoralize themselves like dog on bone with the delusion that someday they will! Those that get a piece of the crumb and pray they'll get a bigger one! And then there are those that have the tenacity and are lucky enough that hit the big jackpot and get the whole box of cookies! The whole shebang! And you, your number one, groping for the crumb but can't even reach it! Pearls before swine!

JOHN   I'm the pearl and you're the swine, baby!

ROSALIE   YOU'VE DUG YOUR OWN FUCKING GRAVE, NOW LIE IN IT!

JOHN [*He gets up and raises his coat pocket like the gangster pointing the gun towards her.*] Watch how I'm going to lie in it!

ROSALIE I did slaughter you in front of the New York casting world! And yes, I did tell Richard Crane and anyone that mentions your name that I will never see you for another role as long as I live! Now shoot me or get the hell out my office!

JOHN You hate men, don't you?

ROSALIE On the contrary, I love real men.

JOHN Real men, huh!?

ROSALIE Men of substance. Men of success. Men who have something to offer the world! You're impotent.

[*A man yells from the audience area.*]

JOHN Your gonna die now!

ROSALIE Do it.

JOHN I'm gonna do it!

ROSALIE Do it then!

JOHN You want me to do it, Rosie!?

ROSALIE Go on! Shoot the load!

JOHN Shoot the load, huh!?

ROSALIE Right now!

JOHN Right now!?

ROSALIE Right now!

JOHN Oh yeah!?

ROSALIE DO IT NOW!

JOHN Do it now!?

ROSALIE YES! NOW! NOW! NOW! NOW!

[*He puts the gun to her temple and strains. He then lifts her out of the chair and kisses her wildly!*]

No…let go…

[*He angles her against the desk and practically mounts her.*]

. . . of…me….

[*She pulls away and takes a fierce look at him, then pulls him onto her kissing him hard. They kiss like two hungry animals and wind up against the wall.*]

JOHN   I've never seen you before!

[*He kisses her face, down to her neck.*]

I'm so lonely!

[*He then kisses her ear.*]

ROSALIE   Oh, yes, no!

[*He stops.*]

No! Yes! Makes me crazy!

[*He goes back to her ear, kissing it.*]

No! Yes! Ohhhh!

[*She pulls away as her body starts to twitch, like quick electric shocks! He takes a step back and observes. She's raw! He can't contain himself and starts kissing her. She positioned her pubic bone on his thigh, positioning him. He looks down and watches how she positions herself. She starts to gently rub up on him in unison.*]

Ouhhhh God. No, yes, right, there.

[*He rubs his leg on her pubic bone in perfect motion.*]

Oh, yes, and my ear.

[*He starts at her ear and rubs up on her at the same time.*]

JOHN   Your eyes, they're so black, I mean a dark chestnut brown color. Fierce in a sexy way.

[*They rub harder.*]

ROSALIE   You think I'm sexy!?

JOHN   Yes.

ROSALIE   How sexy?

JOHN   Very sexy.

ROSALIE   How very sexy?

JOHN   Very, very, very sexy!

ROSALIE   You think I'm a bad girl?!

JOHN   Yes!

ROSALIE   How bad?

JOHN   Very bad.

ROSALIE   Very, very bad…?

JOHN   Very, very, very bad!

ROSALIE   Bad to the bone!?

JOHN   Yes!

ROSALIE   Say it!

JOHN   You're a very, very, very sexy…

ROSALIE   No! Bad to the bone, just that!

JOHN   You're bad to the bone.

[*They are headed for ecstasy!*]

ROSALIE   Again!

JOHN   You're bad to the bone.

ROSALIE   Over and over again!

JOHN   Bad to the bone, bad to the bone, bad to the bone.…

ROSALIE   Faster!

[*They grind faster!*]

JOHN   You're bad to the bone, bad to the bone, bad to the bone, you're bad to the bone.

ROSALIE   With anger now!

JOHN   You're bad to the bone, you're bad to the bone, you're bad to the bone, bad to the bone!

ROSALIE   Such a bad man, I am!

JOHN   I think I might be falling in love with you.

[*Still pumping and kissing.*]

I think I am in love with you! I've been in love six times! Bad to the bone! My therapist told me there's at least seven loves in your life, maybe this is lucky seven! Bad to the bone, bad to the bone. Could you love me!??

ROSALIE   Huh…?

JOHN   Could you love me, Rosie!?

[*Kisses her madly.*]

Huh!? Could you!?

ROSALIE   Ah…sure.

JOHN   Could you marry me!?

ROSALIE   Hah! Don't stop!

[*He grinds hard and kisses her ear!*]

JOHN   Could you marry the right man!?

ROSALIE   The right man, well, does he exist!?

JOHN   Will you marry me!?

ROSALIE   Marriage is a tough word.

JOHN   Marry me, baby!

[*She gets turned on. He likes it.*]

Would you marry me, baby?

ROSALIE   Huh, yeah, sure.

JOHN   Say it!

ROSALIE   Say what!?

JOHN   I'll marry you, baby.

ROSALIE   Yes, I'll marry you, yeah, sure, baby!

JOHN   Through thick and through thin.

ROSALIE   Yes!

JOHN   Till death do we part!?

ROSALIE   Oh mother of God, yes! Till death! Through death! Through fucking death do we part!

[*She is orgasmic! Yes! She explodes! Her body contracts like crazy as she cums! There is a loud banging at the door!*]

AMBER   [*Offstage.*] Rosalie, are you in there!?

[ROSALIE *lands under the table.* JOHN *looks towards the door.*]

JOHN   Oh shit!

AMBER   [*Offstage.*] Rosalie, are you there!

[JOHN *starts pacing.* ROSALIE *starts to drag herself up on one knee.*]

JOHN   I chloroformed your assistant!

ROSALIE   You what!?

AMBER   [*Offstage.*] ROSALIE, IF YOU'RE THERE, PLEASE SAY SOMETHING!

JOHN   I did extensive research online about it!

ROSALIE   [*Calling.*] I'm here!

AMBER   [*Offstage.*] YOU'RE ALIVE! ARE YOU OKAY!?

ROSALIE   YES! YES! HOLD ON ONE SECOND. I'M ON A LONG-DISTANCE CALL!

JOHN   You're right. I am reaching for the crumb I'll never touch! I am a loser!

[*She gets up to her feet.*]

ROSALIE   Don't say that.

JOHN   You said it! I mean, look at me! I'm forty-six....

ROSALIE   [*Fixing herself.*] I thought you said you where forty-five.

JOHN   I'm forty-eight.

AMBER   [*Offstage.*] OPEN THE DOOR, PLEASE!?

JOHN   Why can't I just be a normal person and get a job at Starbucks and be done with it!

ROSALIE   You're a fine actor.

JOHN   But you haven't really seen my work.

ROSALIE   I have your tape. You're very good.

JOHN   You said the camera doesn't like me!

ROSALIE   You're sexy!

[ROSALIE *grabs a mirror and lipstick from her purse, fixing her lips as she heads towards the door.*]

AMBER   [*Offstage.*] ROSALIE, SOMETHING TERRIBLE HAS HAPPENED! THE POLICE ARE ON THEIR WAY UP HERE, SO OPEN THE DOOR RIGHT AWAY OR I'LL HAVE TO BREAK IT DOWN!

ROSALIE   I'M COMING!

[*To* JOHN.]

Why do you think I brought you in on that pilot…?

JOHN   Why!?

ROSALIE   Because of your goddamn talent!

[*More banging.*]

AMBER   [*Offstage.*] I SAID, OPEN THIS FUCKING DOOR RIGHT NOW!

ROSALIE   For Jesus sakes Christ, Amber, it's open!

[ROSALIE *throws open the door.* AMBER *stands there holding a fire extinguisher in her hands.* AMBER *notices* JOHN.]

AMBER   Oh my God! He's got a gun…!

[AMBER *starts spraying* JOHN *with the fire extinguisher, chasing him around the room.*]

ROSALIE   What are you doing!?

JOHN   [*Grabs the gun, holding it up.*] It's a prop from a Sam Shepard play!

[*He throws the gun on the couch as* ROSALIE *tries to grab the fire extinguisher from* AMBER's *hands.*]

ROSALIE   Give me that!

[*They struggle.*]

What's gotten in to you?

[ROSALIE *finally yanks it away.* AMBER *falls to the ground.*]

AMBER   He tried to kill me!

ROSALIE   [*To* JOHN.] Did you try to kill her?

JOHN   Of course not! I'm an actor!

[ROSALIE *gets her to her feet.*]

AMBER   But he dragged me into the mail room and put this chemical over my mouth....I, I feel nauseous.

[*She flops onto a chair. Faints.*]

The room, it's...faint.

[AMBER *starts to fall out of the chair.* ROSALIE *grabs her and holds her up.*]

ROSALIE   [*To* JOHN.] Hand me that water.

[*He looks around.*]

On the desk! Hurry!

[*He grabs it and hands it to* ROSALIE. *She puts it up to* AMBER's *lips.*]

Come on now.

[AMBER *drinks.*]

A little more.

[*She drinks.*]

Take a deep breath now.

[*She does.*]

That a girl. In and out. Like a fighter in the twelfth round. Again.

[*She does again.*]

Better? The police! When did you call the police?

AMBER I…like five minutes ago.

ROSALIE Alright, let's all be very clear on this, huh…? It's a joke! A big joke, you see! John did something very stupid, very dumb, didn't you, John!?

JOHN Sort of, yeah.…

ROSALIE You see, he's preparing for a role, a play about an actor whose got it out for this casting director, and he, well, they, anyway, it's a work in progress! Now, basically, nothing really happened! You understand what I'm saying?

AMBER No.

ROSALIE What don't you understand!? This! Him! Me! You! It's deleted! Delete! You got that!? People deleted, over! Now when the police arrive, you tell them it was a prank call.

AMBER But I…

ROSALIE There are no buts! Listen to me! I know your mother how long?

AMBER Many years.

ROSALIE I changed your diapers! Barmitsvaed you! The whole deal! It's over! This farce! You get it!? Now, come on, get up.

AMBER I…

ROSALIE Shhhhh! What!? Nothing! Cut!!

[*She gets* AMBER *to her feet.*]

AMBER I'm still dizzy.

ROSALIE Join the world! Breathe!

  [*She does.*]

  And again.

  [*She does.*]

  Okay now…you've been at ABC how long?

AMBER March will be three years.

ROSALIE The Capone series. I'm making you a producer. How's that sound?

AMBER I…huh!?

ROSALIE It's a done deal!

AMBER I'm, I, I don't know what to say.

ROSALIE Business as usual. Huh!?

[ROSALIE *walks her to the door.*]

How's it feel to be a producer?

AMBER I'm not sure.

ROSALIE You think you're dizzy now!? A little brevity! A bit of laughter! They say laughter takes years off! Huh!? Let's laugh!

[ROSALIE *looks at* JOHN, *then* AMBER. *They all start laughing.*]

Hah! Hah! Hah!

[*They sort of laugh.* AMBER *looks down the hallway.*]

AMBER Oh my God! They're here!

[ROSALIE *checks it out, grabs* AMBER, *and closes the door.*]

ROSALIE Alright! What happened!?

AMBER Huh!?

ROSALIE Fucking here!? Come on! You're a producer now! Think quick! Be ruthless! What happened here!? Nothing! Just a normal day at ABC!?

AMBER Normal. Just a normal day at ABC.

ROSALIE What kind of call was it?

AMBER A prank call.

ROSALIE Go now!

[ROSALIE *pushes her out. She goes.* ROSALIE *stands there, takes a few breaths.* JOHN *doesn't move. She finally walks to her desk adjusting her underwear on the way, sits, looks up at him. All is quiet.*]

What's whatchamacallit's number…?

[JOHN *stands there.*]

Your manager there…!?

JOHN   Andrew?

[*He takes out his cell phone.*]

It's 917- 222-2222.

[*She dials.*]

ROSALIE   [*Into phone.*] Rosalie Weinstein here. Yes. Fine, thanks. Yes, it was. The coleslaw was great, I know, listen, I'd like to see John Marane for the Capone series on Monday first thing in the morning at, say, around ten.

[*He shakes yes. ROSALIE into the phone.*]

That's right. Just to meet the director and if he feels it's a fit, we'll have him read. That's right. I know. You got it. Okay, of course, bye now!

[*She hangs up.*]

JOHN   *I don't know what to say.*

[*She grabs a script sitting on her desk and tosses it to JOHN.*]

ROSALIE   Top of page 33. From "You think it's easy being me?"

JOHN   [*He looks it over.*] It says with an Italian dialect.

ROSALIE   Just be you.

JOHN   [*He looks it over. From script.*] You think it's easy being me!? Every day I gotta stand up for my right! Sure, I fight, I scratch, I claw my way up the ladder of success, and when they try and knock me down, I get back up even harder! And now that I'm at the top, everybody wants a piece of me! The cops! The Feds! Every low-level mug tryin' to make a name for himself! But guess what!? I ain't goin nowhere! Try and take away what I've worked so hard for all my life! Try and take away who I am! This is America, boys! Land of opportunity! This is show business! I'm Lucky Luciano and my story's just begun! I got more tales to tell! You got that right!

[*Silence.*]

ROSALIE   Take it home. Learn it.

JOHN   I was just reading it....

ROSALIE   Shhh!

JOHN   Well...

[*He grabs his hat, glasses, the gun.*]

It's wood....

[*He heads toward the door, turns, looks at her.*]

ROSALIE   I'm not promising you anything, but at least you'll get a shot at it.

JOHN   No. Yes. I'm grateful!

[*He stands there.*]

You know, I once invited you...

ROSALIE   For dinner.

JOHN   And I promised...

ROSALIE   You'd make me spaghetti and meatballs, yeah, and...?

JOHN   You do have a memory like a dinas...I mean, you have a great memory.

ROSALIE   No, I take pride in being a dinosaur.

JOHN   If you'd like, can I make dinner for you? Can I make spaghetti and meatballs for you sometime?

[*She gets up and walks to him, gets close up.*]

ROSALIE   You want to make spaghetti and meatballs for me, John?

JOHN   Yes. I do. I definitely do.

[*She goes to him and starts kissing. The script falls to the ground as he puts his arms around her as the lights start to fade on them making out.*]

• • •

Irish Stew

Cary Pepper

Cary Pepper

Cary Pepper has had work presented throughout the United States and internationally. Among his full-length plays, *How It Works* won the 2012 Ashland New Plays Festival and *Cufflinked* was a semifinalist for the 2014 Ashland New Plays Festival. Among his one-act plays, *The Walrus Said* won the Religious Arts Guild Playwriting Competition; *Small Things* won the Tennessee Williams/New Orleans Literary Festival 2006 One-Act Play Contest; and *Stealing Melissa* won the 2012 Doc Jim Martin Playwright Competition. He is a member of the Dramatists Guild and a past contributor to the *Best American Short Plays* series (*Small Things; House of the Holy Moment; Come Again, Another Day*).

···production history···

A ten-minute version of *Irish Stew* was performed at 2014 Short + Sweet Sydneyand 2013 Short + Sweet Auckland.

2014 Short + Sweet Sydney (Sydney, Australia)

Directed by Aishveryaa Nidhi

LAURETA   Ann Elbourne

CARLTON   Owain James

3rd Place—People's Choice Showcase

2013 Short + Sweet Auckland (Auckland, New Zealand)

Directed by Alex Lee

LAURETA   Maggie Tarver

CARLTON   Jason Greenwood

characters

LAURETA   old, but still agile

CARLTON   old, but still agile

···

[*A living room. Quite well lived-in, but neat and clean. There's a couch, a coffee table with various items on it. CARLTON and LAURETA sit in chairs. They are old, but still agile. Words no longer come easily to them. However, they are always loving with each other, and they enjoy each other.*]

LAURETA   Have you seen my Irish shoe?

CARLTON   The Irish who what?

LAURETA   The Irish shoe I wear.

CARLTON   *Where* are the Irish?

LAURETA   That's what I want to know. Have you seen it?

CARLTON   What's the question?

LAURETA   My Irish shoe. That's the whole question.

CARLTON   It has a hole?

LAURETA   No, it's in very good condition. I want to find it.

CARLTON   Find what?

LAURETA   My Irish shoe. It's green.

CARLTON   The Irish who grin. They must be very happy.

LAURETA   I've read that they are.

CARLTON   Red? You said it was green.

LAURETA   What is?

CARLTON   The Irish who grin.

LAURETA   That's what I'm looking for. The Irish shoe.

CARLTON   The Irish who what?

LAURETA   It keeps me warm.

CARLTON   The Irish keep you warm?

LAURETA   The Irish shoe.

CARLTON   Green.

LAURETA   Yes.

CARLTON   Not red.

LAURETA   Read? It's not a book. It's worn.

CARLTON   Worn out?

LAURETA   Sometimes. But today I'll wear it in.

CARLTON   So it's worn in.

LAURETA   And very comfortable. Do you know where it is?

CARLTON   You want to wear it.

LAURETA   I want to find it.

CARLTON   Discover it.

LAURETA   It doesn't have a cover. It's a shoe, not a book.

CARLTON   A book. Has it been read?

LAURETA   It was never red. The whole thing has always been green.

CARLTON   The *hole* is green? Or just the cover?

LAURETA   It doesn't have any holes. That's one reason I've saved it for so long. But not the sole reason.

CARLTON   Ah, you're saving its soul.

[*Pause.*]

LAURETA   Do you know where it is?

CARLTON   What?

LAURETA   My Irish shoe. Green. No holes. No cover. Keeps me warm.

CARLTON   Have you looked in the closet?

LAURETA   No.

[*She gets up, goes to the couch, and looks under a cushion. Then she returns to her chair.*]

It's not there.

CARLTON   Maybe it's in the bedroom. I'll see.

[*He gets up, goes to the front door, opens it, and looks around. He closes the door and returns.*]

It's not there. Should I try the bathroom?

LAURETA   The bathroom?

CARLTON   Yes. Perhaps it's under the bed.

LAURETA   I don't think it would be there.

CARLTON   It's worth a try.

LAURETA   If you say so.

CARLTON   Be right back.

[*He exits stage right.* LAURETA *gazes after him for a few seconds, then points upstage.*]

LAURETA   The bathroom's that way.

[*After a bit,* CARLTON *returns. He hands her an old shoe.*]

Thank you.

CARLTON   My pleasure.

LAURETA   [*She stares at it.*] What's this?

CARLTON   What you asked for.

LAURETA   I don't want this.

CARLTON   You said you did.

LAURETA   I did?

CARLTON   Your Irish shoe.

LAURETA   I don't want a shoe.

CARLTON   You said you did.

LAURETA   I did?

CARLTON   Yes.

LAURETA   I don't want *this*.

CARLTON   It's not red. No holes. And it has a sole.

[CARLTON *turns the shoe over and shows her its sole. Pause.* LAURETA *stares at the shoe.*]

LAURETA   [*Sighs.*] I did it again, didn't I?

CARLTON   Apparently.

LAURETA   Sorry.

CARLTON   No need. Last week it took us half an hour to find my magnifying glass.

LAURETA   [*Laughs.*] You kept asking for your cup.

CARLTON   [*Laughs.*] I knew it had something to do with drinking.

[*Their laugher grows during the following lines.*]

LAURETA   So we tore through the entire kitchen!

CARLTON   We sure did! We found a mug, a bottle…

LAURETA   A jar…a shot glass!

CARLTON   The best was the straw!

[*Their laughter softly subsides.*]

But we finally found it. And laughed ourselves silly for another half hour.

LAURETA Well, it's funny when it's you!

CARLTON So you keep saying.

LAURETA But today it's me.

CARLTON You win some you lose some.

LAURETA [*Indicates the shoe.*] Where did you find this?

CARLTON [*Pointing stage right.*] In the bathroom.

LAURETA [*Pointing upstage.*] The bathroom's there.
  [*Points stage right.*] That's the bedroom.

[*Pause.*]

CARLTON Apparently I'm not having the best day, either.

LAURETA You're not looking for your Irish shoe.

CARLTON Tomorrow I might be.

LAURETA I hate when it's me.

CARLTON I hate when it's *me*.

LAURETA You win some, you lose some.

CARLTON We'll just have to start over.

LAURETA All right.
  [*She hands him the shoe. Short pause.*]
  Have you seen my Irish shoe?
  [*He gazes at the shoe, which he's still holding. Then hands it to her.*]
  What's this?

CARLTON Your Irish shoe.

LAURETA My Irish who what?

CARLTON Keep you warm.

LAURETA This isn't it.

CARLTON It's not red.

LAURETA It's not green.

CARLTON It's worn.

LAURETA What am I going to do with this?

CARLTON Save its sole.

LAURETA Do I need to save its sole?

CARLTON You knead bread.

LAURETA This sole's a bit worn. In and out.

CARLTON I've always liked sole. It's not as fishy as other fish.

LAURETA [*Looking at the shoe.*] There's something fishy about this.

CARLTON Maybe if you had some bread.

LAURETA Do I need bread?

CARLTON That's how you make bread.

LAURETA If I made bread, I might have to lie in it.

CARLTON I've never known you to lie.

LAURETA I lie in bed.

CARLTON And I lie with you.

LAURETA [*Indicates shoe.*] What am I supposed to do with this?

CARLTON Wear it.

LAURETA I know where it is. Right here in my hand.

CARLTON Put it on your foot.

LAURETA Which foot?

CARLTON Your left.

LAURETA I haven't left. I'm right here.

CARLTON Your right, then.

LAURETA I'm often right. Should I put it on the other foot? It looks like it fits.

CARLTON Then wear it.

LAURETA Yes. Where is my Irish shoe?

CARLTON The Irish who do what?

LAURETA Keep me warm. And comfy. Like a good Irish stew.

CARLTON Who's Irish Stu?

LAURETA You love Irish stew.

CARLTON I don't remember him.

LAURETA Every Sunday, it was Irish stew for dinner.

CARLTON I must have liked him.

LAURETA You insisted on it.

CARLTON Our house or his?

LAURETA You couldn't wait for dinnertime.

CARLTON I must have liked him a lot.

LAURETA You loved Irish stew.

CARLTON What did he look like?

LAURETA Who?

CARLTON Irish Stu.

LAURETA It was usually a very handsome stew.

CARLTON Handsome, huh? Funny, I don't remember him.

LAURETA It's not a hymn. You don't sing it. You eat it.

CARLTON Eat what?

LAURETA Irish stew. It was beefy.

CARLTON Oh, Irish Stu! Now I remember! Yes! He was beefy. Haven't seen him in years.

LAURETA   Sometimes, with the right onions, it came out sweet.

CARLTON   He was sweet.

LAURETA   And sometimes it was a little salty.

CARLTON   He could be salty. If he had a little too much to drink.

LAURETA   Have you seen mine?

CARLTON   Your what?

LAURETA   Irish shoe.

CARLTON   Irish who what?

LAURETA   Keep me warm.

CARLTON   Of course! I'll always keep you warm.

[*He lovingly puts his arms around her and snuggles her.*]

LAURETA   Thank you. I liked that. But I'd still like my Irish shoe.

CARLTON   You're holding it.

[*She gazes at the shoe in her hand as if seeing it for the first time.*]

LAURETA   What's this?

CARLTON   Your Irish shoe.

LAURETA   No, it's not.

CARLTON   It's not?

LAURETA   No.

CARLTON   Okay, we'll start over.

LAURETA   Again?

CARLTON   You'll get there.

LAURETA   But in the meantime…This sucks.

CARLTON   Got that right. But it's funny when it's *you*.

LAURETA   I could get so angry.

CARLTON   We said we wouldn't.

LAURETA [*Smiles.*] We did.

CARLTON No matter how bad it got. We agreed.

[*Pause.*]

LAURETA [*Staring at* CARLTON.] Who are you?

CARLTON [*Getting concerned.*] Laureta?

LAURETA Kidding!

CARLTON [*Laughs.*] That's my girl! We can do this.

LAURETA There's no consistency. Some days, sharp as a tack. Other days, dumb as hammers.

CARLTON Some days it's moment to moment.

LAURETA Trade you one of my mixed days for two of your clear moments, back to back.

CARLTON We did that. A minute ago.

LAURETA We did?

CARLTON Kidding!

LAURETA It's maddening.

CARLTON It's what it is. We'll get there.

LAURETA Start over?

CARLTON Start over.

LAURETA Yes. Or I'll never get my Irish shoe.

CARLTON What does it look like?

LAURETA What?

CARLTON Your Irish shoe.

LAURETA It's green. And it has…leaves.

CARLTON Sounds like a tree.

LAURETA Yes, it does.

CARLTON   Have you looked in the backyard?

[*She gets up, goes to front door, opens it, looks around, and returns.*]

LAURETA   I didn't think it would be there. I looked anyway, but it's not.

CARLTON   If there's a knot, we'll untangle it. But we have to find it first.

LAURETA   Yes.

CARLTON   Perhaps it's in the kitchen. On the table.

[*She gets up, goes to the table, peers at it, moves items around, and returns to her chair.*]

LAURETA   Not there.

CARLTON   I'll try the bathroom.

LAURETA   The bathroom?

CARLTON   Yes. Perhaps it's hanging on the door.

LAURETA   I didn't see it there this morning.

CARLTON   It's worth a try. How many leaves does it have?

LAURETA   Two

CARLTON   A little threadbare, isn't it?

LAURETA   It's winter.

CARLTON   Ah.

LAURETA   And chilly.

CARLTON   Yes.

LAURETA   That's why I want my Irish shoe.

CARLTON   Irish who what?

LAURETA   Look for my shoe.

CARLTON   Your what?

LAURETA   Shoe.

CARLTON   I'm going. I'm going.

[*He gets up.*]

LAURETA Carlton.

CARLTON Yes, dear?

LAURETA We can do this.

CARLTON Yes.

[*He turns to her.*]

It's getting harder.

LAURETA Yes. But we can.

CARLTON We'll get there.

LAURETA [*Laughs at herself good-naturedly.*] At the rate I'm going today, who knows how long that'll take.

CARLTON Want to scream? Or kick a wall?

LAURETA We said we wouldn't.

CARLTON [*Smiles.*] We did.

LAURETA We'll get there.

CARLTON We will.

LAURETA Sorry it's me today.

CARLTON Today, you. Next week, me again.

LAURETA What if it's both of us together?

CARLTON It'll always be both of us together.

LAURETA I like that.

CARLTON Be right back. Gonna see if it's hanging on the bathroom door.

[*He exits stage right.* LAURETA *gazes after him for a few seconds, then points upstage.*]

LAURETA The bathroom's that way.

CARLTON [*From the other room.*] I can't find your Irish shoe.

[*He returns, holding a green sweater.*]

But I did find this.

[*He hands her the sweater.*]

It's green.

LAURETA [*Examining the sleeves.*] And it has leaves.

CARLTON Yes.

LAURETA My Irish sweater! I've been looking for this all day.
[*She puts it on.*]
Ah! That's much better. Thank you. You're a dear.

CARLTON [*Playfully looking at his hands, feeling his head for antlers.*]
When did I become a deer?

LAURETA [*Playfully.*] Yesterday.

CARLTON Why didn't you tell me?

LAURETA I did. And I'll always love you, no matter what you become.
You're my sweet.

CARLTON And you're my lamb.

LAURETA Like Irish stew!

CARLTON Good old Irish Stu!

LAURETA I made a great Irish stew.

CARLTON *We* make a great Irish stew.

LAURETA We're us.

CARLTON What are we gonna do with each other?

LAURETA What would we do *without* each other?

• • •

Last Call

Weldon Pless

Weldon Pless

Weldon Pless is a Brooklyn-based playwright and screenwriter. He received a master's degree in Irish and Irish American studies from New York University and a master's degree in English from the University of Georgia, where he studied Samuel Beckett's early work. While in Georgia, he was a member of the Athens Playwrights' Workshop. He also works as a freelance editor and an adjunct professor of English in New York City. He is currently at work on a feature-length screenplay and a full-length play.

···production history···

Last Call was part of an evening of staged readings under the auspices of Rising Sun NYC's Under Rehearsed series in Brooklyn, New York, March 18, 2014. Directed by Elizabeth Burke.

> **DIANE** Kim Rios Lin
>
> **CARL** Jak Prince
>
> **BARRY** Dennis Demitry

characters

> **DIANE** a Ph.D. student short on sleep.
>
> **BARRY** and **CARL** been drinking beer since Diane was in diapers.
>
> **LEON** wheelchair-bound and unable to speak; a hell-raiser in his day.

setting

A small college town at 2 a.m., present day.

···

[BARRY *and* CARL *sit in picnic chairs, drinking beer and singing loudly over the blasting twang of a boom box on the ground, playing something like Willie Nelson's "Whiskey River." Both men have BB pistols, and* BARRY *shoots his in the air on the chorus like he's Yosemite Sam.* LEON *sits silently in his wheelchair beside them.*]

[*A cooler sits beside* BARRY, *and cans litter the ground around them.* DIANE *approaches. She's groggy, wearing sweatpants and an oversized T-shirt.*]

DIANE Excuse me....

> [*The men keep singing.*]
>
> HEY!
>
> [*Nothing. She cuts the music.*]

[BARRY *and* CARL *sing a line before they realize they've lost their accompaniment.*]

CARL What in the hell—

BARRY Hey, why'd you kill the Willie? We were havin' ourselves a sing-along.

DIANE   Can you keep it down? I live next door, and—

CARL   Is that your dog I always hear barkin'?

DIANE   Um…no, that's…on the other side, I think. Would you—

BARRY   Hang on there, darlin'. Are you that house with the big shit pile in the back?

DIANE   What?

BARRY   The shit pile? In the back? You can admit it, you're among friends here.

DIANE   Compost. It's not shit—

BARRY   Looks like shit. Smells like shit.

DIANE   That's…It's not shit, Okay? That's not…do you mind just keeping the noise down?

BARRY   Do we mind?

DIANE   Do you mind.

BARRY   [*Looking at* CARL.] Do we mind?

CARL and **BARRY**   [*A pause, then in unison.*] YEP!

[*They laugh hysterically at themselves.* LEON *bobs his head in silent laughter.*]

DIANE   This is seriously not happening.

CARL   What's your name, sweetheart?

DIANE   Diane.

BARRY   Diane, you're not half-bad-lookin' for 2 a.m.—

[CARL *shoots* BARRY *with his BB pistol.*]

BARRY   Ow! Shit!

CARL   Have some manners, you old pervert. Sorry there, Denn…a…what was it?

DIANE   Diane.

CARL   Diane. It's nice to meet you. I'm Carl, and this ugly sommbitch here is Barry.

BARRY Greetings.

CARL And this quiet fella in the portable recliner, that's Leon, our guest of honor tonight.

DIANE I'm really *thrilled* to meet you but—

CARL You know why we're drinking tonight, Diane?

DIANE I'm going to bed.

CARL Leon here is dying.

[*Pause.*]

DIANE Oh my God…I'm really—

BARRY We're all dying if you think about it. You know, the great circle of—

DIANE I thought you meant like tonight.

CARL Oh, I did, I did. Barry's just in a philosophical mood tonight.

DIANE Jesus…I…I'm really sorry.…

CARL Oh, believe me, nobody's sorrier than me. When he starts talking all philosophical and shit I just about—

DIANE I mean about him dying. Are you serious or not?

CARL Course I'm serious. Why would I joke about that?

BARRY Diane, this man has one dying wish. He told me a few years back, he says, "Barry, don't let me die in no goddamn hospital."

CARL He was sick, y'know, Lou Gehrig's disease.

BARRY And you know what we did? We made a pact. Right then. Wasn't none of us gonna die in no goddamn hospital.

CARL Leon here looked like he'd probably be the first of us to go, you understand. I mean exceptin' an act of the Almighty. So we asked him, "Leon, how you wanna go, if you get the choice?"

BARRY And you know what he said, Diane? He said, "I want to have one last night, like old times. Just the three of us. Gettin' drunk and talkin' shit. Maybe some music. And then that'd be it. I'd just drift off and never come back."

[*To* LEON.]

Ain't that right?

[LEON *nods his head down and blinks hard.*]

That's right.

CARL   See, one blink means yes and two means no.

BARRY   BEER!

[BARRY *fishes a beer out of the cooler and throws it to* CARL, *who catches and opens it with surprising agility.* BARRY *tosses another one at* DIANE, *who fumbles and drops it. Then he opens a third and begins to drink.*]

DIANE   Thanks, but—

BARRY   How you doing there, Leon? Ready for another?

[LEON *nods and blinks once.*]

DIANE   Can he, you know…*drink*?

CARL   Think we dragged him out here to watch? Check this shit out.

[BARRY *pulls a tube from* LEON'*s lap that runs under his shirt and presumably into his stomach.* BARRY *slowly empties a beer into the tube.*]

BARRY   Down the hatch. Feelin' tipsy yet?

[LEON *blinks once.* BARRY *and* CARL *laugh.* DIANE *is dumbstruck.*]

Ready to call it a night? Turn in?

[LEON *blinks thrice this time.* BARRY *and* CARL *laugh their asses off.*]

DIANE   What does three blinks mean?

CARL   Three means beer!

[BARRY *and* CARL *laugh some more.* LEON *rocks and his face glows with mischief.*]

CARL   Let me tell you something, Diane. What Leon wants is the perfect night. Can you imagine? To drink all night and never have a hangover?

BARRY   That's the dream, ain't it? Little piece of heaven.

CARL [*Reverently.*] They shall run, and not grow weary. They shall walk, and not grow faint. They shall drink a case of beer, and not awaken with a headache!

[*They laugh hysterically.*]

DIANE Okay, I'm sorry but this is a really bad idea. For one thing, it's… there's no way this is legal. It's like…assisted suicide or something.

BARRY Leon here was the police chief for forty-one years, so I don't think you gotta worry about legal.

DIANE That doesn't change anything…I mean, it's still—

CARL Oh, he's just messin' with you, sweetheart. Leon was a damn plumber. What do you do, Diane?

DIANE What…? I'm a doctoral student. Look—

BARRY Ho, ho. Doctor Diane. Hey, that's good—can you tell me if this tube is working right? I can't quite figure out Leon's little doohickey here—

DIANE Ph.D. Not M.D., but—

BARRY Damn.

DIANE Listen—

CARL Tell me somethin'—what does Ph.D. stand for?

DIANE What? Ph…it…

BARRY You don't know what Ph.D. stands for?

DIANE Philosophy. It stands for doctor of philosophy.

BARRY [*A pause, as he considers.*] Shouldn't it be D.Ph. then? If it's doctor of philosophy?

[CARL *shoots* BARRY.]

Ow!

CARL Quit givin' the poor girl hell, Barry.

[BARRY *shoots* CARL *back.*]

Ow, shit!…so philosophy, huh?

DIANE   It's in literature. Listen—

BARRY   Hell, is it philosophy or literature?

CARL   That don't make no sense, darlin'.

DIANE   Listen to me. Okay? Just *listen*. I'm only gonna ask you one more time. Please keep the noise down out here. I'm not trying to mess up your little...thing, I just want some peace and quiet. Okay? I'm going back to bed.

[BARRY *and* CARL *are silent. They stare at* DIANE. *A long pause.*]

BARRY   BEER!

[*He fishes around in the cooler for a cold one, and* DIANE *looks like she's about to explode.* BARRY *tosses another to* CARL, *but as he reaches up to catch it* DIANE *dives and snatches the BB pistol from his lap, grabs* LEON *by the shoulders, and puts the pistol to his temple.*]

CARL   What the—

DIANE   Shut up! I asked nicely, but you ignored me. So shut the hell up and listen to me right fucking now.

[*The men are stunned.* LEON's *eyes show fear.*]

I came out here to ask you one simple thing: keep the noise down. And you wouldn't. I didn't ask about what you were doing, or meddle with your affairs, I just asked one simple favor. One neighbor to another. But now I'm in it, I'm involved in your sick little suicide pact, and you know what? I don't like it. I think it's wrong, and it's twisted. Now you're gonna be honest with me, right now. Is this man dying?

[*Off their silence.*]

Is this man dying?!

BARRY   I mean, if you think about it—

DIANE   Not philosophically goddamnit! I mean really. Is he gonna die tonight?

CARL   No.

DIANE   [*Relieved.*] Okay.

BARRY   We were just yankin' your chain a little bit.

CARL   He wanted a night out, that's all.

DIANE   [*To* LEON.] Is that true?

[*He blinks once.*]

CARL   It's a goddamn awful disease. We just…he…It's been years of this. Watching him…wither. And Leon, that ain't Leon. He's the best.…He…

BARRY   You shoulda heard him talk, Diane. He was the loudest sommbitch you ever heard. And the funniest. And when his voice finally went…I swear to God, the world ain't…it ain't been the same.

CARL   Two of us can only talk so much shit, you know? We're just trying to fill up his space. It's just so…quiet.

DIANE   [*Softening.*] So you're…you're just drinking.

BARRY   Yes, ma'am.

DIANE   Okay. Will you keep it down? Just a bit? So I can sleep?

CARL and **BARRY**   Yes, ma'am.

[*She lowers the gun.*]

BARRY   Can I tell you something, Diane? You got balls.

CARL   Barry!

BARRY   I don't mean, you know. It's just a…what's the word? I mean you're courageous. You got balls. I'm speaking…I'm speaking…

CARL   You're speaking disrespectfully.

BARRY   No, I mean…Oh, you know what I'm saying. I'm speaking…

DIANE   Metaphorically.

CARL and **BARRY**   Metaphorically!

CARL   Doctor Diane! Ph.D.!

DIANE   Damn right.

CARL   What've you got to sleep for anyway, Dr. D.?

DIANE   What?

CARL   Why you gotta sleep?

DIANE   Because it's 2 a.m.

BARRY   That ain't no reason. Why besides 2 a.m.?

DIANE   I've got...I have research to do tomorrow, and...

BARRY   Research.

CARL   Diane. What you see before your eyes here is an accumulated one hundred and...no let's see...two hundred and...and...two...Over two hundred years of accumulated worldly wisdom.

BARRY   Other than math, of course.

CARL   Shut your ugly mouth, you old fart.

[CARL *pats his lap, looking for his pistol. Then he remembers.* BARRY *points his at* CARL.]

BARRY   Young lady stole your piece, friend.

[DIANE *aims hers at* BARRY.]

DIANE   Quit givin' the man hell.

[BARRY *freezes. A pause.*]

BARRY   Under one condition.

DIANE   What's that?

BARRY   Tell her, Leon.

   [LEON *blinks thrice.*]

   That's right—BEER!

[BARRY *slides the cooler with his foot toward* DIANE. *She considers.*]

DIANE   Okay. Just one, though.

   [*As she grabs her beer,* LEON *rocks in silent laughter. The other men catch on and laugh too.*]

   What's so funny?

CARL   Leon said the same thing first time we met him. And he hadn't stopped drinkin' beer since.

BARRY   One more request, Dr. D. You mind resuscitating the Willie?

[*She flips on the boom box and takes a seat on the cooler. The blasting twang of country music.*]

[*Lights out.*]

• • •

Daffodils

Daniel Guyton

Daniel Guyton

Daniel Guyton is a playwright and screenwriter from just south of Atlanta, where he lives with his wife, two dogs, and a cat. He has won numerous writing awards, has had over 200 productions of his plays throughout the world, and has over thirty publications under his belt, including *Best American Short Plays 2012–2013*.

··· production history ···

Daffodils premiered at the Out of Box Theatre (Carolyn Choe, artistic director) in Marietta, Georgia, in May 2014 as part of the Playing in the Dark festival. It was directed by Jerry Jobe. The set and prop designer was Raymond Fast. The music was designed by Paige Garwood and Chris Owenby. The cast was as follows:

JEREMY   Ian Gibson

RAIN   Lauren Coleman

• • •

[JEREMY *and* RAIN *cross an open field. Both are in their twenties, with jackets and mittens on. It is fall. He scans the ground carefully, as she watches for unwanted company.* JEREMY *stops.* RAIN *stops. The remnants of a stone pillar sticks out of the ground.* RAIN *looks around.*]

RAIN   Is it here?

JEREMY   Yeah.

[*She nods, uncomfortably.*]

RAIN   Okay.

[*He points to the stone.*]

JEREMY   That stone was a…cement pillar. A…land marker, I guess.

[*He kneels.*]

Maybe a fence? It's sort of worn down now. Into nothing.

[*Pause. She puts her hand on his shoulder.*]

I remember looking up at it. It was…taller than this. I think.

[*Small pause.*]

In the spring, this whole field is covered with daffodils. A…yellow sea. Could lie beneath it, beneath the waves. And no one would ever find you.

RAIN   I'll bet it's beautiful.

[*He glares at her.*]

I know. I'm…sorry. I…

[*He stands.*]

JEREMY It's okay. My dad would take me out here every time. The…

[*Small pause.*]

The stone was the only thing you could see. The…

[*He stands.*]

No barn. No…road. You can't see the neighbor's house from here. Just…this pillar, and fourteen acres of daffodils blowing in the wind.

[*She stands next to him.*]

RAIN I'm really proud of you, you know.

JEREMY I'm glad he's dead.

[*Pause.*]

RAIN I know.

[*She touches his chest.*]

I know you are.

[*He moves away.*]

JEREMY I don't want to be here.

RAIN Well…

[JEREMY *is almost offstage.*]

Jeremy?

[*He stops.*]

What…what are you feeling now?

JEREMY I'm . . I don't know.

RAIN Are you angry? Scared?

JEREMY I don't…

RAIN Because you're safe, you know?

[*Small pause.*]

With me.

JEREMY I know.

RAIN   You can tell me anything.

JEREMY   I know.

RAIN   So we'll come back later then? I…I really want to talk about…

JEREMY   No. I don't ever want to see this place again.

RAIN   I know. But…you're in charge of the estate now, so…

JEREMY   So what? So what does that *mean*? The…

[*He marches back to her.*]

To be in charge? Who was in charge when I was…?

[*He starts to tear up.*]

When he was…?

[*Small pause.*]

I hope this whole fucking place burns to the ground!

[RAIN *looks away from him.*]

You think that'll get us anywhere? You think…?

[*Pause.*]

If I burned it all? Would that accomplish anything?

[*He sits down on the ground.*]

Solve anything?

[*Small pause.*]

I have baggage, honey. Suitcases after suitcases of overflowing baggage. Underwear falling out. Can't even find my toothbrush. Grand Central Station in a *year* doesn't see as many suitcases as I've got.

[*Small pause.*]

And if you don't want to marry me anymore because of my luggage, I'll understand.

RAIN   I have suitcases too, Jeremy. You know what happened to my mother. And yes, I would marry you right now, if you had…*eighteen* Grand Central Stations worth of suitcases.

[*She touches him.*]

You're the man I've been waiting for, Jeremy. My entire life. I will walk with you, follow you....Whatever you need. And these are not your suitcases anyway. These are his. You can dump all of these suitcases out, right now, in this field, and no one would ever be the wiser. And if burning this field to the ground will help you empty the suitcases, then I will help you, Jeremy. I will light the matches.

[*She touches his face.*]

Okay?

[JEREMY *nods.*]

However, I think we'll get a lot more money if we sell it, honey. Unscathed.

[*He starts to pull away.*]

Fourteen acres is a lot of land. We can move to LA. Have that honeymoon in France like we always wanted....

JEREMY But it's blood money! This whole field is covered in blood. And then...shielded by a golden sea. No one knows the fertilizer that's in this ground! It's me! It comes from me! My spirit pouring out of me like a garden hose, watering the fields. I...couldn't stop it. I couldn't make it stop. I just...hid beneath the ocean. And fed the angry daffodils my soul. In the morning, they were bigger, stronger. The color of the sun. Blood red mixed with lemon petals like an orange grove. A...flame. The entire ocean burning. Searing off my skin.

[*Small pause.*]

I walked a mile in the morning. Red...blood...running down my legs. I showered. For centuries I showered. Scrubbing off my skin like...

[*Small pause.*]

And still, the blood kept running. Like Charybdis circling the drain. My body fell, in tiny droplets, on the green linoleum tiles in the kitchen. Up the stairwell. Seeping through the wooden steps. When finally I slept, my father cleaned it. He wouldn't look at me for years. But...when finally I slept, my father cleaned it.

[*Small pause.*]

As if I'd never bled at all.

[*After a moment,* RAIN *sits down on the grass.*]

RAIN   If he wasn't in that coffin, I would shoot him.

JEREMY   I've thought about that many times.

RAIN   I wish I could have met you sooner, Jeremy. I…I wish I could have…

JEREMY   What?

RAIN   Protected you.

[JEREMY *looks away.*]

I don't know how, I…Killed him, maybe? Screamed at him? Yelled at him to stop?

JEREMY   Believe me, I've tried all that. I…After Momma died, he…

[*Small pause.*]

He just kept telling me I had her eyes. He…said I smelled just like her. I…

[*He starts to cry.* RAIN *looks away.*]

RAIN   Do you have any gasoline? The ground'll never burn like this.

[*She stands. He looks at her.*]

Come on, let's torch this son of a bitch.

JEREMY   Why?

RAIN   Hmm?

JEREMY   Why are you willing to help me?

RAIN   Because it hurt you. I'll destroy anything that ever hurts you, Jeremy. From now until the end of days, I will protect you, you understand me? If anyone tries to hurt you, I will…

[*She clenches her fists, then calms them, and takes his face in her hands.*]

You are everything to me, you know?

[*She starts to tear up.*]

The thought of what he did to you…The…

[*Small pause.*]

I'm really glad he's dead.

[JEREMY *hugs her*.]

JEREMY I know.

[*She looks up at him.*]

RAIN I'm sorry I made you come here, Jeremy. I...

JEREMY I know.

RAIN I love you so much.

[*They kiss.*]

We'll do whatever you want, okay?

[JEREMY *nods and smiles.*]

JEREMY I know. I just...I'm really angry, that's all. We don't need to burn it. I...just need some time to think, that's all.

RAIN You have a right to be.

[*Small pause.*]

Angry.

JEREMY He wasn't always awful. You know? And that's what hurts the most, I think. I remember playing baseball when I was younger. He'd be watching in the sidelines. Smilin' and...being pretty happy for me. I think. I remember being happy. Really happy for a while. And then Momma got sick, and...he stopped paying attention to me after that. We stopped going to baseball. I...stopped playing, and he stopped even looking at me until...

[*Small pause.*]

August 17, 1992. Those nights I spent out here staring at this stone. This...Feeling like I...

[*Small pause.*]

I remember him crying in his bedroom all day long. He...Momma planted daffodils, one by one. In a tiny corner of the yard—way out past the hickory. That was...Daddy planted cabbage, corn, potatoes. Ran a local market up in town. But after Momma died, he...The daffodils grew wild. He never trimmed them. Never...cut them....

They ran rampant through the cabbage plants. Choked out all the corn. Daddy said that shouldn't happen, that the daffodils were weak. But he never cut them down. He...he said they reminded him of her.

[*Pause.*]

I think that's why he took me out here. Back behind this pillar, because...they reminded him of her....

[*She tries to hug him, but with a growl, he kicks the stone with the bottom of his shoe. It doesn't budge. He kicks it again repeatedly. He then kneels and tries to lift it with his hands. It is primal, rageful, but the stone will not be moved. Eventually, he gives up in a heap of sweat and breath.* RAIN *calmly wraps her arms around him.*]

RAIN   If I could blast that stone into a million pieces, I would. If I could reverse the mortar and the flow of time, I would return that stone to dust. And water. From whence it came. For you to have to look at something so unmoving, so...cold...

[*Small pause.*]

But if I did that, Jeremy, if...I destroyed that stone...

[*Small pause.*]

What if I lost you in the process? What if I never met you? What if...?

[*Long pause.*]

When my mother died I...She was holding me just like this. Her arms across my chest. The tornado flattened everything. Our house, our...neighbors.

[*Long pause.*]

She held me many hours before I realized she was gone. I couldn't talk because...she was holding me so tightly. I couldn't move because...she was holding me so tightly. For sixteen hours, I couldn't move. I was...pinned in this position. From the time the twister hit until...

[*Small pause.*]

I thought that she was mad at me. I thought that she was...

[*Small pause.*]

She wouldn't let me go. It took twenty men to get us out of there. Twenty men to lift a house from off of my mother's back. The refrigerator....Stove....

[*Small pause.*]

Even after she was gone, she...protected me. She shielded me. She kept my body warm.

[*She caresses his face.*]

Your mother loved you, Jeremy. She never left you. She couldn't stop the storm from coming, but she never left your side. The daffodils were protecting you, shielding you. Keeping your body warm.

[*She whispers in his ear.*]

I'll never let you go, Jeremy. I'll never let you go.

JEREMY   Rain?

RAIN   I'll wash away your tears.

[*He smiles sadly.*]

JEREMY   I would like that very much.

[*They kiss. Lights fade.*]

• • •

March Madness— Shhhhhh!

Jules Tasca

Jules Tasca

Jules Tasca is the author of over 125 (full-length and one-act) published plays that have been produced worldwide. He has also written for radio and television, including *The Hal Linden TV Special*, *La Llorona*, and *Maria*.

He was the national winner in New York's Performing Arts Repertory Theater Playwriting contest for his libretto *The Amazing Einstein*. His libretto for C. S. Lewis's *The Lion, the Witch and the Wardrobe* is currently touring nationwide.

For his play *Theater Trip*, he received a Thespie Award for Best New Play, and *Old Goat Song* won a drama critic's award in Los Angeles. His plays *The Spelling of Coynes*, *The Death of Bliss*, *Deus-X*, *Birth of Theater*, and *If Hamlet Had Been a Reading* have been included in the *Best American Short Plays* series. His tragic piece *The Balkan Women* won the Barrymore Award for Best Play. *The Grand Christmas History of the Andy Landy Clan* was broadcast on forty-seven national Public Radio Stations.

His tragedy *Judah's Daughter* received the Dorothy Silver International Playwriting Award. He won first prize in the Bucks County Writers' Club Screenwriting Contest. His piece *Live Drawing* has been published by the Dramatic Publishing Company. Tasca's play *The Mission* received a Silver Palm Award from the South Florida Theatre League for best new play. *Art Lover* was produced as part of the 2011 Philadelphia International Festival of the Arts. His latest anthology, *Chekhov's Ladies*, has been accepted for publication by Samuel French Inc.

···production history···

World premiere, Theater Three, New York, February–March 2014, directed by Jeff Sanzell.

DR. PHILIP FEIN   Ed Brennan

TROY McWIGGIN   Mark T. Cahill

JOE BELALE   Odell Cureton

characters

DR. PHILIP FEIN   President of Midwest University.

TROY McWIGGIN   Assistant Basketball Coach.

JOE BELALE   Head Basketball Coach.

time

Present

setting

Office of the President

···

[*Lights come up on* DR. PHILIP FEIN *sitting at his desk. His office door opens and* TROY McWIGGIN *enters, wearing sweat pants and a Midwest University hoodie.*]

FEIN   Troy….

TROY   Dr. Fein….

FEIN   How'd the practice go today? I hope you worked the three-point shot with Jenkins and with…

TROY   Dr. Fein, I'm not here to discuss the basketball team.

FEIN   What is it, Troy?

[*He rises.*]

What's the matter? Your face is ashen.

TROY   Before I say anything…Could you…Could you send Hope Williams home?

FEIN What? What is this?

TROY Please, sir, just get her out of here....

FEIN You walk into the president's office and tell him to send his secretary home? Just like that?

TROY Shhhh, sir, please....

FEIN I beg your pardon.

TROY You don't want Hope Williams hearing any of this. You don't even want to chance that she might hear through closed doors.

FEIN What're you whispering about? Troy, explain yourself.

TROY It's horrible....It's terrible....It's not hot water; it's boiling acid, Dr. Fein.

FEIN Be frank with me, Troy. Did one of your basketball players get injured? God, don't tell me that.

TROY Dr. Fein....

FEIN You're the assistant coach. Did the Reynolds boy re-injure his...

TROY Shhhhh....

FEIN Troy, Jesus...what're we shushing about?

TROY Sir, just don't talk so loud. No, this is not about Reynolds or any other team member.

FEIN Then what could be so horrible as to frighten you like this?

TROY Please, send Hope Williams home.

FEIN Why must I....

TROY You know how emotional she is. If she hears us, I tell you flat out, she'll call the police.

FEIN The police?

TROY Shhhhh....Yes. And before anything is reported, I wanted to consult with you.

FEIN What in the name of God is it then?

[TROY *looks around, listens at the door. Then he crosses to* FEIN *and whispers in his ear.*]

FEIN   No! No! Oh no!

[FEIN *is nonplussed and backs away from* TROY. TROY *follows* FEIN *and whispers further information in his ear. Finally,* FEIN *stares at* TROY *and drops into his chair.*]

Good God…Good God Almighty, Troy. Where is our good God? I'm…I'm stunned.…I'm absolutely…what would possess Joe Belale, our basketball coach, to…

TROY   Shhhhhh.…

FEIN   Where is Coach Belale now?

TROY   I have him hiding in the men's room across from your office. I wanted to break it to you first.…

FEIN   Get him in here. Tell him to act normal. I don't want Hope Williams to get an inkling that he…

TROY   I understand, Dr. Fein.

FEIN   And try to look less…less shaken than you did when you walked in here. Hope can't know.…

TROY   I knew you'd understand how serious this is…

FEIN   Shhhh.…Go get him.

[TROY *exits.* FEIN *rises and wipes his brow. Then he paces.*]

How? How could he? How could this happen? The coach? Coach Belale? Now? In the middle of March Madness? With our team soaring? How could he be so…

[TROY *re-enters with* COACH JOE BELALE. JOE *sits and puts his head in his hands.*]

Did Hope suspect that anything's wrong?

TROY   She did ask if everything's set for the Villanova game. I said yes. We're just working out logistics for the team's trip to Pennsylvania.

FEIN   Good.…

TROY   Don't you think you should send her home, sir?

FEIN   No. That's a sure way to make her suspicious. We'll just keep our voices down.

[FEIN *crosses to* JOE.]

Coach?…Coach Belale?

TROY   My instinct was to call the police, but I…

FEIN   Shhhhhh!

TROY   [*Sotto.*] I just had a gut feeling that you'd know what to do.

FEIN   Coach?…Joe…Joe…For Christ's sake, Joe, look at me.

[JOE *sits up.*]

Is what Troy McWiggin told me…well…what's your explanation?…Joe?…Joe?

JOE   What do you want me to say?

FEIN   So you're saying that what Troy reported is…

JOE   He walked in on…on…

FEIN   Have you done this before?

JOE   Look…I'm…I'm sorry.…

FEIN   It's habitual?

JOE   I don't want to talk about it. Troy, couldn't you just've kept your mouth shut?

TROY   Kept my…Coach Belale; you…God…you know how much I respect you…your skill…your guts…you know I'd do anything for you.…But this.…This is something where…where you…you need help.…We need to call the police and…and, well, if you need help and a lawyer and if you…

JOE   Why did you have to come back to the locker room? Goddarnit. The lights were out. Hell, practice had been over an hour ago. Everyone had gone…I thought.…

TROY   I stayed in my office watching the tape of Villanova's last game to study their offence. I came back for my cell phone and my car keys and I see you…see you…

FEIN   Shhhhhh! Voice down, please. What difference does it make if Troy came back or why he came back? Jesus Christ, Joe, he caught you...

TROY   Shhhhhh....

FEIN   I'm in shock, Joe....

TROY   We're all in shock, Coach. My mind's run out of bounds over this....Are we...Are we waiting too long to call the police?

JOE   Why do you need to call the police, Troy?

TROY   Coach, if I don't...If I don't, I'll be just as guilty if I don't....If we don't....If...

JOE   Understand. I'm not average...I'm...I'm a very complicated person. Dr. Fein—Phil—think of some of the thoughts you've had since you got up this morning...you must've had...

FEIN   Stop, Joe. I...I never acted on any of those...assuming I had any thoughts....

JOE   Everyone has...

FEIN   This is not a justification for...

TROY   Shhhhhh....

FEIN   When you decided to pursue this sordid activity, did you, Joe, ever consider the basketball team? Huh? The Trojans? Our Trojans? The Midwest University Trojans? Huh? Did you ever once consider that if it leaked out that you...

TROY   Shhhhhh....

FEIN   [*A quieter voice.*] If this gets out, think how it impacts...impacts...Joe...Jesus, we're in March Madness....And the Trojans could go all the way this spring.

JOE   Could? Hell, we will....

FEIN   But this now...This...

JOE   The let's just forget the whole business.

TROY How? Coach, how could we....The authorities....Some authority should be notified that....Look, I'm just being honest. If we don't report this. . . As I said...I could go to jail myself....

FEIN Shhhhhh...Jesus, Troy....

JOE Troy, do you know what you're saying?

TROY Coach, be honest here. It's criminal what you...

JOE Shhhhhh!

FEIN He's right....The sad part, Joe, is that Troy's right....Troy, please go out and check on Hope. Make sure she heard nothing....

[TROY *exits, and* FEIN *crosses close to* JOE.]

I wanted to get him out of here for a minute, Joe, to tell you that what Troy caught you doing with...with...Let's just say that it's perverted.

JOE Phil, I...

FEIN Someone like Troy—an Irish Catholic—would call your behavior...evil, Joe...evil...egregiously evil....

JOE I am not evil. I am...I am just a nuanced person who...who, well, sometimes lives...lives out of the box.

FEIN Shhhhhh! You call what you did with that...

[TROY *re-enters.*]

TROY Hope's out of the picture, Dr. Fein. She's playing solitaire on her computer.

FEIN Good. I just told Coach Belale that we have to do the right thing.

TROY That's all I'm saying. We need to call the...

FEIN Troy, I agree with you. This...this is a grave matter, but we need to keep our heads level.

TROY We are keeping our heads....

FEIN I'm simply saying, let's approach this matter rationally....

TROY As we're doing. The Coach could get a good lawyer and maybe some psychiatric...

FEIN Shhhhhh!

JOE I don't need any psychiatrist. Look, I said I'm a complicated person....

TROY But a crime has been committed and I...

JOE Shhhhhh!

TROY If I look the other way, Coach, I'll never be able to sleep again. You understand?

FEIN Be that as it may, Troy, let us deconstruct our equation. Think. If we notify the police, what happens to Coach Belale? Think. The goddamned sports arena is named after him—Belale Field House. Think. There's a bronze statue of Coach Belale at the entrance of the field house. Think. What happens to the team when they drag our coach out in handcuffs—and by God they will.

JOE I've never been in handcuffs...myself. Listen. I admit I have outlandish desires....

FEIN Shhhhhh, Joe, shhhhhh.... Think, Troy, Joe Belale is a campus god, more highly esteemed than our doctors in the science complex doing cancer research.

TROY But...

FEIN Think. What happens to the reputation of Midwest University if they find out that this revered teacher and coach has...

JOE Shhhhhh....

FEIN Think. Would the NCAA let him continue coaching?

TROY I don't think they...

FEIN Think. The NCAA would pull the basketball team out of the competition for this perversion....

JOE I'm a very complex human being....

FEIN Think For what this...this complex human being has done, they could sanction the university....Could sanction me....Think, Troy. What would happen to the assistant coach if this all falls apart? Think.

What the fuck would the media do when it gets hold of this blatant immorality that you cast your eyes upon in the Trojan locker room?

TROY I…I…I come back for my cell phone and my keys and my…

JOE We're all dead if this… God…The whole world will die with me if…

TROY Shhhhhh!

FEIN My big…Our big worry is the victim. How do we know the victim hasn't gone to the police? Huh?

JOE Victim? Come on.…

FEIN How did you get the victim into the locker room? Joe?

[JOE *whispers into* FEIN's *ear.*]

Oh…Ohhhh…So the victim…

JOE Shhhhhh.…

TROY Dr. Fein, the victim can't go to the police because…

[TROY *whispers into* FEIN's *ear.*]

FEIN Jesus…Oh…I see.…So there's no way the victim could go to the…would want to go to the…the…

TROY No. But we can.…I mean, a crime's been committed.…I walked in…I saw…I'm a witness and…and…

JOE Tory, I have more wins than any active basketball coach in this country.…

TROY And you're admired, yes, but, Coach, if…if Dr. Fein and I do nothing, we're…we're complicit in…in a serious crime.…

FEIN Troy, everything you're saying is correct.…

TROY That's the only reason, Joe, I say we should call the police.…

JOE And ruin my life? I'm a role model in the community.…

TROY But if we don't tell the truth and say if this happens again and they…they investigate and learn that I…That you…Dr. Fein, we've got to tell the truth.

FEIN Shhhhhh…Troy, this obsession you have with the truth.…

TROY Obsession? How could a person have an…

FEIN Sometimes being…Troy, being humane is a…a greater good than the truth that hurts so many. Do diplomats always tell the truth? Senators? Presidents? No. They know that, at times, it's wiser and more compassionate to hold a sordid truth in our hearts and bear the pain, carry the burden of another's trespass than…Jesus, all I'm asking is that we be merciful.…

TROY Dr. Fein, how can we…

JOE The governor of the state, Troy, is going to present me with the Citizen of the Year Award at graduation.

TROY He is?…

JOE Yes, but shhhhhh…I wasn't supposed to spill that, Phil, I know, but I…I'm telling Troy because I want him to know the kind of man I am.

TROY Dr. Fein, I still feel…I still feel…

FEIN Troy, the basketball team of Midwest University is the university. The money. The sports scholarships. The national notice. The alumni fund. The team that Coach Belale has created here trumps even academics at our school. The Trojans. The team is the good earth that grows all of this, all of us. Think. Anyway Joe spins it or his lawyer spins it, the truth will only damn us along with Coach Belale.

TROY I understand that…that…well, that—that could happen.

FEIN Will happen.…

JOE I just have some unusual peccadilloes.

FEIN Shhhhhh.…

TROY So…

FEIN So…

TROY So…Then…How do we proceed?

[FEIN *paces a few beats.*]

JOE   You don't understand, Troy, that complicated men have strange interests....

TROY   I do. But, Coach, when those interests are a...a felony, we must notify...

FEIN   I've got it.

JOE   What?

FEIN   In my judgment I say...I say we don't notify anyone about this...this indiscretion....

TROY   You mean the Coach just turns himself in to the....

FEIN   Shhhhhh...Troy, after today, you know the Coach will never do anything like this again. Joe? Joe? Isn't that so? Joe, for Christ sake!

JOE   Well...I'll...I'll try...I will try....

FEIN   There, Troy. You want more honesty than that?

JOE   We've got a big game to prepare for....

TROY   I...I...

FEIN   When Coach Belale retires, Troy, my man, there'll be no search committee. No. The head coaching position is yours.

TROY   No...No search committee?

FEIN   None....That's what I said....

TROY   You mean that I...that I...

FEIN   Yes, I do. Troy, as a reward for uncovering these depraved acts....

JOE   Reward....

FEIN   And putting an end to Coach Belale's unacceptable behavior, you deserve full credit. You saved this university, Troy McWiggin....Yes, you did....

TROY   How did I...

FEIN   So forget today. Think. Think ahead! Coach—head coach—Troy McWiggin. Think of when Coach McWiggin is the honcho of some future March Madness. Listen to the cheers. Gather in the accolades…Hold high that trophy, man!

TROY   I've always fantasized.…

JOE   You're a complicated person too, Troy. I can see you are. Yes.…

TROY   Well, I…I think we—all of us—are capable of falling to temptation and I.…

FEIN   I'm proud of your loyalty, Troy. I won't forget this.

TROY   Oh, I know. We all know you're a man of your word. A man's man. Yes.

FEIN   So let's just wrap this up, huh? Let's concentrate on the game. Are we sure Reynold's hamstring will be okay for him to play?

TROY and JOE   Absolutely.…

TROY   I've been working with him. Deep tissue massage. Stretching. Twice a day in the whirlpool.

[*Lights begin a slow fade.*]

FEIN   God bless your commitment, Troy.

JOE   Reynolds'll be ready.

TROY   He will.…

FEIN   I can't wait for Saturday.…

JOE   If we beat Villanova, the rest of the chart is cake, I tell you, pure cake.…

FEIN   Gives me goose bumps even thinking about this game.…Almost makes me forget what Coach Belale did in the locker room with that poor…

TROY and JOE   Shhhhhh!

[*Lights are out.*]

• • •

Acknowledgments

The authors in this collection are the ones who make this book what it is, and for that they really deserve all the credit. I would like to thank several people who helped me locate these excellent pieces of theater, especially Dan Gallant, John Bolen, and John Patrick Bray. And thanks to everyone who submitted their work for me to read and review, making this project, once again, a joyful but also challenging undertaking.

Thanks always to the folks at Applause Theatre & Cinema Books, especially John Cerullo, Bernadette Malavarca, and Carol Flannery. Thanks also to June Clark, my agent, for supporting this project. And thanks to Jean and Erin, always in my corner.

THE BEST AMERICAN SHORT PLAYS SERIES

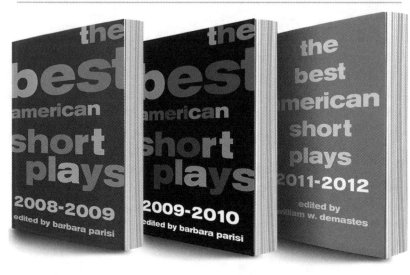

2013-2014

978-14803-9548-0 Paperback $19.99

2011-2012

978-1-4768-7734-1 Hardcover $32.99
978-1-4768-7733-4 Paperback $19.99

2010-2011

978-1-55783-835-3 Hardcover $32.99
978-1-55783-836-0 Paperback $18.99

2009-2010

978-1-55783-763-9 Hardcover $32.99
978-1-55783-762-2 Paperback $18.99

2008-2009

978-1-55783-761-5 Hardcover $32.99
978-1-55783-760-8 Paperback $18.99

2006-2007

978-1-55783-747-9 Hardcover $34.99
978-1-55783-748-6 Paperback $18.99

2005-2006

978-1-55783-713-4 Hardcover $32.95

2003-2004

978-1-55783-695-3 Hardcover $32.95

2002-2003

978-1-55783-720-2 Paperback $18.99

APPLAUSE
THEATRE & CINEMA BOOKS

AN IMPRINT OF

HAL•LEONARD®
www.applausebooks.com